Integrating Sophisticated Standards and Systems of Support for Elementary Readers

Elizabeth L. Jaeger

Routledge
Taylor & Francis Group
NEW YORK AND LONDON

Designed cover image: © Getty Images

First published 2026
by Routledge
605 Third Avenue, New York, NY 10158

and by Routledge
4 Park Square, Milton Park, Abingdon, Oxon, OX14 4RN

Routledge is an imprint of the Taylor & Francis Group, an informa business

© 2026 Taylor & Francis

The right of Elizabeth L. Jaeger to be identified as author of this work has been asserted in accordance with sections 77 and 78 of the Copyright, Designs and Patents Act 1988.

All rights reserved. The purchase of this copyright material confers the right on the purchasing institution to photocopy or download pages which bear a copyright line at the bottom of the page. No other parts of this book may be reprinted or reproduced or utilised in any form or by any electronic, mechanical, or other means, now known or hereafter invented, including photocopying and recording, or in any information storage or retrieval system, without permission in writing from the publishers.

For Product Safety Concerns and Information please contact our EU representative GPSR@taylorandfrancis.com. Taylor & Francis Verlag GmbH, Kaufingerstraße 24, 80331 München, Germany.

Trademark notice: Product or corporate names may be trademarks or registered trademarks, and are used only for identification and explanation without intent to infringe.

ISBN: 9781032861470 (hbk)
ISBN: 9781032861463 (pbk)
ISBN: 9781003528234 (ebk)

DOI: 10.4324/9781003528234

Typeset in Palatino
by codeMantra

Access the Support Material: www.routledge.com/9781032861463

Contents

Support Material. vi

1 Introduction. 1

2 Introduction to the Integration of Sophisticated
   Standards and Response to Intervention (RtI)/
   Multi-Tiered Systems of Support (MTSS) 9

3 Research Base for Strong Curriculum that
   Integrates Standards-Based Curriculum and MTSS 27

4 Tier 1, 2, and 3 Curriculum and Instruction 42

5 Developing Curriculum for Reading Instruction 72

6 Developing Curriculum for Writing Instruction 88

7 Additional Curriculum Units. 100

8 Integrated Units 135

9 Tier 2 and Tier 3 Units Based on Informal Reading
   and Writing Assessments 143

10 Conclusion. 187

   Appendix A: Reading Workshop Minilessons 189
   Appendix B: Literature Circles Supplement 196
   Appendix C: Writing Workshop Supplement 206
   Appendix D: Supporting Materials for Curriculum Units. . . .211
   Appendix E: IRI and IELI Materials 281
   Appendix F: Tier 1 and 2 Research 289
   Appendix G: Tier 3 Research 308
   Index. 331

Support Material

The following tools from the book are also available on our web-site as free downloads, so you can easily print and reproduce them for classroom use. To access the materials, go to the book product page at www.routledge.com/9781032861463 and click on the link that says Support Material.

Appendix A: Reading Workshop Minilessons	189
Appendix B: Literature Circles Supplement	196
Appendix C: Writing Workshop Supplement	206
Appendix D: Supporting Materials for Curriculum Units	211
Appendix E: IRI and IELI Materials	281
Appendix F: Tier 1 and 2 Research	289
Appendix G: Tier 3 Research	308

1

Introduction

One characteristic of the Wisconsin farmland where I grew up was the ubiquity of silos. Driving the backroads, you couldn't go a mile without seeing one. Each held its assigned grain: field corn for cows, soybeans for pigs, and oats for chickens. Keeping the grains separate seemed logical. But we now know that livestock benefit from a mixed diet (University of Minnesota Extension, 2025)—like any good meal, there is a mixture of flavors and nutrients fused into a single dish.

The landscape of education typically reflects the same logic as its agricultural counterpart: keep math separate from literacy, assessment from instruction, theory from practice. But in the educational context—as in the farm context—failing to integrate subjects and practices makes little sense (Hannigan & Hannigan, 2020). Students require a range of both content and instructional strategies that are often best in combination.

There is another parallel between the farm and educational contexts. As the National Hog Farmer journal notes a "preference for shiny, new things is pretty universal throughout the animal kingdom" (University of Illinois College of Agriculture, Consumer, and Environmental Sciences, 2017). When provided with a choice between a familiar toy and a bright, new one, piglets chose the latter.

Similarly, schools invest time and energy into a given program, but when it turns out to be less successful than originally hoped, substituting a new program looks more enticing than adjusting the old one (Hall, 2018). As McIntosh and Goodman (2016) note, this often leads to "initiative fatigue" (p. 3) and, ultimately, only surface-level change. Rarely do we imagine something in a new initiative that could be integrated with the previous one—with the strengths of one making up for the weaknesses of the other.

Educational Content and Educational Structure

It is the primary argument of this book that an important area in which educators have responded with a silo-like approach—failing to see and develop the need for integration—is with literacy content and the structures needed for all children to access that content. I refer specifically here to the sophisticated content standards students are expected to master and systems of support for readers who struggle. Rather than discussing these initiatives as complementary and interdependent and attempting to integrate them, most educational researchers focus on one or the other. And when the isolated initiatives prove less than fully successful in increasing student achievement and engagement, the field discounts the benefits of these programs and moves on to the next "shiny" educational object. Integrating these two initiatives increases the likelihood that all students will succeed.

Sophisticated Standards
The Common Core State Standards (CCSS) were published in 2010 and widely adopted across the United States. Not all states adopted the CCSS, and many that did revised them later. I would argue that the standards that are now in place across the country are more challenging than the state standards that preceded them and, even in states where these standards have been altered, they are not dramatically different than the CCSS. As a result, I feel comfortable selecting from the CCSS for the examples included in this text.

Structures of Support
Systems designed to support those students who need extra assistance are typically referred to as response to intervention (RtI) or multi-tiered systems of support (MTSS). RtI was the

original term, focusing on the academic aspects of schooling. As the role of the affective facets of learning became more evident, MTSS—which emphasizes the integration of academic, behavioral, social, and emotional supports—became the predominant term. I will employ this term throughout the text except when quoting researchers who specifically reference RtI.

Goals of This Text

There are a range of books addressing various aspects of CCSS and MTSS, and I will not attempt to replicate the strengths of those books. For example, CCSS-related texts cover recommendations for curriculum at the middle and high school levels (Berry & Aldrich, 2021; Tucker, 2015) and for mathematics (Gojak & Miles, 2015; Muschla et al., 2014); this book focuses on literacy at the elementary level only. Several MTSS-related books do a wonderful job of walking the reader step-by-step through initiating and developing an MTSS program from the ground up, offering a range of strategies for building MTSS teams and improving collaboration (e.g., Hannigan & Hannigan, 2020; McIntosh & Goodman, 2016; Novak & Rodriguez, 2013). This is a crucial aspect of MTSS and I would urge any schools and districts to review and learn from these texts, but due to page constraints, that is not the focus of this book. Finally, the connection between MTSS and placement in special education has been fraught with challenges. It is my belief that, if a child does not progress after some months of individualized instruction, a referral to special education is warranted, but I spend little time in this text addressing that issue because other texts treat this topic in depth (e.g., Spear-Swerling, 2014).

What This Text Does That Others Do Not

This text has four primary components. First, I describe the ways in which the CCSS and MTSS can be effectively integrated to raise achievement for students. This can be accomplished by providing appropriate instruction for children who are challenged, children who achieve with relative ease, and children who have already mastered much of what we would typically teach them. Second, the text provides practical instructions to guide professional development for teachers and administrators in screening and assessing students for placement in a tiered system of supports and in developing CCSS-based lessons and assessments at those various tiers: classroom, small group, and individualized instruction. Third, the text provides examples of these assessments and lessons to serve as models for those that can be developed at the school and/or district level. Finally, because this work is based on academic studies, I provide research support for the efficacy of this project.

Intended Readership

The ideal reader for this book is a teacher or administrator who has a basic familiarity with both their state's literacy standards and MTSS as practiced in their state. In the best of circumstances, this book would be read and enacted by an MTSS team at the school or district level. It might also serve as a supplementary text for a literacy methods course for preservice teachers; ideally, these teachers would have studied the state literacy standards and MTSS in a previous course or courses, so they would be prepared to imagine how these two important aspects of school life could be integrated effectively.

Chapter-by-Chapter Overview

The first chapter of this book explores in detail the need for integrating the two "silos" of sophisticated standards and MTSS. This chapter provides information about the CCSS and MTSS, including goals, development, strengths, and shortcomings. It explains how the strengths of each of these initiatives offset the limitations of the other and how they can be effectively integrated.

Chapter 2 examines the research base for a strong curriculum at each of the three contexts suggested by MTSS: Tier 1 for classrooms, Tier 2 for small groups, and Tier 3 for one-on-one instruction. It also introduces the concept of "Tier 0" instruction:

that is, ways of determining which students have already mastered the content to be presented in Tier 1 and how they might better spend their time.

Chapter 3 describes the reading and writing structures that provide the backbone of the curriculum. These are, for reading instruction: interactive read-aloud, Reading Workshop, shared reading, guided reading, and Literature Circles. The structures for writing are mentor texts within genre study, modeled writing, shared writing, partner/collaborative writing, and Writing Workshop. The chapter also explains several other instructional activities employed in the curriculum units: exit slips, assisted reading, a close reading protocol, the Wheel of Fortune game, and Finger Flash vocabulary practice.

Chapter 4 reviews the process of developing Tier 1, Tier 2, and Tier 3 reading curriculum at the Grade 4 level by teachers and/or administrators using children's literature and/or published core texts (basals). It begins with vignettes of conversations among teachers and support staff as they develop this curriculum. Then it carefully describes the ways educators can work together to develop curriculum: selecting a standard (or multiple standards that might be combined in one unit); developing an optional pre-test which some students may choose to take if they hope to demonstrate that they would benefit from an extension project rather than the regular Tier 1 curriculum; selecting texts to be employed in classroom, small group, and individualized instruction; and producing a unit assessment that will determine which students require additional intervention to achieve mastery. Small group units involve about eight lessons and will be taught only to students who struggle with that unit in the classroom setting; this keeps the group size low and allows most students—even those who struggle with other aspects of literacy—to remain in the classroom so as not to miss instruction in other important subjects. One-on-one instruction will be provided only for students who continue to struggle after small group work and would only require as many sessions as are needed to reach mastery. This chapter also includes a teacher/administrator self-assessment protocol for this work; because this is a collaborative process, it is important that educators work together effectively, efficiently, and cordially, and this protocol helps ensure that group work is productive.

The next several units offer a range of other plans. Writing curriculum at the Grade 2 level is the focus of Chapter 5. It is structured in the same way as Chapter 4, but with a different curricular focus at a different grade level. Because educators often benefit from seeing models prior to embarking on their own curriculum development, Chapter 6 provides example units (one each for literature, information text, foundational skills, and writing at each tier) for two grade levels: 2nd and 4th. Ideally, some units might include more than one standard so as to be as efficient as possible and also to promote the idea that aspects of literacy can be interrelated and that literacy learning is nuanced and multi-faceted; so Chapter 7 provides Tier 1/Tier 2/Tier 3 units at the 2nd- and 4th-grade levels that incorporate multiple standards.

Each standards-based unit ends with an assessment, and data from this assessment will determine which children will require additional support to master that standard. In many cases, however, students who struggle with literacy may also need small group or individualized instruction related to standards assigned to a grade level below that of the student's current placement (e.g., a 5th grader who fails to use context clues in decoding) or with some aspect of literacy that is not covered in the standards (e.g., use of comprehension strategies). I advocate that children who struggle with reading and writing text be assessed with an individual diagnostic assessment so that their literacy strengths and challenges can be readily delineated and addressed. Chapter 8 explains how to use diagnostic information to select students for this type of small group or individualized instruction and provides units for the areas of sight words, basic decoding, multi-syllable decoding, use of context clues, fluency, answering questions, and retelling.

Appendices A through E provide supplementary materials related to curriculum development. Appendices F and G present two research studies that served as the foundation for this book. The first reviews findings from a study that included Tier 1 and Tier 2 work; 4th grade struggling readers missed only

20 hours of classroom instruction to attend Tier 2 classes and made so much progress that none required Tier 3 individualized support. The second reviews findings from a study that focused on Tier 3 instruction; a 4th grader who began the year about two years below grade level made two years gain in reading over the course of a single school year, missing only 40 hours of classroom instruction.

Our educational system is fraught with challenges: teaching to sophisticated standards in ways that meet the needs of all learners first among them. By offering a road map for the ways in which initiatives can be integrated, this text offers direction, instructional support, and a ray of hope.

Bibliography

Berry, G., & Aldrich, C.K. (2021). *Literacy for learning: A handbook for content area and disciplinary literacy practices for middle and high school teachers* (2nd ed.). Rowman and Littlefield.

Gojak, L.M., & Miles, R.H. (2015). *The Common Core mathematics companion: The standards decoded, Grades K-1*. Corwin.

Hall, S.L. (2018). *10 success factors for literacy intervention: Getting results with MTSS in elementary schools*. ASCD.

Hannigan, J.D., & Hannigan, J.E. (2020). *The MTSS start-up guide: Ensuring equity, access, and inclusivity for all students*. Corwin Press.

McIntosh, K., & Goodman, S. (2016). *Integrated multi-tiered systems of support: Blending RtI and PBIS*. Guilford Publications.

Muschla, J., Muschla, G., & Muschla-Berry, E. (2014). *Teaching the Common Core math standards with hands-on activities: Grades 3–5*. Jossey-Bass.

Novak, K., & Rodriguez, K. (2013). *In support of students: A leader's guide to equitable MTSS*. Jossey-Bass.

Spear-Swerling, L. (2014). *The power of RtI and reading profiles: A blueprint for solving reading problems*. Brookes Publishing.

Tucker, C.R. (2015). *Creatively teach the Common Core literacy standards with technology: Grades 6–12*. Corwin.

University of Illinois College of Agriculture, Consumer, and Environmental Sciences (2017). *We all like new things: Pigs share same *desires*. National Hog Farmer, n.p. Retrieved at https://www.nationalhogfarmer.com/hog-welfare/we-all-like-new-things-pigs-share-same-desires

University of Minnesota Extension (2025). Feeding total mixed rations. Retrieved from https://extension.umn.edu/dairy-milking-cows/feeding-total-mixed-rations

2
Introduction to the Integration of Sophisticated Standards and Response to Intervention (RtI)/Multi-Tiered Systems of Support (MTSS)

The Common Core State Standards (CCSS)—developed by the National Governors Association Center for Best Practices (NGACBP) and Council of Chief State School Officers (CCSSO) and in conjunction with Achieve, Inc.—were adopted and implemented by 46 states and the District of Columbia between 2010 and 2013. Even among those states that never adopted the CCSS, state alternatives were not radically different. For example, Alaska's objective was to develop standards that were similar enough that they could purchase and implement CCSS-based instructional materials (ADEED, n.d.). At the current time, the CCSS remain in place in 36 states and D.C. In recent years, several states have revised and/or renamed these standards, but most changes have been relatively minor (Korn et al., 2016; O'Day & Smith, 2019). Arizona, for example, changed the name of its standards to Arizona College and Career Readiness Standards in 2014 and "replaced" them in 2016, but the most significant revision was the addition of cursive writing (Hinton, 2016). Despite former Secretary of Education Betsy DeVos's comment that "at the U.S. Department of Education, Common Core is dead" (Tampio, 2018), these standards and their close cousins continue to drive instruction nationwide, so they are the point of reference for this text.

Response to intervention (RtI) is a protocol for providing strong core instruction for all students (Tier 1), additional support for the 10%–20% of students who need it (Tier 2), and more intensive and individualized support for a small number of students (about 5%) who still do not succeed (Tier 3) (Brown & Doolittle, 2008). This framework first emerged on the educational scene with the 2004 re-authorization of the Individuals with Disabilities Education Act (IDEA) (O'Day & Smith, 2019). RtI also offered an alternative to the ability/achievement discrepancy formula process for enrollment in special education; if a student continued to struggle after receiving Tier 3 support, they might automatically qualify for special education services without further testing.

As educators came to understand that behavioral, social, and emotional supports played a significant role in educational achievement, the term multi-tiered systems of support (MTSS) assumed priority in the educational conversation, with RtI seen as the academic subset of MTSS (Pullen et al., 2018). This book does not discuss behavioral programs such as Positive Behavioral Interventions and Supports (PBIS), nor does it reference counseling within the school context and other social and emotional supports. Nevertheless, I have chosen to employ the term MTSS throughout the book—except when citing authors who use the term RtI—because I wish to acknowledge the importance of aspects of school that are not specifically academic and because it is now the more commonly referenced term (Brown-Chidsey & Bickford, 2016; Hall, 2018). Because it reflects the focus of this book and references the CCSS, I have adopted California's definition of MTSS: "an integrated, comprehensive framework that focuses on CCSS, core instruction, differentiated learning, student-centered learning, individualized student needs, and the alignment of systems necessary for all students' academic, behavioral, and social success" (California Department of Education, 2025).

The California Department of Education website provides a list of ways in which RtI and MTSS are similar, all of which are also applicable to this text:

- "Supporting high-quality standards and research-based, culturally and linguistically relevant instruction with the belief that every student can learn including students of poverty, students with disabilities, English learners, and students from all ethnicities evident in the school and district cultures.
- Integrating a data collection and assessment system, including universal screening, diagnostics and progress monitoring, to inform decisions appropriate for each tier of service delivery.
- Relying on a problem-solving systems process and method to identify problems, develop interventions and evaluate the effectiveness of the intervention in a multi-tiered system of service delivery.
- Seeking and implementing appropriate research-based interventions for improving student learning.
- Implementing a collaborative approach to analyze student data and working together in the intervention process" (California Department of Education, 2025).

The website goes on to describe ways in which MTSS differs from RtI, also applicable here:

- "Focusing on aligning the entire system of initiatives, supports, and resources.
- Promoting district participation in identifying and supporting systems for alignment of resources, as well as site and grade level.
- Systematically addressing support for all students, including gifted and high achievers.
- Enabling a paradigm shift for providing support and setting higher expectations for all students through intentional design and redesign of integrated services and

supports, rather than selecting a few components of RtI and intensive interventions.
- Endorsing Universal Design for Learning instructional strategies so all students have opportunities for learning through differentiated content, processes, and product.
- Integrating instructional and intervention support so that systemic changes are sustainable and based on CCSS-aligned classroom instruction.
- Challenging all school staff to change the way in which they have traditionally worked across all school settings" (California Department of Education, 2025).

The CCSS and MTSS have much to offer for teachers and students in contemporary classrooms. They have the potential to increase achievement, as well as serving the socio-emotional needs of children.

Lack of Clear Success in These Two Initiatives and Potential Reasons

Despite their many strengths, there is no clear evidence that either of these ambitious and heavily promoted educational initiatives has been wholly successful. Polikoff (2017) reported that no current analysis "provides convincing causal evidence of the impact of the CCS on any student outcome" (p. 2). Considering his finding that 41 states did not fully implement the CCSS until the 2013–2014 or 2014–2015 school year, data collected in 2013 and 2019 offer a useful comparison. During this period, the average 4th-grade reading score on the National Assessment of Educational Progress (NAEP) dropped from 222 to 220 and the average 8th-grade reading score dropped from 268 to 263. In addition, the achievement gap between whites and students of color did not diminish and the spread of achievement widened (Loveless, 2021).

The impact of RtI (now MTSS) implementation is also questionable. On the positive side, in a meta-analytic review of RtI research published before the 2004 iteration of the IDEA,

Burns et al. (2005) found that RtI implementations seemed to produce stronger student outcomes than previous approaches, with fewer students identified as having a learning disability. In a single-site study, VanDerHeyden et al. (2007) determined that, when RtI data were included in the referral process, fewer evaluations were conducted and, of those assessed, a higher percentage qualified. There were, however, no significant gains in reading scores on the NAEP between 2005 and 2019, and the only large-scale experimental study of RtI implementation (Balu et al., 2015) failed to demonstrate any positive impacts.[1] Teachers are motivated to implement approaches that lead to gains in student achievement (Shingles et al., 2024) and that motivation may wane if improvement is not evident.

What accounts for these distressing results? Lack of commitment on the part of teachers does not seem to be the answer. Kane et al. (2016) found that 85% of teachers polled assessed their knowledge of the CCSS as good or excellent and most claimed to employ teaching practices in line with the standards, ranging from 49% emphasizing intertextuality to 88% requiring students to provide evidence for their assertions (Opfer et al., 2017). Most teachers surveyed by Barrett-Tatum and Smith (2018) supported the CCSS, with 87% viewing the English language arts (ELA) standards as good or better than earlier standards. Teachers also believe they have at least a basic understanding of the way RtI works (Al Otaiba et al., 2019), and many classroom teachers (Bester & Conway, 2021; Nichols et al., 2017) and special educators (Werts et al., 2014) view the protocol as beneficial.

Researchers offer other reasons for these initiatives' lack of success. With respect to the CCSS, it appears the standards have been poorly implemented (Lee & Wu, 2017; Polikoff & Dean, 2021). Loveless (2021) addressed CCSS implementation and his statement is relevant for RtI as well: he claimed that large-scale educational projects are affected by the challenges of "navigating multilayered systems of governance" (p. 3) in which individuals and agencies—inside and outside government—have "the power to disrupt a policy's implementation" (p. 4).

In terms of student support systems, the complexity of the MTSS process can be overwhelming (Nichols et al., 2017;

Werts et al., 2014), especially if school leadership lacks vision, fails to provide necessary resources, and communicates ineffectively (Morse, 2024). Mechanisms sometimes focus more on checking off the correct boxes than on improving instruction (Reyes, 2017) and districts that depend on state funding "may prioritize compliance with regulation over pursuing innovative MTSS policies" (Lee & Dunham, 2025). Additionally, more culturally relevant approaches to the MTSS process are needed (Gomez-Najarro, 2019).

Isolated Initiatives as a Root Cause of Failure

Without minimizing the factors described above, I argue here that a major cause of this problematic outcome is the failure to integrate the MTSS framework with the CCSS by developing and implementing strong, standards-based curricular materials for Tiers 1, 2, and 3. In 2017, a colleague and I found that there was very little effort in the CCSS literature to offer a clear path for readers who struggle as they work toward mastery of complex standards. Similarly, there was little attention in the MTSS literature to focusing on sophisticated ELA standards within a framework of supports (Jaeger & Pearson, 2017). Brown-Chidsey and Bickford (2016) suggested that there have been efforts to align the two initiatives but provide no examples.

A review of these literatures in the ensuing eight years demonstrated little change in this regard (e.g., Bleiberg, 2021; Neitzel et al., 2022): this despite the fact that in a survey of teachers and administrators about CCSS barriers, 71% of teachers specified the wide range of student abilities as their top challenge (Center on Standards, Alignment, and Instruction, 2019) and, in a three-state study, Polikoff et al. (2020) found that 70% of teachers said their evaluations were based in part on the extent to which they modified instruction for low-achieving students. Blackburn and Witzel (2018) noted that, as lessons become more challenging, differential scaffolding is necessary; yet neither the CCSS guidelines (Haager & Vaughn, 2013) nor state websites (Hodge et al., 2020) reference substantive advice on scaffolding.

The Role of Weak Curriculum Materials

Standards—what should be taught—are the foundation for instruction. Curriculum—documents that describe how to teach those standards—traces the path to achievement. Even if standards are of high quality, instruction will not be effective if the curriculum is weak. And since many districts purchase ELA textbooks, these texts should align with standards and curriculum documents as well. There are issues with ELA textbooks at all tiers referenced in MTSS.

Tier 1 Issues

In general, elementary classroom ELA textbooks (i.e., texts used at Tier 1) are problematic. Pak and colleagues (2020) found that claims by textbook companies of alignment to CCSS appear to be overstated. Only 44% of the published K-5 ELA texts are aligned with standards (EdReports, 2024). So, a large majority of teachers feel they need to alter the curriculum materials they use (Kane et al., 2016) to increase engagement, align better with the standards, improve cultural relevance, adjust difficulty, and improve usability (Polikoff, 2021). Opfer et al. (2017) found that virtually all elementary ELA teachers surveyed turned to online materials to supplement these texts. Polikoff and Dean (2019) could find no review of online materials developed for CCSS use but, alarmingly, their assessment of high school ELA materials led them to assert that two-thirds of these texts should never be used. As Loveless (2021) claimed: "Common Core is a set of standards, not a curriculum. Others develop curriculum materials. Some will be good and some will be bad. And some of the bad materials might be very bad" (p. 105). As a result, 65% of teachers employ standards-aligned materials once per week or less (EdReports, 2024).

I have too often witnessed a disconnect between content standards and curriculum textbooks, with the instructional *how* mismatched with the instructional *what*. Texts do not always complement standards documents, and, when forced to choose, teachers tend to select texts over standards because beginning with standards instead places an undue burden on their time. Sometimes a district curriculum map has been carefully developed directly from the state standards and the two correspond nicely. But then there is the question of purchasing a program that may or may not jive with standards and curriculum.

Detailed recommendations about developing curriculum maps are beyond the scope of this text; there are other authors who cover this topic well (e.g., Great Minds, 2011; Heflebower et al., 2021). I will assume that a school or district employing this book has at least a basic curriculum map in place; that is, they have decided which standards are to be emphasized at which grade levels, which standards are best taught on their own (Chapters 4–6 cover this) and which might be integrated (the topic of Chapter 7), and a general order of instruction. I will also assume that the school or district has a relatively engaging anthology of readings such as a basal text and/or multiple copies of trade books appropriate for each grade level (i.e., picture books, easy readers, short stories/novels, and information texts), and a range of single copy trade books that would likely be found in school or classroom libraries.

With these "givens," I make the argument that, rather than worry about whether a basal claims to be standards-based or worry that trade books do not explicitly address standards at all, school and district educators are fully capable of developing literacy curriculum that carefully attends to standards. I also argue that they can do so in less time than it would require to take a mediocre or even average program and wrangle it into rich instruction.

Tier 2 Issues

With regard to curriculum employed to support students who struggle, I examined all peer-reviewed intervention studies focused on reading in English at the elementary level published between 2019 and 2025 ($n = 9$). Of these studies, only two described the intervention in enough detail that it could be replicated in another context. None of the manuscripts provided any indication that the intervention(s) described focused on higher-level thinking such as that demanded by the CCSS. Just six MTSS and MTSS-like studies published between 1989 and

2025 included measures of higher-level thinking, with only one referencing the CCSS.

Tier 2 instruction plays a vital role in supporting readers who struggle, but there are concerns about these interventions as commonly implemented. Because the CCSS emphasize integration of the ELA with content area curriculum, it is crucial for readers who struggle to miss as little classroom instruction as possible (Kramer et al., 2021). Yet, students receiving Tier 2 services often work with a pull-out teacher on a daily basis, missing as much as 130 hours of regular class time over the course of a year (Vaughn et al., 2010). This despite the fact that Wanzek and colleagues have demonstrated that effect sizes for Tier 2 interventions of greater than 100 sessions had weaker mean effect sizes (0.28) than do those of fewer than 100 sessions (0.54 for foundational reading skills and 0.36 for language and comprehension) (Wanzek et al., 2016; Wanzek et al., 2018).

In addition, many Tier 2 interventions offer the same instruction for all students who qualify for assistance, either by providing a combination of approaches including decoding, fluency, vocabulary, and comprehension (Wanzek & Vaughn, 2008) or by teaching only one specific aspect of reading (Faggella-Luby & Wardwell, 2011) which may be mismatched to individual student need. Research suggests, however, that not all readers who struggle do so for the same reasons. Buly and Valencia (2002) studied 4th-grade students who failed the state standardized test, assessing each reader using measures of word identification, fluency, and comprehension. They found that only 9% of students demonstrated difficulties in all three areas. The remaining children exhibited strengths in at least one major aspect of reading. Their research served as the theoretical foundation for the Tier 2 recommendations I make in this text.

Tier 3 Issues

We know quite a bit about one-on-one tutoring. In a recent review study, Nickow et al. (2024) found that "tutoring interventions rank among the most widespread, versatile, and potentially transformative instruments in today's educational toolkit" (p. 75). They found an estimated pooled effect size of 0.288

with stronger scores for those studies that employed teachers and paraprofessionals rather than volunteers, that focused on the earlier elementary grades, that took place within the school day, and that occurred at least three times per week. Dietrichson et al. (2017) found an even greater mean effect size of 0.36 for tutoring (as compared with that of small group instruction at 0.24). Shanahan (1998) attributes the effectiveness of tutoring to more intense student involvement, the ability of tutors to individualize by connecting to the student's prior knowledge and academic needs, appropriate pacing, immediate and relevant feedback, and a personal connection between tutor and child. In terms of tutoring session content, Morris et al. (1990) emphasized the importance of employing interesting texts with natural language, individualized word study, writing with invented spelling allowed in drafts to be revised later, and reading aloud to the child. Juel (1996) focused on scaffolded reading and writing experiences that occurred with the child's Zone of Proximal Development and cognitive modeling of reading processes.

The primary issue associated with Tier 3 instruction is that there is so little research at all; we know very little about how Tier 3 intervention emerges logically, effectively, and efficiently from Tier 2 and Tier 1 instruction. Gersten et al. (2020) frequently reference MTSS, but their descriptions of Tier 2 and Tier 3 interventions are, in fact, simply small group instruction and one-on-one tutoring; their manuscript provided no clear indication that these interventions were situated within an MTSS framework, much less that the tutoring approach and content emerged from that found in the small group and/or the large group instruction that preceded it. Austin et al. (2017) examined studies in which Tier 3 interventions were, in fact, part of a Tier 1 through Tier 3 continuum and found that "Tier 3 interventions can help inadequate responders [at Tier 2] make statistically significant gains in reading" (p. 207). Unfortunately, what counted as Tier 2 and Tier 3 approaches in their review was defined by which came first in time rather than the size of the group—this despite clear indications that one-on-one tutoring produces stronger results with mean effect sizes of 0.59 as compared to 0.33 for small groups (Wanzek et al., 2018). In addition, all the instructional protocols at both tiers incorporated multiple components, with each including a focus on phonics and most including attention to fluency and comprehension; only three of the 12 studies attended more fully to specific student needs.

"Tier 0" Issues

While there are most certainly issues related to classroom instruction and intervention for readers and writers who struggle, we know next-to-nothing about how to meet the needs of children who have mastered sophisticated literacy standards prior to classroom instruction. I could find exactly zero peer-reviewed articles in my university's database addressing the needs of advanced readers in the CCSS context and only nine speaking about gifted students and CCSS. Of these, seven were less than three pages in length and none were reports of research. The available articles argue that the CCSS are well-aligned with the National Association for Gifted Children (NAGC) standards but that a more advanced developmental scope and sequence is needed (VanTassel-Baska, 2012) and that both tasks and products need to be differentiated. There are also texts written to assist teachers in meeting the needs of gifted students (e.g., Hughes et al., 2013; Kasten, 2016).

In addition, the students whom I identify as Tier 0 earn that status not because they have been defined with a label such as "gifted" but because they have demonstrated mastery of a given standard. For one standard, this may be a gifted and talented designee, for another a child enrolled in special education. Carol Ann Tomlinson (2013, 2014), a strong advocate of differentiation, recommends the use of pre-assessments to determine which children have already mastered content, but her work does not appear in the CCSS research literature. While referencing gifted students rather than those I refer to as Tier 0, VanTassel-Baska (2012) supports the idea of pre-assessment, especially performance-based and portfolio approaches. Johnsen (2012) notes that the NAGC recommends the following approaches, which also seem applicable to Tier 0 learners:

1. Provide pathways to accelerate the CCSS for gifted learners. For example, cluster and compress discrete skills across grade levels and incorporate higher-level skills and concepts.
2. Provide examples of differentiated task demands to address specific standards.
3. Create interdisciplinary product demands to elevate the learning for the gifted and to efficiently address multiple standards at once (p. 81).

I argue here that the lack of clear success in approaches to the teaching of sophisticated standards and structuring supports for those children who need it has two primary causes. First, that they are viewed as two separate endeavors, and second, that curriculum developed for each of the MTSS tiers is not as strong as it might be. This chapter provides a picture of what a strong and integrated curriculum and instruction might look like.

Note

1   It is important to note that there have been important methodological critiques of this study (Fuchs & Fuchs, 2017; Gersten et al., 2017).

Bibliography

Al Otaiba, S., Baker, K., Lan, P., Allor, J., Rivas, B., Yovanoff, P., & Kamata, A. (2019). Elementary teacher's knowledge of Response to Intervention implementation: A preliminary factor analysis. *Annals of Dyslexia, 69*, 34–53. doi: 10.1007/s11881-018-00171-5

Alaska Department of Education and Early Development (n.d.). Alaska Reading/Language Arts Standards Retrieved from https://education.alaska.gov/standards

Austin, C.R., Vaughn, S., & McClelland, A.M. (2017). Intensive reading inventions for inadequate responders in grades K-3: A synthesis. *Learning Disability Quarterly, 40* (4), 191–210. doi: 10.1177/0731948717714446

Balu, R., Zhu, P., Doolittle, F., Schiller, E., Jenkins, J., & Gersten, R. (2015). *Evaluation of Response to Intervention practices for elementary school reading.* U.S. Department of Education.

Barrett-Tatum, J. & Smith, J.M. (2018). Questioning reform in the standards movement: Professional development and implementation of Common Core across the rural South. *Teachers and Teaching: Theory and Practice, 24* (4), 384–412. doi: 10.1080/13540602.2017.1401534

Bester, S., & Conway, M. (2021). Foundation phase teachers' points of view on the viability of Response to Intervention in their school context. *South African Journal of Education, 41* (1), 1–12. doi: 10.15700/saje.v41n1a2058

Blackburn, B.R., & Witzel, B.S. (2018). *Rigor in the RtI and MTSS classroom: Practical tools and strategies.* Routledge.

Bleiberg, J. (2021). Does the Common Core have a common effect? An exploration of effects on academically vulnerable students. *AERA Open, 7* (1), 1–18. doi: 10.1177/23328584211010727

Brown, J. E., & Doolittle, J. (2008). A cultural, linguistic, and ecological framework for Response to Intervention with English language learners. *Teaching Exceptional Children, 40* (5), 66–72. doi: 10.1177/004005990804000509

Brown-Chidsey, R., & Bickford, R. (2016). *Practical handbook of multi-tiered systems of support: Building academic and behavioral success.* Guilford Press.

Buly, M.R., & Valencia, .S.W. (2002). Below the bar: Profiles of students who fail state reading assessments. *Education Evaluation and Policy Analysis, 24* (3), 219–239. doi: 10.3102/01623737024003219

Burns, M.K., Appleton, J.J., & Stehouwer, J.D. (2005). Meta-analytic review of responsiveness-to-intervention research: Examining field-based and researcher-implemented models. *Journal of Psychoeducational Assessment, 23,* 381–394. doi: 10.1177/073428290502300406

California Department of Education (2025). Definition of MTSS. Retrieved from cde.ca.gov/ci/cr/ri/mtsscomprti2.asp.

Center on Standards, Alignment, Instruction, and Learning (2019, April). *Common challenges to implementing college-and-career-readiness standards.* Author.

Dietrichson, J. Bog, M., Filges, T., & Jorgensen, M.-M.K. (2017). Academic interventions for elementary and middle schools with low socioeconomic status: A systematic review and meta-analysis. *Review of Educational Research, 87* (2), 343–382. doi: 10.3102/00346543166687036

EdReports (2024). *State of the instructional materials market: 2023.* Retrieved from https://www.edreports.org/resources/article/state-of-the-instructional-materials-market-2023

Faggella-Luby, M., & Wardwell, M. (2011). RtI in a middle school: Findings and practical implications of a Tier 2 reading comprehension study. *Learning Disability Quarterly, 34* (1), 35–49. doi: 10.1177/073194871103400103

Fuchs, D., & Fuchs, L.S. (2017). Critique of the national evaluation of response to intervention: A case for simpler frameworks. *Exceptional Children, 83* (3), 255–268. doi: 10.1177/0014402917693580

Gersten, R., Haymond, K., Newman-Gonchar, R., Dimino, J., & Jayanthi, M. (2020). Meat-analysis of the impact of reading interventions for students in the primary grades. *Journal of Research on Educational Effectiveness, 13* (2), 401–427. doi: 10.1080/19345747.2019.1689591

Gersten, R., Jayanthi, M., & Dimino, J. (2017). Too much, too soon? Unanswered questions from National Response to Intervention Evaluation. *Exceptional Children, 83* (3), 244–254. doi: 10.1177/0014402917692847

Gomez-Najarro, J. (2023–2024). Identity-blind intervention: Examining teachers' attention to social identity in the context of response to intervention. *Urban Education, 58* (4), 645–674. doi: 10.1177/0042085919860561

Great Minds (2011). *Common Core curriculum maps in English Language Arts, Grades K-5*. Jossey-Bass.

Haager, D., & Vaughn, S. (2013). The Common Core State Standards and reading: Interpretations and implications for elementary students with learning disabilities. *Learning Disabilities Research and Practice, 28* (1), 5–16. doi: 10.1111/ldrp.12000

Hall, S.L. (2018). *10 success factors for literacy intervention: Getting results with MTSS in elementary schools.* ASCD.

Heflebower, T., Hoegh, J.K., & Warrich, P.B. (2012). *Leading standards-based learning: An implementation guide for schools and districts.* Marzano Resources.

Hinton, M. (2016, December 28). Arizona state school board votes to replace Common Core. Retrieved from https://www.edweek.org/

teaching-learning/arizona-state-school-board-votes-to-replace-common-core/2016/12

Hodge, E.M., Benko, S.L., & Salloum, S.J. (2020). Tracing states' messages about Common Core instruction: An analysis of English/language arts and close reading resources. *Teachers College Record, 122*, 1–42. doi: 10.1177/016146812012200303 language learners. *Language Arts, 81* (1), 52–61.

Hughes, C.E., Kettler, T., Shaunessy-Dedrick, E., & VanTassel-Baska, J. (2013). *A teacher's guide to using the Common Core State Standards with gifted and advanced learners in the English/language arts.* Prufrock Press.

Jaeger, E.L., & Pearson, P.D. (2017). The integration of Common Core and response to intervention: Supporting vulnerable readers in a time of sophisticated standards. *The Educational Forum, 81*, 81–92. doi: 10.1080/00131725.2016.1242676

Johnsen, S.K. (2012). Gifted education and the Common Core State Standards. *Gifted Child Today, 35* (4), 229–230. doi: 10.1177/1076217512456364

Juel, C. (1996). What makes literacy tutoring effective? *Reading Research Quarterly, 31* (3), 268–289. doi: 10.1598/RRQ.31.3.3

Kane, T.J., Owens, A.M., Marinell, W.H., Thal, D.R.C., & Staiger, D.O. (2016). *Teaching higher: Educators' perspectives on Common Core implementation.* Center for Education Policy Research.

Kasten, L. (2016). *Challenging Common Core language arts lessons: Grade 4.* Routledge.

Korn, S., Gamboa, M., & Polikoff, M. (2016). *Just how common are the standards in Common Core states?* The Center on Standards, Alignment, Instruction, and Learning.

Kramer, S.V., Sonju, B., Mattos, M., & Buffum, A. (2021). *Best practices at Tier 2: Supplemental interventions for additional Student support: Elementary.* Solution Tree Press.

Lee, J., & Dunham, H.R. (16 January, 2025). Multiple-shaded or all alike? Local responses to the multi-tiered systems of support implementation in Florida. *Leadership and Policy in Schools.* doi: 10.1080/15700763.2025.2453853

Lee, J., & Wu, Y. (2017). Is the Common Core racing America to the top? Tracking change in state standards, school practices, and student achievement. *Education Policy and Analysis Archives, 25* (35), 1–23. doi: 10.14507/epaa.25.2834

Loveless, T. (2021). *Between the state and the schoolhouse: Understanding the failure of Common Core.* Harvard Education Press.

Morris, D., Shaw, B., & Perney, J. (1990). Helping low readers in grades 2 and 3: An after-school volunteer tutoring program. *Elementary School Journal, 91* (2), 132–150. doi: 10.1086/461642

Morse, T.E. (2024). Revisiting the multi-tiered system of supports framework: An important mechanism for realizing equitable education in urban schools. *Education and Urban Society, 56* (9), 1051–1064. doi: 10.1177/00131245241262013

National Governors Association Center for Best Practices and Council of State School Officers (2010, June). *Common Core State Standards for English language arts and literacy in history/social studies, science, and technical subjects.* Author. Retrieved from corestandards.org/ELA-Literacy/

Neitzel, A.J., Lake, C., Pellegrini, M., & Slavin, R.E. (2022). A synthesis of quantitative research on programs for struggling readers in elementary schools. *Reading Research Quarterly, 57* (1), 149–179. doi: 10.1002/rrq.379

Nichols, S.L., Castro-Villarreal, F., & Ramirez, A. (2017). Response to intervention: Instructional challenges for teachers in high-needs contexts. *Teachers College Record, 119* (9), 1–30. doi: 10.1177/016146811711900906

Nickow, A., Oreopoulos, P., & Quan, V. (2024). The promise of tutoring for PreK-12 learning: A systematic review and meta-analysis of the experimental evidence. *American Educational Research Journal, 61* (1), 74–107. doi: 10.3102/00028312231208687

O'Day, J.A., & Smith, M.S. (2019). *Opportunity for all: A framework for quality and equity in education.* Harvard Education Press.

Opfer, V.D., Kaufman, J.H., & Thompson, L.E. (2017). *K-12 state standards for mathematics and English language arts: Findings from the American Teacher Panel.* The RAND Corporation.

Pak, K., Polikoff, M.S., Desimone, L.M., & Garcia, E.S. (2020). The adaptive challenges of curriculum implementation: Insights for educational leaders driving standards-based reform. *AERA Open, 6* (2), 1–15. doi: 10.1177/233285420932828

Polikoff, M.S. (2017). Is Common Core "working"? And where does Common Core research go from here? *AERA Open, 3* (1), 1–6. doi: 10.1177/2332858417691749

Polikoff, M. (2021). *Beyond standards: The fragmentation of education governance and the promise of curriculum reform.* Harvard Education Press.

Polikoff, M., & Dean, J. (2019). *The supplemental curriculum bazaar: Is what's online any good?* Thomas B. Fordham Institute.

Polikoff, M., Wang, E.L., Haderlein, S.K., Kaufman, J.H, Woo, A., Silver, D., & Opfer, V.D. (2020). *Exploring coherence in English language arts instructional systems in the Common Core era.* The RAND Corporation.

Pullen, P.C., van Dijk, W., Gonsalves, V.E., Lane, H.B., & Ashworth, K.E. (2018). Response to Intervention and Multi-tiered Systems of Support: How do they differ and how are they the same, if at all? In P.C. Pullen & M.J. Kennedy (Eds.), *Handbook of response to intervention and multi-tiered systems of support* (pp. 5–10). Routledge.

Reyes, J. (2017). RTI: Response to intervention or rush to identify. In T. Torres & C.R. Barber (Eds.), *Case studies in special education: A social justice perspective* (pp. 153–171). Charles C. Thomas.

Shanahan, T. (1998). On the effectiveness and limitations of tutoring in reading. *Review of Research in Education, 23,* 217–234. doi: 10.2307/1167291

Shingles, B., Sinclair, C., Weadman, T., Poed, S., Snow, P., Eadie, T., Connelle, J., Goldfeld, S., & Quack, J. (2024). An implementation case study for the Response to Intervention (RtI) approach for oral language and reading instruction in the early years of primary school. *Australian Journal of Learning Difficulties, 29* (1), 97–115. doi: 10.1080/19404158.2024.2335892

Tampio, N (2018, March 26). Betsy Devos said Common Core was "dead"—it's not. Retrieved at https://theconversation.com/betsy-devos-said-common-core-was-dead-its-not-92800

Tomlinson, C.A. (2013). *Assessment and student success in a differentiated classroom.* Association for Supervision and Curriculum Development.

Tomlinson, C.A. (2014). *The differentiated classroom: Responding to the needs of all learners.* Association for Supervision and Curriculum Development.

VanDerHeyden, A.M., Witt, J.C., & Gilbertson, D. (2007). A multi-year evaluation of the effects of a Response to Intervention (RTI) model on identification of children for special education. *Journal of School Psychology, 45*, 235–256. doi: 10.1016/j.jsp.2006.11.004

VanTassel-Baska, J. (2012). A case for Common Core State Standards: Gifted curricula 3.0. *Gifted Child Today, 35* (3), 222–223. doi: 10.1177/1076217512445990

Vaughn, S., Cirino, P.T., Wanzek, J., Wexler, T., Fletcher, J.M., Denton, C.D.,... Francis, D. (2010). Response to intervention for middle school students with reading difficulties: Effects of primary and secondary interventions. *School Psychology Review, 39* (1), 3–21. doi: 10.1080/02796015.2010.12087786

Wanzek, J., Stevens, E.A., Williams, K.J., Scammacca, N., Vaughn, S., & Sargent, K. (2018). Current evidence of the effects of intensive early reading interventions. *Journal of Learning Disabilities, 51* (6), 612–624. doi: 10.1177/0022219418775110

Wanzek, J., & Vaughn, S. (2008). Response to varying amounts in reading intervention for students with low response to intervention. *Journal of Learning Disabilities, 41* (2), 126–142. doi: 10.1177/0022219407313426

Wanzek, J., Vaughn, S., Scammacca, N., Gatlin, B., Walker, M.A., & Caplin, P. (2016). Meta-analyses of the effects of Tier 2 type reading interventions in grades K-3. *Educational Psychology Review, 28*, 551–576. doi: 10.1007/s10648-015-9321-7

Werts, M.G., Carpenter, E.S., & Fewell, C. (2014). Barriers and benefits to response to intervention: Perceptions of special education teachers. *Rural Special Education Quarterly, 33* (2), 3–11. doi: 10.1177/875687051403300202

3

Research Base for Strong Curriculum that Integrates Standards-Based Curriculum and MTSS

Chapter 1 presented two primary problems with the teaching of sophisticated standards in ways that meet the needs of all students. First, efforts to teach to these standards, and to research implementation, are typically viewed as separate from efforts to meet the needs of students for whom differentiation is required (via multi-tiered systems of support [MTSS]) and to research related to this differentiation. Second, curriculum and texts developed for both standards instruction and MTSS support across tiers are not as strong as we might hope. To produce successful outcomes for all students, we need to integrate high-level standards, rich curriculum materials, and effective instructional supports. In Chapter 2, I examine the research base that serves as the foundation for a strong, standards-based curriculum at each tier. Whether in core texts, online lessons, or teacher-developed units, it is rare to find a clear and transparent presentation of the research base behind those curriculum materials. An educator may wonder about the reasoning behind, for example, text choices, instructional moves, and grouping decisions, but

DOI: 10.4324/9781003528234-3

be unable to find the rationale behind those choices. In this next section, I have indicated the research support behind the curriculum that follows in Chapters 3–6.

Tier 1 Curriculum

Because student participants in research that examines classroom instruction span the range of achievement levels, research about teaching and learning, and related practices—especially as they apply to readers who struggle—should serve as the foundation for the curriculum. These mediational tools include:

- Focus on ensuring a positive and collaborative instructional environment (Graham et al., 2015): Positive classroom environments support student engagement and achievement (Reyes et al., 2012). There is little evidence that adding a component of competition is facilitative (Chen & Chiu, 2016 offered the single contrast).
- Adopt a gradual release of responsibility instructional design (Pearson & Gallagher, 1983): During activities early in the unit, the teacher is responsible for most of the "work"; students assume more responsibility as the unit progresses, culminating with independent assignments and/or tests.
- Read authentic texts (McEneaney, Lose, & Schwartz, 2006): The curriculum should employ appropriately leveled high-quality picture books and other whole texts. Most texts would be at students' instructional or independent levels, but those read during shared reading should be more challenging, as recommended by the Common Core State Standards (CCSS; Fisher & Frey, 2014). Many of the reading materials should be selected by students to increase engagement (Graham et al., 2015; Kern, 2014).
- Integrate reading and writing (Frankel, Jaeger, & Pearson, 2013): Students need to learn the various skills and strategies involved in reading and writing as separate

subjects, but they also need to experience the integration of the two subjects by including both reading and writing across a given unit.

- Integrate literacy and content area instruction, when possible (Burke & Kennedy, 2024; Shifflet & Hunt, 2019): Doing so supports learning in content areas, such as science (Senn et al., 2013), and also promotes literacy (Bricker et al., 2010).
- Include comprehensive strategies as a key part of the instructional design (Barrett-Tatum & Dooley, 2015): Although a focus on reading and writing strategies is not part of the CCSS, such strategies assist readers at all levels in developing effective and efficient approaches to text.
- Incorporate student-to-student as well as student-to-teacher interaction (Beecher, 2010/2011): Of the conversation that occurs within classrooms, teachers predominate; in fact, they talk, on average, 70%–80% of the time (Hattie, 2012). As a result, students have very little time to process what they are learning with peers—the very people who are most likely to be able to explain information in ways that may help a student who did not grasp it when delivered by an adult. It is helpful for students to regularly talk with partners prior to sharing out to the whole group and to participate in small group discussions structured by questions they composed themselves. These activities are reflected in the language sub-area of the English language arts (ELA) CCSS.
- Employ systematic assessment (Greenstein, 2013): This includes both formative (Calfee et al., 2014; McLaughlin & Overturf, 2012) and student self-assessment (Graham et al., 2015). These assessments typically focus on one anchor standard but may integrate several specific standards as frequently recommended in CCSS materials (Common Core, 2012).

ELA CCSS documents do not specify the order in which to address the standards, but one review of the CCSS (Pandya & Aukerman, 2014) recommended instruction reflecting Luke and Freebody's

(1999) comprehensive Four Resources Model of literacy practice. This model includes the following roles: code breaker, meaning maker, text user, and text analyst. These roles are, in fact, groups of related literacy tools. Working within and across these roles, readers learn to decode text (including meaning-based strategies such as use of context clues), construct meanings from a combination of text and prior knowledge/experience, learn ways to employ texts for the reader's purposes, and view texts as ideological rather than neutral. Employing this structure emphasizes the process-focused (Mo et al., 2014) and critical/dialogical (Giouroukakis & Cohan, 2014; Grindon, 2014) character of CCSS work.

Tier 2 Curriculum

It is unlikely that all students will fully grasp a standards-based unit taught at the Tier 1 (classroom) level; evidence demonstrates that this may be true for about 15% of any given group of students (Brown & Doolittle, 2008). There may be a range of reasons for this. They may have missed some of the classroom lessons. They may struggle with attention in a large group. They may have misunderstood key vocabulary from the initial lesson and been stymied for the rest of the unit. Or the assessment employed may not be in a format with which they are comfortable. Most of these students will, however, be capable of mastering the standard if taught in a small group.

Curriculum for each Tier 2 unit should be based on the Tier 1 principles listed above and, as far as possible, on the following:

- Employ assessment-based grouping for instruction (Lipson et al., 2011): Teachers should include only students who need help with a particular standard, allowing others—even those who may struggle with other aspects of reading—to be in the classroom for as much instruction as possible.
- Focus on meaning-making (Stephens et al., 2012): Even when the focus of the class is on print-based skills such as decoding, it is important to emphasize text meaning.

- Enact whole-to-part instruction (Dombey & Moustafa, 1998): Intervention settings are often characterized by instruction in isolated skills. But this practice often interferes with the emphasis on understanding. It is crucial for children who struggle with reading to be constantly reminded that the particular skills they are learning overlap and interact with each other and that they are only important to the extent that they serve the ultimate goal of meaning-making.
- Tap personal experience and background knowledge (Smith et al., 2021): Helping students to access what they know and have experienced prior to reading is useful; this is especially true for readers who struggle. Practices like a KWL chart and its variations (Hershberger et al., 2006) and text feature walks (Kelley & Clausen-Grace, 2010) can be beneficial.
- Incorporate student strengths as well as challenges (Watts-Taffe et al., 2012): It is, of course, important to focus on students' challenges and this is, in fact, the organizing principle for the Tier 2 groupings described here. But even readers who struggle typically demonstrate reading strengths as well as weaknesses (Buly & Valencia, 2002). Including activities that draw on those strengths is important for student morale. For example, many readers who struggle with fluency are, nevertheless, competent comprehenders; a teacher read-aloud followed by discussion can serve both as a model for fluent reading and an opportunity for meaning-making.
- Read authentic texts (McEneaney et al., 2006), many of which are self-selected (Ivey & Johnston, 2013): This is important at Tier 1, but I repeat it here because so often decodable texts and those that repeat sight words are often selected in intervention settings. Readers who struggle may also express limited interest in reading, so it is especially important that they select the texts they read whenever possible.
- Include student self-evaluation and tangible evidence of success (Schunk, 2003): Students, particularly those who

struggle, get frequent evaluatory feedback from teachers. What they are rarely taught to do is to seek out evidence of their own progress—evidence that is tangible enough to make that progress clear (e.g., increased ratings on a reading fluency scale). Progress-monitoring assessments are useful; this is typically a brief pretest that establishes that a given student belongs in a particular class (e.g., percentage of oral reading miscues that make sense in context) and is then repeated at the end of class to monitor progress.

In terms of developing plans for Tier 2 classes, the following elements are typically present:

- Note the CCSS that is covered when appropriate (sometimes off-grade level).
- Send an enrollment letter to parent/guardian, typically including recommendations for home practice related to the topic of the class: This keeps families in the loop and offers a specific activity they can practice with their child during the course of the class and potentially beyond.
- Give an enrollment and goal-setting letter to the student: This letter clarifies for the student why they have been enrolled in the class and what they can expect to learn. There is also a place on this document to record the child's score on the pretest and to write in what goal the child has selected for the post-test.
- Develop a general daily plan: It will be easier for students to attend to class content if the general plan for each day is predictable.

The Tier 2 model proposed here differs from others in two major ways: the amount of time children spend out of the regular classroom and the content that characterizes the lessons they attend. The classes initially focus on off-level standards because enrolled students still struggle with these standards (Fuchs et al., 2015). For example, a multi-syllable decoding class for 4th graders addresses RF 3.3C: *Decode multi-syllable words*, and the main idea class addresses RI 3.2: *Determine the main idea of the text; recount the key details and explain how they support the main idea*. Only those

Tier 2 students who exhibit an assessed need in a particular area attend (Lipson et al., 2011). In addition to allowing students to participate more fully in core instruction, this practice keeps class size low and supports focused instruction in the Tier 2 groups. In the research I conducted, most students were enrolled in two or three classes over the course of the year and, as a result, missed somewhere between 9 and 18 hours of class time.

Each unit begins with a progress-monitoring pre-assessment related to unit content (Majeika et al., 2024). For example, for the multi-syllable decoding unit, the teacher counts the number of words correctly pronounced from the Names Test (Cunningham, 1990). Kramer et al. (2021) have noted the importance of student involvement in progress monitoring, so the results of the pre-assessments are shared with the students enrolled in the class and they set goals for improvement. At the end of the class, students are re-assessed using the progress-monitoring measure. In this way, instruction is focused on "a student's progress relative to his previous progress rather than a fixed, global academic achievement standard" (Morse, 2024).

There is a clear path toward more or less support, as needed. In addition to progress monitoring, Tier 2 students participate in Tier 1 unit testing and are also re-assessed using an Informal Reading Inventory (IRI) at mid-year. The teacher considers the results of all three assessments to decide what comes next. Generally speaking, if a child passes unit tests, improves on progress-monitoring assessments, and scores on or above grade level on the IRI, they receive only Tier 1 instruction moving forward. If IRI scores remain below grade level, they continue with Tier 2 support. And if they make little progress on two or more of these measures, they are referred for Tier 3 support. This assessment process forms the bridge among the tiers.

Tier 3 Curriculum

It is possible that, even after the experience of Tier 2 instruction, some students (about 5%) may not demonstrate mastery of the addressed standard (Brown & Doolittle, 2008). In this model, Tier 3 instruction begins with several exploratory sessions in which a range of materials are available to the child; they read and talk informally with the tutor about their interest in and prior knowledge about the texts they select. This is followed by a lengthy interview in which the tutor asks the child about their reading habits, the type of texts they like to read, and their reading history.

Again, Tier 3 sessions should reflect most Tier 1 and Tier 2 principles; in addition, these sessions should be characterized as follows:

- Emphasize individualized student choice to support engagement (Turner & Paris, 1995): It is likely that children who require support at the level of intensity of one-on-one tutoring have experienced considerable failure over the course of their school careers. As a result, it is important to offer them as much control over the interaction as possible: choices of what skills to work on, what texts to read from, etc.
- Teach explicitly (Rupley et al., 2009): Providing very explicit instructions about what to do and how to do it is generally beneficial.
- Model for the student (Fisher & Frey, 2015): Students who struggle with reading may have missed some of the aspects of reading that others seem to learn by osmosis. In this case, modeling by an adult (or competent peer) can be very effective. This is particularly true with respect to strategy instruction (Scharlach, 2008).
- Practice with the child, first using step-by-step directions from the teacher and then based on minimal hints from the teacher, reflecting the gradual release of responsibility model (Pearson & Gallagher, 1983). As the lesson progresses, the student enacts more of the reading process while the teacher observes.
- Encourage independent practice (Rosenshine, 2012): Once responsibility has fully shifted to the learner, they are capable of independently employing what they have learned. This is true in the area of reading comprehension (Marcell et al., 2010) as well as in more discrete tasks.

The tutor designs the upcoming lessons: typically two 45-minute sessions per week over six months or more. Each session has three parts: a self-select reading time of duration chosen by the child, instruction focused on an aspect of reading that the tutor and child agree is an area of need, and instruction on an area the child may not yet recognize as an area of challenge. For the latter two segments, the tutor and child set a goal that will determine when they will move on to another element of reading. The tutor is careful to provide a range of texts for self-select reading and chooses texts for the directed lessons based on the student's interests.

In addition, the tutor watches for any idiosyncrasies exhibited by the child. For example, one reader with whom I worked exhibited strong math skills. I found that if I could present a lesson with clear, written-out steps—much like a computational algorithm found in mathematics—the student more easily grasped reading strategies.

Children who continue to struggle even after receiving small group, targeted instruction are particularly vulnerable to school failure and personal discouragement. As a result, Tier 3 support must be individualized in ways that pick up on the nuances of the student's academic needs but also build a lasting and supportive relationship between the child and a knowledgeable and sensitive adult.

Tier 0

As teachers, we are often so concerned about students who struggle with our curriculum that we fail to remember that there are students within our classroom who may have fully mastered a given standard before we teach it. I want to be clear that I am not necessarily referring to formally designated gifted and talented students—although there may be considerable overlap in the two groups—but to students who, for whatever reason, have had the life experience which results in early mastery of a particular aspect of ELA. These students will vary from unit to unit: one child may have a firm grasp of character analysis but be mystified by the concept of story theme; for another child, it may be the reverse.

As noted in Chapter 1, the research base for work at what I've chosen to call Tier 0 is essentially nonexistent. We simply don't know what it means to provide appropriate opportunities for children who have already mastered content in a context of sophisticated language arts standards structured in an MTSS framework. And although "differentiation" was certainly a buzzword at the time the CCSS appeared on the educational scene, the research base for this practice is actually quite weak and what is available focuses on students who struggle (e.g., Tobin & McInnes, 2008; Walker-Dalhouse et al., 2009). As such, I turn to the work of Carol Ann Tomlinson whose research investigates the ways teachers implement differentiation in their classrooms (Santangelo & Tomlinson, 2012).

Tomlinson (2013) argues for the important role of assessment in differentiation, including pre-assessment. This assessment can be formal—a test, for example—or informal such as student self-assessment (e.g., "How many of you could explain to a partner what it means to figure out the themes of a story?") or one-on-one conversations or observations. In some cases, it makes sense to conduct this pre-assessment shortly after a unit begins—allowing students a quick exposure to content prior to being asked to demonstrate their competence.

I am a firm believer in using pre-assessments to determine which children do not need to sit through my instruction and might better use their time in other ways. This does not generally require a completely new assessment, but rather just using the post-assessment for this additional purpose. These pre-assessments are completely optional—no child is required to take them—and results may suggest that this child may skip a single lesson here and there or the entire unit. Suggestions for how Tier 0 students may spend their time are provided within the specific curriculum units in ensuing chapters. Tomlinson's books, including *Assessment and Student Success in a Differentiated Classroom* (2013) and *The Differentiated Classroom: Responding to the Needs of All Learners* (2014), provide further details.

Bibliography

Barrett-Tatum, J., & Smith, J.M. (2018). Questioning reform in the standards movement: Professional development and implementation of Common Core across the rural South. *Teachers and Teaching: Theory and Practice, 24* (4), 384–412. doi: 10.1080/13540602.2017.1401534

Beecher, C.C. (2010/2011). Response to intervention: A sociocultural perspective of the problems and possibilities. *Journal of Education, 191* (3), 1–8. doi: 10.1177/002205741119100302

Bricker, P., Rogowski, N., Hedt, M., & Rolfe, N. (2010, October). Transporting students into thin air: Using science to enhance reading. *Science Scope, 34* (2), 37–43.

Brown, J.E., & Doolittle, J. (2008). A cultural, linguistic, and ecological framework for response to intervention with English language learners. *Teaching Exceptional Children, 40*(5), 66–72. doi: 10.1177/004005990804000509

Buly, M.R., & Valencia, S.W. (2002). Below the bar: Profiles of students who fail state reading assessments. *Education Evaluation and Policy Analysis, 24* (3), 219–239. doi: 10.3102/01623737024003219

Burke, P., & Kennedy, E. (2024). "Why do you think that?" Exploring disciplinary literacy in elementary science, history, and visual arts. *The Reading Teacher, 77* (5), 642–652. doi: 10/1002.trtr.2283

Calfee, R., Wilson, K.M., Flannery, B., & Kapinus, B. (2014). Formative assessment for the Common Core literacy standards. *Teacher College Record, 116* (11), 1–32. doi: 10.1177/016146811411601106

Chen, C-H., & Chiu, C-H. (2016). Employing intergroup competition in a multitouch design-based learning to foster student engagement, learning achievement, and creativity. *Computers and Education, 103, 99–113*. doi: 10.1016.j.compedu.2016.09.007.

Common Core (2012). Common Core curriculum maps, English language arts, Grades K-5. Jossey-Bass.

Cunningham, P. (1990). The names test: A quick assessment of decoding ability. *The Reading Teacher, 44* (2), 124–129.

Dombey, H., & Moustafa, M. (1998). *Whole to part phonics: How children learn to read and spell*. Heinemann.

Fisher, D., & Frey, N. (2014). Addressing the CCSS anchor standard 10: Text complexity. *Language Arts, 91*, 236–250.

Fisher, D., & Frey, N. (2015). Teacher modeling using complex informational texts. *The Reading Teacher, 69* (1), 63–69. doi: 10.1002/trtr.1372

Frankel, K.K., Jaeger, E.L., & Pearson, P.D. (2013). Embracing complexity: Integrating reading, writing, and learning in intervention settings. In E. Ortlieb & E.H. Cheek (Eds.), *School-based interventions for struggling readers, K-8* (pp. 3–20). Emerald Group.

Fuchs, L.S., Fuchs, D., Compton, D.L., Wehby, J., Schumacher, R.F., Gersten, R., & Jordan, N.C. (2015). Inclusion versus specialized intervention for very-low-performing students: What does access mean in an era of academic challenge? *Exceptional Children, 81* (2), 134–157. doi: 10.1177/0014402914551743

Giouroukakis, V., & Cohan, A. (2014). Common Core, common language: Instructional questioning. *Delta Kappa Gamma Bulletin, 80* (4), 12–18.

Graham, S., Hebert, M., & Harris, K.R. (2015). Formative assessment and writing: A meta-analysis. *Elementary School Journal, 115*, 523–547. doi: 10.1086/681947

Greenstein, L. (2013). Formative assessment for the Common Core: Blending the best in assessment. *Voice from the Middle, 21* (2), 36–42.

Grindon, K. (2014). Advocacy at the core: Inquiry and empowerment in the time of Common Core State Standards. *Language Arts, 91* (4), 251–266.

Hattie, J. (2012). *Visible learning for teachers: Maximizing impact on learning*. Routledge.

Hershberger, K., Zembar-Saul, C., & Starr, M.L. (2006). Evidence helps the KWL get a KLEW. *Science and Children, 43* (5), 50–53.

Ivey, G., & Johnston, P.H. (2013). Engagement with young adult literature: Outcomes and processes. *Reading Research Quarterly, 48*(3), 255–275. doi: 10.1002/rrq.46

Kelley, M.J., & Clausen-Grace, N. (2010). Guiding students through expository text with feature walks. *The Reading Teacher, 64* (3), 191–195. doi: 10.1598/RT.64.3.4

Kern, D. (2014). Digging the Common Core with a helpful tool—text sets. *New England Reading Association Journal, 49* (2), 104–106.

Kramer, S.V., Sonju, B., Mattos, M., & Buffum, A. (2021). *Best practices at Tier 2: Supplemental interventions for additional student support: Elementary*. Solution Tree Press.

Lipson, M.Y., Chomsky-Higgins, P., & Kanfer, J. (2011). Diagnosis: The missing ingredient in RTI assessment. *The Reading Teacher, 65* (3), 204–208. doi: 10.1002/TRTR.01031

Luke, A., & Freebody, P. (1999). Further notes of the Four Resources Model. Retrieved at http://??www.readingonline.org/research/lukefreebody.html

Majeika, C.E., Pierce, J., Smith, H., Lembke, E., & Gandhi, A. (2024). Integrated multi-tiered systems of support in elementary schools: Practical applications. *Intervention in School and Clinic, 60* (1), 53–61. doi: 10.1177/10534512241254031

Marcell, B., DeCleene, J., & Juettner, M.R. (2010). Caution! Hard hat area! Comprehension under construction: Cementing a foundation of comprehension study usage that carries over the independent practice. *The Reading Teacher, 63* (8), 687–691. doi: 10.1598/RT.63.8.8

McEneaney, J.E., Lose, M.K., & Schwartz, R.M. (2006). A transactional perspective on reading difficulties and response to intervention. *Reading Research Quarterly, 41* (1), 117–128. doi: 10.1598/RRQ.41.1.7

McLaughlin, M., & Overturf, B. (2012). The Common Core: Insights into the K-5 standards. *The Reading Teacher, 66,* 153–164. doi: 10.1002/TRTR.01115

Mo, Y., Kopke, R.A., Hawkins, L.K., Troia, G.A., & Olinghouse, N.G. (2014). The neglected "R" in a time of Common Core. *The Reading Teacher, 67* (6), 445–453. doi: 10.1002/TRTR.1227

Morse, T.E. (2024). Revisiting the multi-tiered system of supports framework: An important mechanism for realizing equitable education in urban schools. *Education and Urban Society, 56* (9), 1051–1064. doi: 10.1177/00131245241262013

Pandaya, J.Z., & Aukerman, M. (2014). A four resources analysis of technology in the CCSS. *Language Arts, 91* (6), 429–435.

Pearson, P.D., & Gallagher, G. (1983). The instruction of reading comprehension. *Contemporary Educational Psychology, 8,* 317–344. doi: 10.1016/0361-476X(83)90019-x

Reyes, M.R., Brackett, M.A., Rivers, S.E., White, M., & Salovey, P. (2012). Classroom emotional climate, student engagement, and academic achievement. *Journal of Educational Psychology, 104* (3), 700–712. doi: 10.1037/a0027268

Rosenshine, B. (2012, spring). Principles of instruction: Research-based strategies that all teachers should know. *American Educator,* 11–20.

Rupley, W.H., Blair, T.R., & Nichols, W.D. (2009). Effective reading instruction for struggling readers: The role of direct/explicit teaching. *Reading and Writing Quarterly, 25* (2–3), 125–138. doi: 10.1080/10573560802683523

Santangelo, T., & Tomlinson, C.A. (2012). Teacher educators' perceptions and use of differentiated instruction practices: An exploratory investigation. *Action in Teacher Education, 34* (4), 309–327. doi: 10.1080/01626620.2012.717032

Scharlach, T.D. (2008). START comprehending: Students and teachers actively reading text. *The Reading Teacher, 62* (1), 20–31. doi: 10.1598/RT.62.1.3

Schunk, D. (2003). Self-efficacy for reading and writing: Influence of modeling, goal setting, and self-evaluation. *Reading and Writing Quarterly, 19* (2), 159–172. doi: 10.1080/10573560308219

Senn, G.J., McMurtrie, D.H., & Coleman, B.K. (2013). RAFTing with raptors: Connecting science, English language arts, and the Common Core State Standards. *The Middle School Journal, 44* (3), 52–55.

Shifflet, R., & Hunt, C.S. (2019). "All teaching should be integration": Social studies and literacy integration in preservice teacher education. *Social Studies, 110* (6), 237–250. doi: 10/1080/00377996.2019.1635978

Smith, R., Snow, P., Serry, T, & Hammond, L. (2021). The role of background knowledge in reading comprehension: A critical review. *Reading Psychology, 42* (3), 214–240. doi: 10.1080/02702711.2021.1888348

Stephens, D., Cox, R., Downs, A., Goforth, J., Jaeger, L., Matheny, A.,... Wilcox, C. (2012). "I know there ain't no pigs with wigs": Challenges of Tier 2 intervention. *The Reading Teacher, 66* (2), 93–103. doi: 10.1002/TRTR.01094

Tobin, R., & McInnes, A. (2008). Accommodating differences: Variations in differentiated literacy instruction in Grade 2/3 classrooms. *Literacy, 42* (1), 3–9. doi: 10.1111/j.1467-9345.2008.00470.x

Tomlinson, C.A. (2013). *Assessment and student success in a differentiated classroom.* Association for Supervision and Curriculum Development.

Tomlinson, C.A. (2014). *The differentiated classroom: Responding to the needs of all learners.* Association for Supervision and Curriculum Development.

Turner, J., & Paris, S. (1995). How literacy tasks influence children's motivation for literacy. *The Reading Teacher, 48* (8), 662–673.

Walker-Dalhouse, D., Risko, V.J., Esworthy, C., Grasley, E., Kaisler, G., McIlvain, D., & Stephen, M. (2009). Crossing boundaries and initiating conversations about RTI: Understanding and applying differentiated classroom instruction. *The Reading Teacher, 63* (1), 84–87. doi: 10.1598/RT.63.1.9

Watts-Taffe, S., Laster, B.P., Broach, L., Marinak, B., Connor, C.M., & Walker-Dalhouse, D. (2012). Differentiated instruction: Making informed teacher decisions. *The Reading Teacher, 66* (4), 303–314. doi: 10.1002/TRTR.01126

4

Tier 1, 2, and 3 Curriculum and Instruction

Having described the research base that serves as the foundation for standards-based curriculum within the structures of a multi-tiered support system (MTSS) and the basic format that characterizes this type of teaching, in this chapter I describe the major instructional approaches well-suited to implementing curriculum in each tier and several specific activities that appear across many curriculum units. They are described here as they are applied in the Tier 1 context but can often be employed at Tier 2 and Tier 3 as well.

Structures for Reading

Although the standards and texts will vary, I am suggesting a systematic and relatively standardized process for developing reading curriculum units at Tier 1. This allows for a variety of texts, ways of reading, and activities without forcing those developing lesson plans to reinvent the curriculum wheel for each standard. There is even a similar approach to crafting unit assessments; not only does this save time and energy, but it also makes it likely that a child who understands the content will do well on the assessment because they are familiar with the structure. The structures I recommend employing in most Tier 1 units are interactive read-aloud, Reading Workshop, shared reading, guided reading, and Literature Circles.

Interactive Read-Aloud

We've understood the importance of reading aloud to children—both at home and in school—for a long time (Beck & McKeown, 2001). This practice builds children's oral language vocabulary and their sense of text structure and can also promote empathy when read-alouds include texts that are culturally varied (Young et al., 2020). Most importantly, it introduces young children to reading in a joyful, non-threatening way and allows older students to maintain that happy connection to books long after they have learned to read.

Often, adults read aloud to children without stopping to interact with them. But sometimes we want to get more out of a read-aloud than this. At these times, we stop at various points to discuss the experience; this is called an interactive read-aloud (Fisher et al., 2004). There are many ways to conduct this activity. Described below is a basic version.

Simplest Version

1. Select a reading strategy or literary element you want to focus on. This could be anything from dealing with difficulty while reading to evaluating a character's decisions.
2. Select an age-appropriate picture book; the "reading level" of the book may be higher than that which students could read on their own. The book should be well-suited to what you want to teach. For example, if you are focusing on predicting, you'll need a book with several "cliffhanger" points.
3. Decide where you will stop to interact with students, think about why those points are best, and what you will say. Place Post-its in the text—with reminders jotted on them, if you like—at the places you intend to stop. Include enough stopping points to allow students to

have a significant experience with the element you are focusing on, but not so many that the flow of the text is disrupted.
4. Introduce the text to the children—a bit about the plot, without giving away important details. Explain what you'll be focusing on and, if they've not participated in an interactive read-aloud before, that you'll be stopping at various places during the reading. Tell them that they can also interrupt the reading if they have something to say.
5. It is generally a good idea to "think aloud" at the first stopping place (possibly more) to model the way you are thinking about the text. You might, for example, share your prediction at the first cliffhanger point. After that, plan to call on students to respond.
6. The interactive read-aloud is intended to be focused, but not obsessively so. If students want to talk about things other than the area of focus, be sure to allow for this.

There are several articles that are helpful in planning for and conducting interactive read-alouds. I've listed three here, along with their particular strengths:

- ♦ Fisher et al. (2004). This article reviews seven components of interactive read-alouds recommended by exemplary teachers and how to put these components into practice.
- ♦ Hoffman (2011). Note: This article includes many good ideas for older students as well. It introduces:
  - The idea of collaborative construction of meaning—that teachers and students build meaning together rather than the teacher having a single meaning in mind and attempting to convince students to adopt it
  - Discussion of five types of literary response
  - Recommended attributes for appropriate books
  - Options for managing student talk during the read-aloud
  - How to deal with "misinterpretations"

- The use of follow-up questions
- Differences between these conversations and the traditional teacher-asks question/child-responds/teacher-evaluates response type of interaction

♦ Young et al. (2020). Young and colleagues focus on the ways parents and teachers can promote empathy and cultural awareness through read-aloud texts.

Reading Workshop

One of the most challenging aspects of reading instruction, particularly as children grow older, is finding ways to deal with the range of reading levels that are commonly found within a single classroom. It's equally important to maintain and build engagement by allowing for student choice. Reading Workshop is a structure that helps with both differentiation and motivation.

Some authors use the term Reading Workshop in a very general sense—including a range of practices such as independent reading time, Literature Circles, and end-of-book projects. What I've described below is a more simplified and constrained version, and it assumes that other reading practices are conducted at other times.

Simplest Version

1. Decide on a very specific classroom process (e.g., how to select independent reading books), a reading strategy (e.g., using context to figure out unknown words), or a literary/expository text element (e.g., character traits, use of text features).
2. In most cases, you'll then select a text well-suited to teaching a minilesson for this area of focus. If Reading Workshop is preceded by an interactive read-aloud, you may simply revisit the read-aloud text for the minilesson, reminding students of the way, for example, text features helped them understand a science text the day before. The minilesson should be less than ten minutes in length and will involve primarily "teacher talk." For example, if you

are teaching a minilesson on predicting, you will explain what a prediction is and then make several predictions yourself rather than having students do so. This ensures that the lesson will be very brief. Students will make a number of predictions of their own while they are reading their own text.
3. Students then have time to read in a self-selected reading book, either narrative or expository text, as appropriate. During this time, they should practice enacting the minilesson; usually they will use Post-its to mark places in the text where they noted something related to the focus of the lesson or jot notes on paper.
4. It's good for the teacher to read a text of her/his own choosing for about five minutes and then spend the rest of the time circulating and briefly chatting with students about their reading. As I confer with students, I often specifically ask them if they would be willing to share their experiences of using the minilesson during the debrief time.
5. After students have read for, ideally, at least 20 minutes, call on volunteers to share with the class ways in which they used the minilesson.

Additional Resources
- There are many books on this topic that have been published more recently, but I find most of them to be overly detailed. A wonderful little book is Hagerty's *Readers' workshop: Real reading*. The sections on conferring and assessment are particularly good.
- Another useful resource is Candler (2011).
- I have placed a collection of potential content-based minilessons in Appendix A. The following are procedural minilessons that are necessary to teach as you begin Reading Workshop:
  - Choosing books:
    - Note: This minilesson may be postponed if the books in your classroom have been leveled; you

can initially direct the child to the proper level, rather than insisting that they take the time to do these tests.
- Remind students that they will not be happy with books they select to read if they are not both of interest to them and at a level that is appropriate for them. As they look through your school or classroom library, encourage students to think about what kind of books they enjoy, what authors they like, and what topics they are interested in.
- I recommend the "Five Finger Method" for book selection when the child has more trouble with print than with understanding. It is a technique that allows students to roughly gauge the level of difficulty of a book they might be considering by opening a book randomly and, as they read one page, putting up a finger for each word they cannot pronounce or don't know the meaning of; names of people are not counted.

    0–1 finger = a book which they can easily read with no help

    2–5 fingers = a book which will be moderately difficult if read independently, or quite easy with support

    6 or more fingers = a book which will be very challenging, but may be OK if motivation is high

- For children whose reading is relatively fluent but have difficulty with understanding, I recommend the "Five Page Method." The child reads the first five pages of the book they have selected, and then I ask them to retell what is going on. If the child is unable to do so, we talk it through and I offer the child another chance, since the beginning of the book is often far more difficult than the rest. If they still struggle to retell after another

five pages, I urge—but not demand—that they select a different book.
- Book auction: Ask students if they know what an auction is; link the knowledge they have to "Book Auction." Demonstrate how you will introduce books to them: sharing the title and the author, telling how hard and how good it is (on a scale of 1–10), telling a little bit about the book, and reading a short section. After doing this with several books, ask students to choose one that they'd like to read. If more than one child wants the same book and there aren't multiple copies, "auction" the book off by asking students to choose a number between 1 and 20 and giving it to the closest "bidder." Put a Post-it inside the cover with a list of the other students who wanted the book so that the "winner" knows who to give it to when finished. Encourage students to do their own "Book Auctions" for the class when they complete books that have been enjoyable for them.
- Preparing to read: Discuss what they do to get ready in the morning and what problems would occur if they did not do so. Elicit any strategies they currently have for preparing to read and why it is important to do so. Introduce the following sequence:
  - Read the title.
  - Look at the pictures.
  - Think about what you already know.
  - Make predictions about what you think might happen and ask questions that you are wondering about.

  Go through the process for a picture book. "What they already know" should focus only on things they are absolutely certain of. Predictions and wonderings should take into account the title, pictures, and their background knowledge. Ask students to choose a new book and go through the "preparing to read" steps for that book.

Shared Reading

The term shared reading refers to a range of practices that involve helping children to access text that is too difficult for them to read alone (Fisher et al., 2008). For the youngest children, this is typically done with a Big Book and much of the focus is on mastery of concepts of print such as directionality; concept of word boundary; use of initial sounds; utilizing rhythm, rhyme, and repetition, etc. For older students, each child has a copy of the text.

Simplest Version for Big Books

1. Plan for an area or areas of focus (e.g., concept of word boundary).
2. Introduction
    a. Discuss the topic of the book, eliciting prior knowledge.
    b. Predict from the title and the cover picture.
    c. Do a picture walk—looking through the book and discussing what students see in the pictures.
    d. Introduce area(s) of focus (e.g., "Today we are going to learn how to tell where a word begins and ends").
3. Reading
    a. The teacher reads the text aloud, pointing to the words, and stopping to talk about the area(s) of focus.
    b. The teacher and students read chorally, with the teacher pointing to the words.
    c. Divide pages among students; each student (or pair of students) comes up and reads their page aloud (alone or with the teacher), pointing to the words.
4. Inventions
    a. Go back through the book with the children, using Post-it notes to alter a key word on each page (e.g., in a patterned book where only one word changes on each page, come up with other alternatives to that word).

b. Have the students read the "new" book with you, reminding them that the pictures may no longer help them.
5. Re-readings: Give out small copies of the text for students to practice with partners independently and/or alone. If there are no small copies, make the Big Book itself available for students to re-read.

Simplest Version for Other Texts
1. Prepare for and introduce the lesson as you typically would.
2. During the actual reading, the teacher employs *assisted reading*. In this technique, the teacher circulates around the room reading aloud over children's shoulders. Students are to track along in the text—with their eyes alone, pointing line-by-line in the margin, or pointing to each word. Every now and then, the teacher stops at a word which comes at the end of a sentence or phrase and the students read that word aloud. For example, if the sentence reads *The man went to the store*, the teacher would read *The man went to the...* and students would read *store*.

Additional Resources
- Slaughter (1983). This article discusses:
  - How to make Big Books.
  - Using words from the Big Book for word study.
- Fisher et al. (2008). This article covers:
  - Examples of ways in which teachers discussed text aspects with older students during shared reading.
  - Vocabulary strategies: context clues, word parts, other resources.

Guided Reading

Guided reading is a method of reading instruction in which the teacher meets with a small group of students who share some common characteristic; they are generally either reading at the same level or have the same skill need (Morgan et al., 2024). The focus of this description will be on grouping by reading level, the most common approach. Children who are not with the teacher are assigned work they can do independently. Note: If this is the class's first experience with guided reading this year, teach them the general protocol by having all of them read the same selection.

Simplest Version (Especially for Young Children)

1. Choosing a selection

    a. Choose a book at the instructional level of your group. Particularly good selections are those with pictures which contribute to the text. Both fiction and non-fiction texts can be used.

    b. (optional) Also, choose a second text at the same or slightly lower level.

2. Preparing to teach the selection

    a. Note any words which may be difficult for students, either in terms of pronunciation or meaning; these words will be addressed in Step 3 or 4 of the teaching sequence. Note: If there is a clear picture clue for the word, do not count it as difficult.

    b. (optional) Develop a patterned writing assignment for Step 3i. If the book selection already follows a pattern (e.g., She went to the beach and found a shell. She went to the park and found a leaf …), use that one. If not, compose one of your own.

3. Teaching the selection

    a. Making initial predictions

        - Look at the title and cover picture: Read the title of the book and ask students to describe what

they see in the picture on the cover, pointing to specific things in the picture.
- (optional) Personal connection: Connect what is viewed to the students' personal experience.
- Predict: Then ask them to predict what might happen in the book (fiction) or what they might learn from it (non-fiction).

b. Picture walk/follow-up predictions (only for texts that provide many pictures)

- (optional) Picture walk: Continue as above through the book, having them describe the pictures but not yet reading. If, while offering these descriptions, children use words that are in the text, point these words out to them.
- Other predictions: Elicit additional predictions.

c. Difficult words: If the difficult words you noted in your preparation have not come up, introduce them now.

d. Set purposes for reading: Explain to students what they should look for as they read.

e. Independent reading: Ask students to read independently the full selection; they may read silently, whisper read, or read aloud, as you wish. As they do so, monitor their reading and help as needed by giving clues, rather than just providing the word, whenever possible. If one or more children are really struggling with the text, use assisted reading with these students (i.e., you read aloud quietly as they follow along) and then ask them to try again on their own. Give students a focus question for re-reading if they finish the initial reading before other children.

f. (optional) Read aloud: Allow each child to read a page to the group.

g. (optional) Guided cloze technique: This technique assists students to make use of both phonics and context clues. Read aloud from the text; stop at a word and ask students to try to tell you both what the word is and how they know. For example, imagine you are reading a story about a farm; the text says, "I saw a h_____" and there is a picture of a hen on the page. If a child correctly predicts *hen*, but can give no reason, you might say, "How do you know it's not *horse*?" (by the picture). "How do you know it's not *chicken*?" (by the initial sound). If a child incorrectly predicts *horse*, you might say, "Can you think of an animal that starts like *horse*, but looks like the animal in the picture?" If a child incorrectly predicts *chicken*, you might say, "The picture looks like a chicken. Can you think of another word that means the same thing, but starts with /h/?"
h. Retell/questions: Ask students to tell you what they remember about the selection. Ask direct questions to elicit any information they do not remember spontaneously; these questions may be at different levels of thought (e.g., fact, vocabulary, inference, evaluation, favorite part). Encourage the conversation to go from child to child, not just teacher to child and back.
i. (optional) Writing: Introduce the writing pattern you prepared for the selection. Ask students to write additional example sentences following the pattern. They should keep the books with them for reference.
j. (optional) Introduce second selection: Bring out the second selection and go through Steps 3a–3d.
k. (optional) Work/conference time: During this time, you will listen to each child read individually, both the guided selection (for fluency) and the independent

selection (for strategy use). The child may need to read all or part of the initial selection more than once to build fluency (i.e., relatively accurate, smooth, expressionful reading). While you meet with individual children, other students work through the following sequence of activities:

- Partner read the initial selection (either trading off pages or reading chorally)
- Independent reading of initial selection with focus question
- Independent reading of second selection
- Writing
- Self-select reading (from a collection of books several levels below those used for guided reading)

Additional Resources

- ♦ Fountas and Pinnell (2012). Fountas and Pinnell provide a strong overview of the guided reading practice. This text covers:
  - The idea of *Thinking within the Text*: solving words, monitoring and correcting, searching for and using information, summarizing information, adjusting reading for different purposes and genres, and sustaining fluency
  - The idea of *Thinking beyond the Text*: inferring, synthesizing, making connections, and predicting
  - The idea of *Thinking about the Text*: analysis and critique
  - Systematic assessment
  - Ten characteristics related to text difficulty
  - Using language to facilitate talk and support analytic thinking about text
  - Ways teachers can begin with the more basic dimensions of instruction and progress toward more challenging dimensions

- Burkins and Croft (2011). This article is particularly helpful in noting student behaviors that indicate "reading distress."
- Ascenzi-Moreno and Quinones (2020). These authors focus on guided reading in contexts that serve bilingual students.

Literature Circles

Literature Circles is a process for reading instruction that emphasizes student choice of reading material, independence in the reading process, student choice of discussion topics, growing independence in discussion, and Book Group-like interaction (Brabham & Villaume, 2000).

Simplest Version

1. The teacher selects books—one or two more than the number of groups they hope to have. Not all "good" books work well for Literature Circles. Generally speaking, I look for books which are on the short side, are on the easy side, and have plots and themes that are readily accessible to students. Using short stories is another alternative, especially for students' first experience.
2. The teacher introduces potential books. A typical introduction has the following elements:

    a. Bring up a theme from the book that students may be able to connect to their own experience. For example, with the book *The Chocolate Touch*, I ask students if they have ever wanted something very badly but changed their minds when they actually got it. Sometimes I take the time to discuss their experiences in the total group, ask them to share with a partner, raise their hand if they have had such an experience, or simply ask them to think about the topic.

    b. Then I tell them a little about the book, giving them enough information to pique their interest, but not so much as to give away crucial elements of the plot.

c. Next, I read a short selection from the book to give them a sense of the language and writing style they will encounter.
   d. After introducing the books, give students ample time to peruse them. They should read at least one page from each book before filling out a ballot ranking their choices.
   e. Before the next class session, form groups by putting ballots in piles by first choice and then moving them as necessary to form workable groups and to ensure that no one gets assigned to their last choice.
3. Reading process: Since the teacher cannot be with more than one group at a time, it is important for students to learn the process for reading.
   a. Students read aloud, at least at first. Other students follow along silently.
   b. Students do not "help" each other with words unless asked by the reader to do so. If the reader makes an error that changes the meaning of the text (e.g., *fork* for *forest*), other students may make a gentle knocking sound. If the error does not affect the meaning (e.g., *woods* for *forest*), other students should ignore it.
   c. Students may interrupt the reading to make brief comments, keeping in mind that the time for full discussion comes later.
   d. Anyone can stop the reading to ask for help understanding a word or a passage.
   e. To model the process, select two strong readers to help you. Prepare them to: make some intentional errors; ask questions; make comments; and give help as needed with a sample text. While the group demonstrates, the other students' job is to gather the following information:
      - What do we do when a reader struggles with a word? (nothing; just wait)
      - How do we know when to give help to the reader? (when they explicitly ask for help)

- What do we do when we don't understand the meaning of a word or a part of a story? (stop the reader and ask)
- Should our stops be long or short? (short as possible to maintain the flow of the reading)
- What does it mean when someone "knocks"? (that the reader has made an error that alters the meaning of the text and has kept on reading)

4. Reading: Students read the first section of the book (usually one-fourth to one-third).
5. Preparing for discussion:
    a. One approach is for students to mark parts of the text with Post-its that they'd like to share and discuss.
    b. Another approach is for students to write open-ended questions. Explain that open-ended questions are those to which the answers are found primarily by thinking about what has been read and to which there are multiple answers. These questions may begin with *Do you think _____? And why or why not? What do you think _____? Why do you think _____? How do you think _____?* Each student should come to the discussion having written two open-ended questions and three answers for each that they can imagine other students offering in response.
    c. In both cases, students may talk with a partner prior to meeting with their group.
6. Discussion expectations: Talk with students about how they might facilitate a smooth-flowing discussion: being well-prepared, contributing, showing patience with other students, not repeating what has already been said, etc. Introduce the discussion rules:
    a. Each person must speak once before anyone can speak a second time. After each person has participated, the discussion is then open to all as often as they wish.
    b. Hands must be raised. Interrupting and side conversations are not allowed.

c. The person who has just spoken is responsible for calling on the next speaker. This ensures that a student is not interrupted before completing their thought.
   d. No one is to change the subject until the discussion leader determines that no one has anything more to say on that topic.
7. Discussion: Allow the discussion to proceed, directed as much by the students as possible. If you ask questions, they should evolve naturally from what has been said by them. Your role should be primarily managerial: clarifying what's been said, short-circuiting a premature change of topic, enforcing rules, etc. Discussion occurs two to three more times as students complete the reading of the remaining segments of the book.

Additional Resources

As is true for Reading Workshop, most published texts are overly complex. For this reason, I have placed details about possible during-reading assignments, culminating projects, and student evaluation—as well as frequently-asked questions—in Appendix B. In addition, the following articles are useful:

- The deep-level discussion that results from the process this book describes supports socioemotional growth for participants (Venegas, 2019).
- In traditional Literature Circles, students read fiction texts such as short stories and novels. But studying information texts via this process allows for engagement around content in science and social studies (Barone & Barone, 2016).
- This article addresses ways in which Literature Circles are beneficial for English language learners (Carrison & Ernst-Slavit, 2005).

Structures for Writing

I also recommend a relatively standardized process for developing writing curriculum units at Tier 1. This allows for a variety of genres, ways of writing, and activities without forcing those developing the curriculum to start from scratch for each standard. I'll review the structures I recommend employing, some in Tier 1 units and some at Tier 2 and Tier 3, depending on the standard: mentor texts within genre study, modeled writing, shared writing, partner/collaborative writing, and Writing Workshop.

Mentor Texts within Genre Study

Over the course of a student's elementary years, they will be exposed to, and expected to write in, a variety of genres. Three genres are emphasized in the Common Core State Standards: persuasive, informational, and narrative text. Teachers may include others—such as poetry, plays, how-to, response to literature, etc.—in their curriculum. Some of these genres may be completely unfamiliar to a given child and a detailed analysis of the expectations and process for writing in that genre may be vital. Children may benefit from a study of genres which are more familiar—such as personal narrative—to understand the nuances of that genre.

Simplest Version
Pytash and Morgan (2014) suggest that teachers begin by seeking out strong exemplar texts within the genre of choice. At this point they recommend what they term "active noticing" (p. 96)—a process, initiated by the teacher but turned over to the students as soon as possible, which involves attending closely to all aspects of the text. Dollins (2020) describes this process as following the EASE mnemonic; students:

1. *Examine* the text, asking, "What is the author doing?" in terms of text structure, point of view, use of language, etc.
2. *Assess* the text, asking, "Why did the author write in this particular way?" and how these choices affected the text?

3. *Suggest* alternatives, asking "How could you write the passage in a different way?" emphasizing that there is always a variety of ways to approach a genre
4. *Envision* a new text, considering the question "How is this technique transferrable?" (p. 192)

It has been my experience that, once students have become familiar with a given mentor text, it is beneficial to ask them to seek out other examples of that genre and compare them to the original mentor text. Finally, as Morgan et al. (2012) suggest, students and teacher should craft their own example of the genre—on a topic of their own choice whenever possible—by writing "under the influence" (p. 32) of the mentor texts they have analyzed.

Additional Resources
- Langer (1985) demonstrates that children have a sense of genre early on, which becomes more sophisticated over time.
- Dorfman and Capelli (2007/2009) recommend practices for cultivating genre awareness through both fiction and non-fiction texts.
- This article explores the benefits of genre instruction for English learners (Zohbie & Bhowmik, 2024).

Modeled Writing
Modeled writing is infrequently described in the research literature. Mohr (2017) views this approach as a time when teachers model "planning [and] text generation" (p. 622). This allows students to attend closely to the writing process because they need not shoulder the responsibility of selecting a topic, determining the content and language, and transcribing the text.

Simplest Version
The teacher writes on a piece of chart paper or a document camera so that the children can observe the composition of the text. They conduct a think-aloud while writing: discussing the

genre they are employing, the topic, the organizational structure, the selection of words, etc.—the full range of writing decisions made during the writing process. After the draft is complete, children are asked to reflect on what they observed and to ask any questions they might have.

Shared Writing

While the teacher assumes most of the responsibility during modeled writing, students play a bigger role in shared writing (Button et al., 1996; Fisher & Frey, 2013).

Simplest Version

1. The teacher selects the genre, and possibly the topic, and continues to serve as scribe.
2. Given a topic—chosen by the teacher or collaboratively—children are asked what sentence they recommend to begin the composition. There may be some back and forth until agreement is reached.
3. The teacher records the sentence on chart paper, re-reads the sentence, and asks what should come next; this continues as students negotiate the content.
4. When the group agrees that the text is complete, they read it chorally.
5. Students may recommend changes, and revisions are made via agreement.
6. In some cases—especially for very young writers—the teacher may actually "share the pen" with students who come up to the chart paper and write a letter or a word. This practice is commonly referred to as interactive writing.

Shared writing is particularly well-suited to Tier 3 work.

Additional Resources

- Teachers who have employed this technique with individual struggling writers note that two points are key: the

student and teacher "are required to maintain the topic and determine the direction of the story [or other text] as they take turns adding sentences" (p. 29) and that, ultimately, the sentences flow together seamlessly so that the text appears to be written by a single author. These goals are even more important when multiple children are involved in the composition (Mather & Lachowicz, 1992).
- ◆ Williams's (2018) article focuses on employing this technique with beginning writers.

Paired/Collaborative Writing

Once students are quite familiar with a given genre via mentor texts and modeled and/or shared writing, paired writing can be a great next step—a final bridge to independent writing in the Writing Workshop context. Partners are typically assigned a genre but have full collaborative control over topic and execution. Stratigou (2016) studied 4th graders; she found that texts written by partners were stronger than those written independently and that most children enjoyed writing this way. Working with 6th graders, Matos (2021) found that those students who had the opportunity to write argumentative texts with a partner produced stronger independent texts at the end of the study, "specifically with respect to coordination of evidence with claims" (p. 1337). In other words, the skills students gained by working collaboratively transferred to an assessment situation in which they could not depend on a partner.

Simplest Version

1. Partners may be self-selected or chosen by the teacher; in the latter case, students may be paired with peers of similar or differing skill.
2. Students may do their best if they have had an earlier experience with modeled writing and/or if provided with clear directions and/or a revision/proofreading checklist.
3. They work in pairs to draft and edit their work.

Additional Resources
- ♦ Cross-grade-level partners are also an option (Bajtelsmit & Naab, 1994).
- ♦ This piece examines partner negotiation of text in the wiki context (Doult & Walker, 2014).
- ♦ In a free-flowing writing workshop, some partnering may occur unprompted (Jaeger, 2021).

Writing Workshop

As one can see by reviewing the variety of (often lengthy) texts on Writing Workshop, many authors believe that the more complex the better. I disagree. As a result, I suggest Fletcher and Portalupi's (2001) text *Writing Workshop: The Essential Guide* as a great foundation. As the authors note, "Instead of trying to write an encyclopedic, everything-you-ever-wanted-to-know book about writing workshop, we have worked hard to boil the subject down to the essentials" (p. xi).

Here is the process I use with 2nd graders. For older students, I often include a study of workshop vocabulary and explicit sets of expectations and procedural steps; I have placed those in Appendix C to keep what I cover here as simple as possible. Note: It is important for students to have two-pocket folders in which to keep their work.

Simplest Version (Over Several Days)
- ♦ Ask students to respond in writing to the prompt: I am/am not a writer because _____. Discuss with students. The point here is to convey that a writer is, simply, someone who writes and, therefore, that all of them are writers.
- ♦ Ask students to imagine all the things they can think of that writers do and then talk with a partner. As they share out with the whole group, make sure to introduce planning, drafting, reading work aloud to others, giving/receiving feedback, revising content, proofreading mechanics, and publishing, if the students do not bring up these topics.

- Remind students of the way Reading Workshop works: you teach a minilesson, they read, and they share about their reading. In Writing Workshop, you teach a minilesson (which they may or may not use that day), they write, and they share their writing.
- Teach the Topics List minilesson:
  a. Lesson set: Discuss: What's fun about writing? What's hard about it? If no one mentions "deciding what to write about" and "not having time to write when you have a good idea" as problems some writers have, bring them up. Ask where we can get writing ideas and brainstorm.
  b. From strong feelings: Think of particular times when you have had strong feelings: sadness, delight, embarrassment, etc. Describe times when you experienced each of these feelings. List the topics on your writing topics list, demonstrating how to abbreviate the idea to just a few words. After each example, have students add a time when they had a similar feeling to their list; not every student may have something to add for every feeling.
  c. From books: Think about a book you've read recently. In what ways does that book remind you of something that's happened to you? Read aloud a picture book that will generate ideas (e.g., *Miss Nelson is Missing*). Have students add ideas to their lists.
  d. From each other: Ask one child to read their favorite topic and have other students add a similar experience to their lists, if applicable. Ask for several other topics. Have them read their lists to a partner for other examples.
  e. Have students place this list in the left pocket of their writing folders.
  f. Follow-up: Encourage students to add to their lists regularly and to use them when they are struggling to come up with a topic.
  g. Exit slips (p. 66–67): *Why is it a good idea to keep a topics list?*

h. In ensuing days, teach other procedural minilessons such as those on prewrites (word web, sketching, talking through your ideas with a partner), drafting (focusing only on content, skipping lines, writing on only one side of the page), conferring with a partner during writing time, and sharing their work at Author's Chair time.
i. Over time, teach other minilessons specific to genre (e.g., line breaks for the poetry genre) or process (e.g., using an editing checklist).

Additional Resources

- Technology of various sorts can be integrated within writing workshops (Ciampa, 2016).
- Far from silent places, many writing workshops support students in communicating with each other as they write (Laman, 2011).
- Hubbard and Shorey (2003), Fu and Shelton (2007) discuss writing workshops for students with special needs.

Tier 3 Structures for Reading and Writing

In addition to the specific approaches to writing described above, I employ an overarching structure for most Tier 3 units. The primary characteristics of this structure are that it is highly individualized and explicit, that the tutor is careful to explain how the standard will be useful to the student, and that there are ongoing opportunities for the student to inquire about any aspect of the standard that they do not fully understand (Table 4.1).

TABLE 4.1 Tier 3 Structures

Define/describe	The tutor states the standard that is the focus of the unit, defines what it means, and explains with details.
Why important to be a better reader	The tutor explains why getting better at this standard will make reading/writing easier and more effective.

(*Continued*)

TABLE 4.1 (Continued)

Model	The tutor reads a text aloud, conducting a think-aloud which demonstrates use of the standard and answering any questions the student might have.
Activate prior experience	The tutor asks the student to describe any experiences they have had with the standard.
Student enacts the standard with the tutor directing	The tutor tells the student how to enact the standard by giving step-by-step directions.
Student enacts the standard with only hints from the tutor	As above, but with only one-to-two word hints.
When to use/not use	The tutor explains in what situations it is (in)appropriate to apply the standard.
How to know if it's effective	The tutor tells the student how they will know if they have applied the standard appropriately.
How to transfer to class/home	The tutor helps the student to effectively transfer what they have learned to other contexts; typically, this is via a bookmark with hints recorded on it.
Independent practice and debrief	The tutor and student collaborate to set a goal for achievement (e.g., a specific level on a scale). The tutor provides the student with a text. The student enacts the standard with that text and the two debrief about the process/outcome related to the set goal.

Additional Common Activities

There are several specific activities that I've found to be particularly effective and versatile. They have been referenced above or will be referenced in upcoming chapters, but I describe them here.

Exit Slips

Exit slips are a good way of checking on how well students understood the lesson you have taught. The teacher decides on a simple question which will assess the extent to which students grasp the content of the day's lesson. They write a response on a notecard and hand it in at the end of the lesson. The teacher reviews the cards to determine if they need to adjust the next day's lesson in some way.

Assisted Reading

Each child has a copy of the text to be read. The teacher circulates around the room, reading aloud over the shoulder of one child after another. Every now and then, the teacher stops just before the last word in a phrase or sentence, and all children say that word aloud. Assuming they are fully engaged in this process, children may choose whether to track the text with their eyes or with a finger. This is an especially useful approach when not all children in the class are able to read a text on their own.

Close Reading

Close reading—the practice of attending closely to a relatively short segment of text—is emphasized in the teaching of sophisticated standards because the effort to make connections and to find evidence is key (Ensley & Rodriguez, 2019). The following is a generic activity that I use frequently, and with modifications, across the curriculum presented in this text:

- Ask for a volunteer to read the paragraph (s) aloud. Repeat one more time with another student.
- Ask students to reflect on feelings and thoughts this passage brings up for them, quoting from the text as they explain.
- Ask students to talk about particular words and phrases they notice and what seems important about them.
- Ask students to make connections between two sentences in the passage and tell how they are connected.
- Ask students to connect this passage to another passage in the text and tell how they are connected, quoting from the text.
- Ask students to tell why they think the author wrote the passage/text, quoting from the passage/text as evidence.
- Ask for any last ideas.

Wheel of Fortune

Wheel of Fortune is a game in which the teacher (or sometimes a student) comes up with a sentence that is related to the day's content. The leader puts a short line on the board for each letter in the sentence with a slash in between words. For example, if the sentence is *We will draw self-portraits this morning*, they would put __ __/__ __ __ __/__ __ __ __/__ __ __ __-__ __ __ __ __ __ __ __ __/__ __ __ __ __/__ __ __ __ __ __ __ __. Each person has a turn to guess a letter for the puzzle and, if they are able, a word. If the students are new to this game, the most common letters—*a, e, i, o, u, n, r, s, t*—may be listed on the board as a reminder. When a letter that is part of the puzzle is guessed, the leader fills in all the spaces containing that letter; in the example above, if the letter W was guessed, all three Ws would be filled in. The game continues until someone guesses the full sentence. This game emphasizes decoding, use of context cues, and sentence structure.

Finger Flash Vocabulary Practice

List five challenging words on the board; number them one to five. State the meaning of one of the words. Say "One, two, three, go," at which point students quickly hold up the number of fingers that correspond to the number of the correct word.

Based on the research evidence provided in Chapter 2, Chapter 3 has reviewed the range of instructional structures and specific activities that will serve as the "stuffing" for the curriculum presented and developed in Chapters 4 (reading in 4th grade) and 5 (writing in 2nd grade). In Chapter 4, we will look at a standard that deals with character development.

Bibliography

Ascenzi-Moreno, L., & Quinones, R. (2020). Bringing bilingualism to the center of guided reading instruction. *The Reading Teacher, 74* (2), 137–146. doi: 10.1002/trtr.1922

Bajtelsmit, L., & Naab, H. (1994). Partner writes: A shared reading and writing experience. *The Reading Teacher, 48* (1), 91–93.

Barone, D., & Barone, R. (2016). "Really," "not possible," "I can't believe it": Exploring informational text in literature circles. *The Reading Teacher, 70* (1), 69–81. doi: 10.1002/trtr.1472

Beck, I. & McKeown, M. (2001). Text talk: Capturing the benefits of read-aloud experiences for young children. *The Reading Teacher, 55* (1), 10–20.

Brabham, E.G., & Villaume, S.K. (2000). Continuing conversations about literature circles. *The Reading Teacher, 54* (3), 278–280.

Burkins, J. & Croft, M. (2011). Toolbox: Handy helpers for guided reading. *The Reading Teacher, 65* (2), 147–149. doi: 10.1002/TRTR.01020

Button, K., Johnson, M.J., & Furgerson, P. (1996). Interactive writing in a primary classroom. *The Reading Teacher, 49* (6), 446–454.

Candler, L. (2011). *Laura Candler's power reading workshop: A step-by-step guide.* Compass.

Carrison, C., & Ernst-Slavit, G. (2005). From silence to a whisper to active participation: Using literature circles with ELL students. *Reading Horizons, 46* (2), 93–113.

Ciampa, K. (2016). Implementing a digital reading and writing workshop model for content literacy instruction in an urban (K-8) school. *The Reading Teacher, 70* (3), 295–306. doi: 10.1002/trtr.1514

Dollins, C.A. (2020). A critical inquiry approach to mentor texts: Learn it with EASE. *The Reading Teacher, 74* (2), 191–199. doi: 10.1002/trtr.1928

Dorfman, L.R., & Capelli, R. (2007). *Mentor texts: Teaching writing through children's literature.* Stenhouse.

Dorfman, L.R., & Capelli, R. (2009). *Nonfiction mentor texts: Teaching informational writing through children's literature.* Stenhouse.

Doult, W., & Walker, S.A. (2014). "He's gone and wrote over it": The use of wikis for collaborative report writing in a primary school classroom. *Education 3–13, 42* (6), 601–620. doi: 10.1080/03004279.2012.752022

Ensley, A., & Rodriguez, S.C. (2019). Annotation and agency: Teaching close reading in the primary grades. *The Reading Teacher, 73* (2), 223–229. doi: 10.1002/trtr.1812

Fisher, D., Flood, J., Lapp, D., & Frey, N. (2004). Interactive read alouds: Is there a common set of implementation practices? *The Reading Teacher, 58* (1), 8–17. doi: 10.1598/RT.58.1.1

Fisher, D., & Frey, N. (2013). A range of writing across the content areas. *The Reading Teacher 67* (2), 96–101. doi: 10.1002/trtr.1200

Fisher, D., Frey, N., & Lapp, D. (2008). Shared readings: Modeling comprehension, vocabulary, text structures, and text features for older readers. *The Reading Teacher, 61* (7), 548–556. doi: 10.1598/RT.61.7.4

Fletcher, R., & Portalupi, J. (2001). *Writing workshop: The essential guide.* Heinemann.

Fountas, I.C. & Pinnell, G.S. (2012). Guided reading: The romance and the reality. *The Reading Teacher, 66* (4), 268–284. doi: 10.1002/TRTR.01123

Fu, D., & Shelton, N. (2007). Including students with special needs in a writing workshop. *Language Arts, 89* (4), 325–336.

Hagerty, P. (1999). *Readers' workshop: Real reading.* Scholastic.

Hoffman, J.L. (2011). Coconstructing meaning: Interactive literary discussion in kindergarten read-alouds. *The Reading Teacher, 65* (3), 183–194. doi: 10.1002/TRTR.01025

Hubbard, R.S., & Shorey, V. (2003). Worlds beneath the words: Writing workshop with second language learners. *Language Arts, 81* (1), 52–61.

Jaeger, E.L. (2021). Friends and authors: Spontaneous co-composing in a writing workshop. *Journal of Early Childhood Literacy, 21* (2), 177–207. doi: 10.1177/1468798419833096

Laman, T. (2011). The functions of talk within a 4th-grade writing workshop: Insights into understanding. *Journal of Research in Childhood Education, 25* (2), 133–144. doi: 10/1080/02568543.2011.556518

Langer, J.A. (1985). Children's sense of genre: A study of performance on parallel reading and writing tasks. *Written Communication, 2* (2), 157–187. doi: 10.1177/0741088385002002003

Mather, N., & Lachowicz, B.L. (1992, Fall). Shared writing: An instructional approach for reluctant writers. *Teaching Exceptional Children,* 26–30. doi: 10.1177/004005999202500107

Matos, F. (2021). Collaborative writing as a bridge from peer discourse to individual argumentative writing. *Reading and Writing, 34,* 1321–1342. doi: 10.1007/s11145-020-10117-2

Mohr, K.A.J. (2017). Using modeled writing to support English-only and English-learner second-grade students. *The Journal of Educational Research, 110* (6), 619–633. doi: 10.1080/00220671.2016.1169391

Morgan, D.N., Clark, B., Paris, J., & Kozel, C. (2012). Teaching writers through a unit of study approach. *Voices from the Middle, 19* (3), 32–36.

Morgan, D.N., Valerio, M., & Evans, K.I. (2024). A 20 year guided reading research synthesis: Examining student data. *Literacy Research and Instruction, 63* (3), 193–216. doi: 10.1080/19388071.2023.2267625

Pytash, K.E., & Morgan, D.N. (2014). Using mentor texts to teach writing in science and social studies. *The Reading Teacher, 68* (2), 93–102. doi: 10.1002/TRTR.1276

Slaughter, J.P. (1983). Big books for little kids: Another fad or a new approach for teaching beginning reading? *The Reading Teacher, 36* (8), 758–762.

Stratigou, K. (2016). Enhancing fourth graders' writing skills through collaborative writing tasks: An experimental study. *Research Papers in Language Teaching and Learning, 7* (1), 181–198.

Venegas, E.M. (2019). We listened to each other: Socioemotional growth in literature circles. *The Reading Teacher, 73* (2), 149–159. doi: 10.1002/trtr.1822

Williams, C. (2018). Learning to write with interactive writing instruction. *The Reading Teacher, 71* (5), 523–532. doi: 10.1002/trtr.1643

Young, N., Conderman, G., Jung, M., & Kenney, J. (2020). Promoting empathy, equity, and awareness through read-alouds with young children. *Illinois Reading Council Journal, 49* (1), 4–15.

Zohbie, A., & Bhowmik, S. (2024). Using a genre-based approach to teach writing to elementary ESL students: A boon or a barrier? *TESOL Journal, 15* (4), 1–16. doi: 10.1002/tesj.819

5

Developing Curriculum for Reading Instruction

In Chapter 1, we examined the weaknesses of published English language arts (ELA) curriculum, and I suggested that it is actually more effective and efficient for teachers in a school or district to develop curriculum themselves than it is to take weak curriculum materials and modify them. I will provide examples of reading curriculum units at all three tiers in Chapters 4–6—examples that provide a model for what teacher-developed curriculum looks like—but first I need to convince you that you and your colleagues can develop units of high quality. Ideally, grade-level team members and a librarian—either at the school or district level—will work together. A planning conversation might sound something like this:

Aubrey (4th-grade team lead): "So, we're here today to develop a curriculum unit for Literature Standard 4.3: *Describe in depth a character, setting, or event in a story or drama, drawing on specific details in the text (e.g., a character's thoughts, words, or actions)."*
Ben (another 4th-grade teacher): "This standard is really confusing to me. I don't understand why they combined characters, settings, and events. Describing a character in depth is a much different—and more complicated—thing than describing a setting."

Cai (a third 4th-grade teacher): "And did you notice there's the word OR in there rather than AND? Does that mean that as long as students can do one of the three things, that's OK?"

Aubrey: "That's where the curriculum map is really helpful. We agreed that we would prioritize understanding of characters and that we'd deal with describing setting and events if we have time near the end of the year. I think we're good with developing a character unit for now. Let's talk about what character understanding means for us. I'll take notes."

Derrick (another 4th-grade teacher): "In my mind, it's about noticing what a character thinks, feels, says, and does."

Ebony (librarian): "And what their traits are, too—not just things they think, feel, say, and do on any given day, but the pattern of who they are."

Ben: "And then characters sometimes change over time. By the end of the story, they are not the same person they were at the beginning."

Aubrey: "Anything else?...OK, I think that's a good start. We should keep these ideas in mind as we develop the unit. We know from developing other units that we have several tasks ahead of us. We need to select a picture book with at least one really strong character and develop a lesson around it that introduces the standard via a read-aloud. We all have classroom libraries for students to draw from for the Reading Workshop part of the unit, but someone needs to think about what we want students to look for as they read their self-selected texts. Then someone needs to find a story in the core text, also with a strong character or characters, and plan a lesson around that; some of what is in the teacher's guide might be helpful but don't count on it. We'll wrap up the unit with guided reading groups, so we need a selection of texts at a range of reading levels—maybe 3rd, 4th, and 5th since they'll be reading independently—and an instructional protocol for each. Finally, someone needs to write the unit assessment; that person should probably wait until the other folks have finished their work, so the assessment reflects the work the students have done."

Ebony: "I ran into an older but wonderful picture book the other day and it will be perfect. We don't have it here at school, but I imagine I can get at least a couple copies from the public libraries and plan the initial lesson."

Ben: "I'm swamped right now, so I think I'll take on the assessment next week."

Cai: "I did less than my share last unit, so I can take on Reading Workshop planning as well as the basal story."

Derrick: "That leaves me with the guided reading texts. If Ebony could help me out with finding them in the library, I'll do the rest."

Ebony: "Will do."

Teachers Plan for a Character Unit at Tier 1

In the following pages, I will track the work of the 4th-grade team whom we met above. Ebony begins with the picture book *The Prairie Fire*. The main character, Percy, is a young boy who lives on a farm on the prairie. His family is forced to deal with a fire that threatens their land. Percy must assume tasks that are beyond what he imagined himself to be capable of.

Introductory Read-Aloud

Ebony suggests that teachers tell students that, over the coming weeks, they will be paying attention to story characters and, in some cases, how they change over the course of the story. Teachers will need to discuss with students the term *infer* (to come to a conclusion from evidence—of what the character thinks, feels, says, and does). The teachers will then ask the students to consider what the story tells them about what Percy is like as they read the book aloud. Ebony thinks it might be best for students to stop the teacher when they want to contribute so they won't have to remember their ideas for an extended time, and so they will discuss what Percy was like at the beginning as well as at the end of the story. When students contribute, the teachers will note whether the evidence they provide is something a character thought, said, or did. Ebony is also in charge of deciding on an exit slip question for students to reply to on slips of paper at the end of the lesson; she chooses: *There are three things we can pay attention to in order to understand a character. Name at least one of them.* Ebony then gives her notes to Cai to consider as she plans the Reading Workshop and shared reading lessons.

Reading Workshop

Cai begins by planning the minilesson they will teach at the beginning of Reading Workshop. The teachers will hand out a character traits list (see Appendix D, p. 211) and review traits and evidence they found in *The Prairie Fire* as a model for what students will do as they read their self-selected texts. As students read, they will focus on one character and put Post-its in the book to note traits of that character. They'll share out at the end. On exit slips, students will list a trait that describes the character they focused on and a piece of evidence from the text.

Shared Reading

For the shared reading, Cai selects "Addie in Charge" from their core text. Although this story is included in a grade-level text, not all students will be able to access it without support, so they will use an approach called assisted reading: teachers will move around the room, reading aloud over students' shoulders; the children are to follow along silently and when the teacher stops at a word, they will say it in unison. For example, if the teacher reads *Addie went to visit her ...* the students would end the sentence by saying *cousin*. Every now and then, the teacher will stop and ask students to circle on the character traits list any trait that they attribute to Addie. Next, they will craft a paragraph together, following the pattern: I understand what kind of person Addie is. I know she is _____ (character trait) because _____ (evidence from the story). I know she is ... and so on. To end the lesson, the teacher will lead a close reading activity—as described on p. 67—using a section of text near the end of the story.

Guided Reading

Derrick plans for guided reading groups. Ebony recommends three short stories at a range of levels. For each, he proposes the following instructional protocol:

- Introducing the story by: exploring prior knowledge, predicting from the title and pictures, introducing a few challenging words, setting a purpose for reading, and introducing the writing assignment the students will do when they have completed reading.
- Independent work: reading of text and completing the writing assignment.
- Discussion (at the group's second meeting): each group member contributes to a "round-robin" retell—that is, one child begins the retell and this responsibility shifts to other children until the retell is complete. Then they talk about traits and evidence for one or more characters and how they may have changed over the course of the story.

Ben asks Ebony to recommend a picture book to use for the assessment and she suggests *Mr. Lincoln's Way*. As the teachers read the book aloud, students will circle traits they believe to be true of either Eugene or Mr. Lincoln on a character traits list. They will transfer these traits to a traits-and-evidence form (Appendix D, p. 212) and add information about how they know the character exhibits that trait. Finally, they will write a paragraph following the format they used as a group after the shared reading lesson.

The previous section focused on the *planning* of a unit. In the next section, the emphasis will be on the *teaching* of that unit as conducted by Ben, one of the teachers who participated in developing the curriculum. I offer a description of the instruction that might go on during the initial read-aloud, but the conversations in Reading Workshop, shared reading, and guided reading would not be dissimilar.

What Might Teaching Look and Sound Like at Tier 1?

Ben begins the character unit described above with his students. Over the course of the unit, he will engage students in Reading Workshop, shared reading, and guided reading, followed by a unit assessment, but on this first day, he conducts the interactive read-aloud to introduce the standard.

Ben says: "Remember last week when we read the picture book *I Am the Dog, I Am the Cat*? What do you remember about what the dog was like? Tell the person sitting near you."

Ben asks: "And what about the cat?"

Students describe what they remember about the cat.

Ben asks questions like: "How do you know the dog is brave? How do you know the cat cares about the dog?"

Students talk about things the animals think, say, and do.

Ben says: "We're going to talk today about understanding characters. Animals in books like the dog and the cat demonstrate certain characteristics like bravery and caring. Authors are even more careful when they write about people to make sure that we understand what those characters are like and they do so by letting us know what they think, what they say, and what they do. Turn to a partner and talk about a character in a book you've been reading—what that character is like and how you know." After a few minutes: "Would anyone like to tell the group about a character you remember?"

After several children have a chance to share, Ben explains: "For the next couple of weeks we will be paying careful attention to story characters and, in some cases, how they change over the course of the story. One word that it will be important for you to understand is *infer*: to come to a conclusion from evidence. For example, we *inferred* that the cat cared about the dog because she cleaned his muzzle. Most of the time we have to infer what characters are like. A character doesn't, for example, commonly say, 'I'm smart!' Rather they think up interesting ideas, they answer tricky questions, and they make good choices. It's also important to know the difference between a character's feelings (which come and go) and a character's traits (which are true most of the time)."

I have a book to read to you today called *The Prairie Fire*. It's about a boy named Percy whose family lives on a farm and is forced to deal with a fire that was, most likely, caused by a lightning strike. As I read aloud, think about what Percy is like and how you know. Any time you'd like to share something about Percy, just raise your hand. I'll stop reading and call on you.

When students contribute, Ben notes whether the evidence they provide is something a character thought, said, or did.

Exit slips: At the end of the lesson, Ben hands each child a blank slip of paper and asks the students to write an answer to this question: *There are three things we can pay attention to in order to understand a character. Name at least one of them.* Later, he reads these exit slips to see if he needs to review today's topic before moving on.

As strong as curriculum and instruction in a classroom may be, some students will likely need additional support. The next sections examine what planning and teaching for these children might look like in the Tier 2—small group—setting.

A Reading Specialist Plans for a Character Unit at Tier 2

Among Aubrey, Ben, Cai, and Derrick's 4th-grade classrooms, the work of eight students who took the character trait assessment was not considered adequate. Three seemed to grasp the idea of character traits and evidence but struggled with the writing aspect of the assessment. Hasan, the school reading specialist, meets with these three students and, after a brief explanation, they demonstrate proficiency. The other five students, however, struggled more fundamentally.

Hasan is responsible for designing and teaching Tier 2 units. In circumstances in which classroom teachers are responsible for Tier 2 and Tier 3 instructions, they can certainly design the units themselves in much the same way. Note: In the plans that follow, words in italics reflect the principles of a strong Tier 2 curriculum described in Chapter 2.

The ability to understand characters is a relatively high-level skill. Hasan wants to offer students an activity which will *emphasize student strengths*—in this case, decoding—so he begins each lesson by playing the game of Wheel of Fortune with students; in this game, students guess letters of a sentence until the sentence is complete (p. 68 for a full description of the game). This sentence also tells students what their next task will be.

For the first class session, Hasan will ask the students to draw a self-portrait; this activity *taps into personal experience.* He will give out a list of character traits and ask the students to write words that apply to them (from the list or others) around their picture. After this, they will share their picture and words with peers who suggest other traits they believe to be true of that student, allowing for *student-to-student interaction.* Finally, they will write a paragraph with sentences following the pattern: "I am an interesting person! I am _____. The way I show this is _____" and so on ... This task *emphasizes meaning-making* and the *integration of reading and writing.* During the second class session, the students will draw and write about a friend or family member they know well.

For the third session, Hasan will shift away from personal experience to a character in a picture book—an *authentic text.* Students will circle traits about the main character on the traits list. Then, for each trait, the group will list at least one piece of evidence from the text. Finally, as a group they will write a paragraph about the main character in the pattern they've been using.

For the fourth session, Hasan will read another picture book, and the students will chart traits and evidence as a group and then write individual paragraphs. By the fifth session, they will assume full responsibility for selecting a trait, providing evidence, and writing the paragraph. This plan allows for a *gradual release of responsibility.* They will *assess their own* paragraphs by answering the questions: Did I name the character I was writing about? Did I write about at least three character traits? Did I provide evidence for each trait? Then they will exchange paragraphs with a partner for feedback, allowing for *student-to-student interaction.* Students will end the unit by talking about what they learned in the class, as well as when/where they might use what they've learned.

In the next section, I will provide a vignette of the first day of Tier 2 instruction. Again, student/teacher interactions in the remaining days of the unit have the same flavor.

What Might Teaching Look and Sound Like at Tier 2?

Hasan begins with an open-ended question: "We will be talking in this class about how to understand characters. Why do you think it's important to pay attention to what characters are like?"

Students may respond that it helps them to understand the story, that it makes the story more interesting, that they can imagine what it would be like to be in a similar situation, etc.

Hasan notes: "We're going to do an activity in a moment, but first we're going to play a game called Wheel of Fortune." He puts the following lines on the board: __ -__ __ __ __ __ __ __ __ __ __. The game goes on until someone can guess the whole puzzle: *You will be drawing a self-portrait.*

Hasan gives out paper and crayons or markers, as well as a character traits list, and says: "The words on the list are character traits. Please review the list and ask me if there are any traits you are not familiar with. You may feel you have some of these traits and not others. In addition to drawing your self-portrait, please write traits that are true of you in the space around your picture."

After students have had time to draw and write words on their paper, Hasan asks a student to hold up their picture and read the words. He asks: "Please look at your character traits list. Who can find another word that is true for Charlie?" Charlie adds the additional words if she wishes and other students have turns.

Hasan points to the following writing pattern that he has placed on the board: I am an interesting person! I am _____. The way I show this is _____. I am also _____. The way I show this is _____. "Please write about yourself using this pattern so we can learn more about who you are."

Even after a solid Tier 2 experience, a student or two may need further follow-up. The next sections examine what planning and teaching might look like in the Tier 3—one-on-one—setting.

A Reading Specialist Plans for a Character Unit at Tier 3

In the case explored above, one child, Charlie, struggled with the character standard even after Tier 2 instruction. In developing Tier 3 curriculum for Charlie, Hasan focused on several things: ensuring that the lessons were individualized to reflect Charlie's interests, were developed collaboratively, attended to motivation, included a mnemonic, and were intensely goal-oriented.

Hasan suspects that Charlie may have difficulty remembering the THINK/SAY/DO aspects of understanding characters, so he develops a mnemonic and visual of this: TWO SMALL DOGS (as in TWO in place of THINK, SMALL in place of SAY, and DOGS in place of DO). After he teaches the mnemonic, he will define understanding characters as being aware of what they think, say, and do and coming to conclusions about what kind of people they are. He will also explain why it is important to understand characters and model how to do that using the wolf from Little Red Riding Hood as an example. To activate prior experience, he'll ask Charlie to talk about Little Red herself. At the end of the first lesson, because he knows that Charlie is very interested in sports, he decides he'll offer texts that have sports players as major characters. He asks Charlie if she'd prefer a book about soccer or about baseball; Charlie chooses soccer and they spend some time reading silently, keeping the "two small dogs" mnemonic in mind.

In ensuing lessons, Hasan provides an instructional frame for Charlie. She will: *Read. Notice thinking, saying, or doing. Ask what the character is like.* At first, Hasan assumes responsibility for deciding when Charlie will stop in her reading. He asks what the character is thinking, saying, or doing, and what Charlie now knows about the character. Gradually, Charlie will take responsibility for the whole process: choosing a stopping point and reflecting on character development without prompting.

By the end of the unit, Hasan and Charlie have discussed when to use this process (when losing interest, when confused) and when not to (when she is fully understanding and caught up in the story). They agree that Charlie will know when she is doing this effectively: if she is growing more and more interested in the character. Hasan provides Charlie with two bookmarks—one for home and one for her classroom—that will remind her about the mnemonic (two small dogs) and the process. (*Read. Notice thinking, saying, or doing. Ask what the character is like.*)

Hasan may or may not decide that it will be productive for Charlie to re-learn the paragraph writing process. It may well be that being able to talk fluently about characters is an important enough gain because Charlie will continue to be exposed to structured writing assignments like that employed in the character unit in the classroom context.

In the next section, I will provide a vignette of the first day of Tier 3 instruction. Student-teacher interactions in the remaining days of the unit are similar.

What Might Teaching for Integration Look and Sound Like at Tier 3?

Hasan: "You may remember that we have been working on understanding characters. At the end of the class, it seemed like you might need a bit more help with that. I want you to remember that understanding characters means seeing what they are like—for example, *brave*—and noting how you know that—by what they think, what they say, and what they do. It might help you to remember those ideas by making a picture in your head of two small dogs. Can you do that? So, there's two of them, right? Two begins with T like Think. And they are small. Small begins with S like Say. And they are dogs. Dogs begin with D like Do. T goes with two and …?"
Charlie: "Think."
Hasan: "S goes with small and …?"
Charlie: "Say."
Hasan: "And D goes with dog and …?"

Charlie: "Do."

Hasan: "So make the picture of the two small dogs in your head again. What are the three ways we understand what characters are like?"

Charlie: "Two is Think; small is Say; dogs is Do."

Hasan: "You've got it! Now I want to talk with you about why it's important to understand characters if you want to be a strong reader. One reason is because it helps us understand the story; for example, if we understand that a character is brave, then it won't surprise us if they stand up for a friend who is being bullied. Another reason is because stories are often more interesting if we think about what kind of people the characters are and compare them to what we are like. Here's an example: I noticed that the wolf in Little Red Riding Hood was sneaky; he dressed up like the grandmother and fooled Little Red when she came to visit. Now, your turn. Were you surprised when Little Red Riding Hood went off the path on the way to see her grandmother?"

Charlie: "Yeah—I thought she'd listen to her mother."

Hasan: "And do you think you are like Little Red or not?"

Charlie: "Actually, yes—I don't always do what my mother says!"

Hasan: "So you can probably understand the way Little Red behaves because you sometimes make the same choices she did. Now I'd like you to select a book from the ones I have here, and we'll do some quiet reading. As you're reading, think about the two small dogs which stand for ..."

Charlie: "Think, say, and ...?

Hasan: "And do. Let me know when you've read for as long as you like, and we'll talk about one of the characters in the story."

So far we've focused on children who learn at a relatively easy pace within the classroom and on children who need additional support to be successful. There are, however, students in most classrooms who, for whatever reason, have already mastered the content to be covered in class. They may be designated as gifted and talented, but it may also be the case that they have no such label. Typically, these students are treated the same as those who are likely to learn the content with ease. I recommend that additional options be provided for what I term "Tier 0" children—options which challenge them to make better use of their time than sitting through lessons they do not need.

Teachers Plan for a Character Unit at Tier 0

One approach to selecting which children will be considered "Tier 0" for a particular unit is through use of a pre-assessment. A pre-assessment of character knowledge can be found in Appendix D (p. 212). So, how do students spend their time if they choose to take and pass a unit pre-assessment on, say, character analysis? Some students may choose to read in a novel of their choosing (connected to the character analysis unit in the focus on characters), read aloud to a younger child and talk with that child about characters, or make a puppet based on a book character. These activities are directly related to the unit at hand.

The following section offers a vignette of the class session in which Cai explains the way pre-assessments work; allows students to decide whether they wish to take the assessment, as well as the decisions Cai makes once she has reviewed these assessments; and how students who do well may then spend their time for the remainder of the unit.

What Might Teaching Look and Sound Like at Tier 0?

Cai introduces the idea of pre-assessments to her 4th-grade class; she says, "Have any of you ever been sitting in class and realized that you already knew what I or some other teacher was teaching?"
Several students raise their hands.

> Cai: "How did that make you feel?"
> Students suggest that it felt frustrating—like they weren't going to learn anything.
> Cai: So, here's an idea. We are going to be studying how to understand characters. How many of you feel you already know quite a bit about that?

Again, several hands go up.

Cai: At the end of the unit, there will be an assessment in which you will write about a book character, what you know about what that character is like, and how you know. Anyone who would like to may take that assessment *before* the unit starts. If you do very well, you can skip my teaching and use that time to do other work which you and I will decide on together. If you do well in some areas of the assessment but not others, you may be able to skip a lesson or two but not the whole unit.

Ten students decide to take the assessment. Five students demonstrate complete mastery of the skill, two clearly grasp the idea of character analysis but struggle with the writing, and the results from three of the assessments show that these students need to attend instruction for the whole unit. Of the five who passed the assessment, four decide to choose other work by selecting options from a contract that includes silent reading with written reflection, developing an art project based on a character in a book they have read, or writing a short story with strong characters. One student knows his friend may have difficulty with the unit and wants to be there to support him, so declines the alternative work option. Of the two who were challenged only by the writing part of the assessment, one decides to read during the early lessons and return to the group for the writing instruction, while the other worries she will not fully understand the later lessons without the earlier ones, so will attend for the full unit. All students are pleased to know in advance what aspect of the curriculum—if any—will serve them. And the teacher believes she is meeting the needs of all students: the main point of MTSS.

Assessments have their place for students, of course, but they are also important for teachers. This is especially true when teachers assume the role of developing as well as implementing curriculum units. It is crucial that teachers reflect on the work they and their colleagues are doing. In the next section, I offer a simple and straightforward process to support teachers in monitoring ways they are thinking and feeling about planning and teaching.

Teacher Self-Assessment

Curriculum development should be effective, efficient, and, at least to some degree, socially nourishing. One way to do that is by taking time to conduct a group self-assessment at regular intervals (Zaqiah et al., 2024). Here are some possible questions you may wish to address. Teachers would rate the first six items listed below on a scale from 1 = poor, 2 = OK, 3 = good, 4 = great, and provide answers to the remaining questions. Leaving space on the rating form for teachers to provide details for each question and also a larger space for general comments is also a good idea. The grade-level team lead can review these assessments, summarize them for the group, and initiate a discussion, or each team member can bring their own ratings to a meeting and present to the group prior to discussion.

How do you feel about:

1. The length of time spent developing a unit?
2. The amount of the work *you* are doing?
3. The amount of the work *others* are doing?
4. The quality of the curriculum developed?
5. The quality of instruction that occurred?
6. The quality of interactions among team members?
7. What aspects of the curriculum and its development need improvement?
8. What goal will you set for yourself moving forward?
9. What goal do you feel *the group* should set for itself moving forward?

If teachers complete these assessments after each unit, they can track progress and reflect on personal and group growth over time.

Chapter 5 will address what this process might look like for writing curriculum development. We will look at a 2nd-grade standard that deals with the personal narrative genre.

Bibliography

Zaqiah, Q.Y., Hasanah, A., Heryati, Y., & Rohmatulloh, R. (2024). The impact of in-service teacher education program on competency improvement among Islamic religious education teachers using self-assessment. *Education Sciences, 14* (11), n.p. doi: 10.3390/educsci14111257

6

Developing Curriculum for Writing Instruction

Like their 4th-grade colleagues who planned a unit for reading instruction, a group of 2nd-grade teachers will work together to develop a writing unit. A planning conversation might sound something like this:

> *Ivan (2nd-grade team lead):* "So, we're here today to develop a curriculum unit for Writing Standard 2.3: *Write narratives in which they recount a well-elaborated event or short sequence of events, include details to describe actions, thoughts, and feelings, use temporal words to signal event order, and provide a sense of closure.*"
>
> *Jade (another 2nd-grade teacher):* "So, I thought we were going to plan a personal narrative unit—but maybe it has to be fiction? The standard doesn't say."
>
> *Kenneth (a third 2nd-grade teacher):* "Yeah, I noticed that, too. It's the same for kindergarten and 1st grade. Beginning with 3rd grade and all the way through high school, though, it refers to narratives that are "real or imagined," so I think we're good either way. And I'm more inclined to personal rather than fictional narrative because it will be much more straightforward for our kids."

Ivan: "Agreed. Unless there are any objections, let's move forward with personal narrative. Also, there are a lot of pieces to this standard and we don't want to overwhelm the kids. Since we'll be teaching fictional narrative later in the year, let's not tackle the whole idea of temporal words—hold off on that for later. Come to think of it, that might fit better in our unit on how-to writing anyway."

Lydia (yet another 2nd-grade teacher): "A teacher at another school just told me about modeled writing—when the teacher writes on chart people in front of the students, doing a think-aloud as they go. I think that, since it's near the beginning of the year, that would be a great way to start the unit. Then we could go back over what we wrote and have the students check to see if we included all the aspects of personal narrative: first-person point of view, a story about something that really happened, an interesting lead, events in order, an ending that wraps things up, and some idea about what the narrator is feeling along the way."

Jade: "I like that. And then maybe the next day students could write a narrative of their own, read them aloud in groups, and check for those same things."

Ivan: "Beginning with modeled writing sounds great, but let's bring in a published narrative, too."

Ebony (librarian): "A Curve in the River"—you know that short story with Julian and his brother—would be a good one.

Kenneth: "Once the kids have drafted their first personal narrative, I think adding a bit more structure might move them forward. Maybe they could fill out a pre-write form to plan a little more."

Lydia: "Yes—and maybe a revision and proofreading checklist."

Ivan: "Anything else? OK, I think that's a good start. Sounds like you might develop the modeled writing plan, Lydia? And you'll plan for the shared reading, Ebony? Kenneth the planning form and Jade the revision and proofreading checklist? I think I may have some forms that would just need to be adjusted from a previous genre. I'll fill in if anyone gets stuck and also look ahead to our next writing unit."

All: Agreed.

Teachers Plan for a Personal Narrative Unit at Tier 1

In the following sections, I will track the work of the 2nd-grade team whom we met above. Lydia will plan for the modeled writing. Each teacher will choose their own topic, but Lydia will suggest ideas for the think-aloud that accompanies the drafting. Teachers will:

- Begin by talking to the students about several topics they are considering—all events that really happened—and going through the process of deciding which one is best.
- Mention that, since they are telling their own story, they'll be using I/me/my pronouns.
- Craft a lead that will not only encourage a reader to keep reading but also remind the students that they can revise the lead later.
- Regularly ask, "What happened next?" to emphasize that the story should be told predominantly in chronological order.
- Regularly ask, "What was I thinking and how was I feeling?" as the story unfolds.
- Note how they are bringing the story to a close.

Lydia will also develop a reference list for students to use when they read their initial personal narratives in a small group: first-person pronouns, strong lead, events in order, including thoughts and feelings, and closing the story.

Ebony will plan for teaching the personal narrative mentor text using shared reading, "The Curve in the River." Once again, the students will use Lydia's reference sheet to analyze the short story.

Kenneth and Jade will work together to develop the planning form (see Appendix D, p. 214 for an example) and the revision and proofreading checklist (see Appendix D, p. 215 for an example) because it is important for these documents to parallel each other. The planning form will focus on where and when the events occurred, listing main events in order, remembering thoughts and feelings, and writing an ending. The checklist will focus on the lead, events in order, thoughts and feelings, and proofreading skills students have already learned: capital letters at the beginning of sentences, end punctuation, and circling possible spelling errors.

The previous section described *planning* of a unit. In the following section, the emphasis will be on the *teaching* of that unit as conducted by Lydia, one of the teachers who developed the curriculum. I offer a description of the instruction that might go on during the modeled writing, with similar conversations occurring in Writing Workshop and shared writing.

What Might Teaching Look and Sound Like at Tier 1?

Lydia begins the unit with modeled writing: drafting a personal narrative on chart paper as the students observe.

> *Lydia:* "We're going to begin a new writing unit today. The genre we'll be studying is personal narrative. That means you write about something that actually happened to you. I'm going to draft my story on chart paper so you can see it and I'll stop as I go along to tell you what I'm doing and why. I have two ideas for what to write about and I can't decide. Maybe you'll be able to help me. One idea is to write about what happened when I took my dog to the doggie beauty salon to get washed and clipped. The other idea is to write about a trip I took to Disneyland. What do you think?"
>
> *Lane:* "I've been to Disneyland and I've heard about a hundred other stories about Disneyland. I'm sure the dog story will be funny. Do that one!"
>
> The group generally agrees that they'd prefer to hear about Lydia's dog.
>
> *Lydia:* "OK. I'm going to be telling a story about myself. So, do you think you'll hear more I/me/my words or more she/her/hers words?"
>
> *Mark:* "I/me/my I think."

Lydia: "Yup. I'm going to begin by writing: *My dog Max was looking a little scruffy. His fur was matted and stuck out all over the place. He needed a bath and a haircut, for sure.* Can you make a picture in your head when you hear that?"

Nedra: "For sure. My dog sometimes looks like that, too."

Lydia: "Hmm, I need to remember what I did first. Oh, I know—*I called Good Looks for Dogs. They said they had an appointment later that day, so I booked it. Things were looking up!*"

Oscar: "Things were looking up means you were feeling glad, right?"

Lydia: "I was—and it's important to include what I thought and how I felt in my story. Lydia continues this back-and-forth with the students: scribing the narrative herself but engaging the students in discussion along the way."

As noted earlier in Chapter 4, it is unlikely that all students will fully grasp a standards-based unit taught at Tier 1. Small group instruction at Tier 2 will, however, provide the support needed for most of these students.

A Reading Specialist Plans for a Personal Narrative Unit at Tier 2

A Tier 2 personal narrative writing unit focuses, by definition, on meaning-making, personal experience, and writing authentic texts with self-chosen topics. It is also important to focus on strengths (and, therefore, enjoyment), as well as weaknesses; move from whole to part in instruction; employ a gradual release of responsibility model; integrate reading and writing; include student-to-student interaction; and demonstrate success via self-evaluation.

Among Ivan, Jade, Kenneth, and Lydia's 2nd-grade classrooms, ten students struggled with personal narrative writing. Four of these students experienced trouble only with the proofreading aspect of the assignment and spending a few minutes one-on-one with each of these children seemed to resolve that problem; plus, they will have the opportunity to practice these skills in upcoming genres, as well. The teachers believed that the other six students, however, would benefit from additional work.

Hasan, the school reading specialist, developed a Tier 2 unit for personal narrative writing. Completing an assignment like this is a relatively complex endeavor, so Hasan wants to begin each class with an activity that is writing-based but relatively simple. He decides to employ dictation. Hasan collects a single paragraph from each student's previously written personal narrative. He will begin each class period by dictating one of the paragraphs, clause by clause, to the students. Then he will provide them with a typed copy of the paragraph and have students work in pairs to make corrections to their work. This assignment allows for additional exposure to the personal narrative genre without students assuming full responsibility for drafting.

Because the students attending this group struggled with personal narrative writing in their classrooms, it might be tempting for Hasan to switch to part-to-whole instruction: having them focus on changing pronouns to first-person on a worksheet, re-organizing a list of events presented out of order, etc. But Hasan is committed to basing the Tier 2 work on students' own writing. He believes the best way to do this is to have students work in pairs to craft a personal narrative. He asks the students to think about places in their school that they would most like to know something more about, and they agree that the cafeteria is of interest. He carefully explains the purpose of the visit to the cafeteria staff: to support the students in writing about that visit. He also explains to the students that, upon return, they will be working in partners to write about the visit.

After they return from the cafeteria, Hasan reintroduces the planning form that they used in their classrooms. He asks them to work in pairs to complete the form while he circulates to help them. Attending to six students rather than 30 is among the benefits of small group work.

During ensuing sessions, partners craft personal narratives about the cafeteria and use the revision and proofreading checklist for editing. They complete this assignment with a discussion about what they now understand better about personal narrative writing and any questions they still have.

Hasan sends a note home to parents/guardians asking if it might be possible for them to take their child to a place they've never been before—a new park, a museum, etc.—and to discuss the experience with their child. This allows for a very recent experience the child can write about. If this isn't possible, Hasan meets with each child and talks through with them a recent experience. Additional sessions involve planning for, drafting, and editing an individually written personal narrative.

In the next section, I provide a vignette of the second day of Tier 2 instruction, beginning after the dictation. Again, student/teacher interactions in the remaining days of the unit have a similar quality.

What Might Teaching Look and Sound Like at Tier 2?

The class is in the cafeteria:

> *Paul (the lead cafeteria worker):* "So, I hear you are interested in what happens here in the cafeteria—the parts that you can't see—and that you're going to be writing about it when you get back to your classroom, right?"
>
> *Hasan:* "As you can imagine, Paul, the children will probably be saying 'I this' and 'We that.'"
>
> *Paul:* "Oh, I get it. *I couldn't wait to see all the food* and *We had so many questions.* So, do you really have questions?"
>
> *Quinn:* "How do you keep the cold food cold?"
>
> Paul shows them the large refrigerator and explains how it works.
>
> *Rona:* "When we have pasta, how do you cook it—enough for all of us? Is there one ginormous pot?"
>
> Paul shows them the many burners and pots they use.
>
> The children continue to ask questions. When time is nearly up, Hasan asks the students to review all the things they've done together, in the order they happened.

He also asks them about the thoughts and feelings they had. Finally, he asks them to come up with exciting ways to begin their narratives. They talk with their partners to come up with ideas.

Sierra: Trevor and I want to say, "Our visit to the cafeteria was awesome!"

Umberto: Viraj and I will begin with, "Paul helped us learn about the cafeteria."

The group returns to Hasan's classroom to work on their planning sheets.

It is possible that, even after the experience of Tier 2 instruction, some students may not demonstrate mastery of the addressed standard. The next sections examine what planning and teaching might look like in the Tier 3—one-on-one—setting.

A Reading Specialist Plans for a Personal Narrative Unit at Tier 3

In the case described above, one child, Rona, continued to struggle with personal narrative writing. In developing Tier 3 curriculum for Rona, Hasan focused on several things: making sure that the lessons acknowledged Rona's growing frustration, were individualized to reflect Rona's interests, were developed collaboratively, and attended to motivation via daily goal setting. He will continue using the planning and editing forms she has grown familiar with.

Kenneth has told Hasan that not only has Rona continued to struggle with personal narrative writing, but she is becoming more and more frustrated as she sees her peers mastering this genre. He decides that he will make no advance plans for this unit. Rather, he will begin with an open conversation with Rona and take things from there. By the end of that conversation, Hasan will be better prepared to tailor their work.

Hasan and Rona will agree on a topic for a personal narrative, one that he knows enough about that he can contribute. They will use the planning form to get ready to write. Rona will dictate and Hasan will record the information. Then they will collaborate using shared writing—talking together to figure out what she wants to say and trading off scribing the text.

In the interim, Hasan will write a personal narrative of his own, including a weak lead, incorrect use of a pronoun or two, placing an event out of order, failing to include thoughts or feelings, just stopping rather than fully ending the story, and several mechanical errors that Rona is likely to notice. They will sit together with their drafts and editing checklists, trading off working on the two drafts (e.g., Rona notices Hasan's weak lead and then they evaluate hers).

Finally, Rona and Hasan will discuss another episode related to the topic of the previous shared writing and he'll help her complete the planning form. Rona will draft her narrative independently. When it comes to the revision and proofreading checklist, Hasan will sit with Rona as she goes step-by-step through the checklist but will not help her with it.

In the next section, I will provide a vignette of the first day of Tier 3 instruction. Student/teacher interactions in the remaining days of the unit are similar.

What Might Teaching Look and Sound Like at Tier 3?

Hasan: "Hey, Rona. Kenneth told me that you're feeling a lot of frustration about personal narrative writing."

Rona: "No kidding. I'm just stupid. All the other kids get it."

Hasan: "Tell me more about what working on personal narratives was like in Kenneth's class."

Rona: "First of all, nothing interesting ever happens to me. Other kids do fun stuff, but I just stay home. So, I don't have anything to write about."

Hasan: "That must be hard. Can you think of something you've done at school that you've enjoyed?"

Rona: "No ... well last year, my teacher Yolanda had this pet rabbit in class, and I was the only kid it wasn't afraid of, so I got to take care of it."

Hasan: "Is the rabbit still there? Yes? Because I'd like to stop by and see it."

Rona: "I still remember all about it."

Hasan: "Can you imagine writing about your experiences with the rabbit?"

Rona: "Yup."

Hasan: Anything else about writing personal narratives with Kenneth?

Rona: "Well, I'm sure he thought he was being nice, partnering me with Wendy who's a really good writer. But she just went ahead and did all the planning and all the writing and all the fixing and I didn't learn a thing."

Hasan: "Wow—no wonder you've had trouble. How about this? I'll meet the rabbit and talk to Yolanda so I can be more helpful, and we'll do something called shared writing where we talk together as we write—with you doing some of it and me doing some of it. Do you think that might help?"

Rona: "Maybe ..."

As is true for reading standards, some students may fully understand writing in some genres before they are taught. This is especially likely for personal narrative writing because it is fully based on a child's experience and has a structure—narrative—with which children are commonly familiar. The next section examines how students who have mastered this genre prior to classroom instruction might spend their time.

Teachers Plan for a Personal Narrative Writing Unit at Tier 0

Again, teachers may offer their students the opportunity to submit a genre piece, and those who demonstrate mastery of that genre may be allowed to take on other work during instruction time. If a student has not fully mastered the genre, they may attend some lessons and not others. For example, in personal narrative writing, a student might grasp the major parts of the genre but may fail to include thoughts and feelings. That child could bring a pre-drafted narrative to the thoughts and feelings minilesson and work on inserting those into their draft before returning to work on their alternative project.

What Might Teaching Look and Sound Like at Tier 0?

Lydia opens the discussion, much as Cai did for her 4th graders, and also finds that several students have had the experience of being taught something they already knew.

> *Lydia:* "So, here's an idea. Beginning next week, we are going to be studying how to write personal narratives: that is true stories about yourself. How many of you feel you already know quite a bit about that?"

A few hands go up.

> *Lydia:* "In this unit, your classmates will write a personal narrative. They will draft it, make changes to it, and then proofread it. Some of you may feel like you might be able to do all or part of this already. Anyone who would like to can write and edit a personal narrative *before* the unit starts. If you do very well, you can skip my teaching and use that time to do other work which you and I will decide on together. If you do well in some areas—like maybe you write a strong draft but have some trouble editing it—you may be able to skip a lesson or two but not the whole unit."

Five students decide to craft a personal narrative. Three of them draft and edit it effectively, one drafts well but struggles to edit, and one has trouble drafting, writing a fictional narrative instead. Of the three who passed the assessment, two decide to choose other work by selecting options from a contract that include writing in whatever genre they choose or developing an art project based on the personal narrative they wrote. One student feels less confident than he appears, so he declines the alternative work option. The student who was challenged by editing worries will not fully understand the later lessons without the earlier ones, so she will attend for the full unit. All students are pleased to know in advance what aspect of the curriculum—if any—will serve them. And the teacher believes she is meeting the needs of all students: the main point of multi-tiered support system (MTSS).

I recommend that, at the end of teaching the personal narrative unit, teachers complete a self-assessment like that described in Chapter 4.

It was the intent of Chapters 4 and 5 to carefully introduce how reading and writing curriculum may be developed at Tiers 0–3 and at two grade levels, and what instruction of all aspects might look and sound like. To reduce the time spent on curriculum development by teachers employing this text, I provide in Chapter 6 additional curriculum units in skeletal form: Tier 1–3 units in literature, informational text, foundational skills, and writing for each of the two grades. These units should serve as additional supports for instruction and further curriculum development.

7
Additional Curriculum Units

In the following pages, there are Tier 1–3 units addressing a literature, an information text, and a foundational skills standard at Grade 2, followed by Tier 1–3 units addressing an information text, a foundational skill, and a writing standard at Grade 4.

Grade 2

Literature Standard RL 2.1: *Ask and answer such questions as who, what, where, when, why, and how to demonstrate understanding of key details in a text.* Note: This unit also includes lessons on eliciting prior knowledge because I've found they are best taught in conjunction.

Tier 1

- Day 1: Introduction and interactive read-aloud: Describe research about which readers learn the most from a given text (those who know the most about the topic prior to reading). List on the board one thing that you already know about the topic of the read-aloud; ask students to talk in pairs and then share out what knowledge they already have about that topic. List a question that you think might be answered in the text; ask students to talk in pairs and then share their questions with the group. Read the book aloud. As they listen, have them hold up one finger if they hear something they already knew, two fingers if they hear the answer to a question they listed, or three fingers if they heard some other new information. Exit slip (pp. 66–67): *Why is it helpful to think about what you know before reading non-fiction texts?*

♦ Day 2: Reading Workshop: Model how to use the Know-Questions-Learn (KQL) form using the read-aloud text from the previous day. Each student needs an expository text SSR book. Give out individual KQL forms (Appendix D, p. 216). Have them list at least three bits of prior knowledge and three questions about the topic of their book before they begin to read. Set a group goal for how many additional bits of information they will learn. As they read (20+ minutes), they record on the form what they learned. Debrief, first with a partner and then share out. Exit slip: *Why is it helpful to think of questions before you read non-fiction texts?*

♦ Day 3: Shared reading: Use a chart-paper size KQL form for a shared reading text. Then do a close reading activity, following the protocol on p. 67 as a class or in small groups.

♦ Days 4–5: Guided reading: Students are divided into three groups. There are six "time slots" in the guided reading process which extends over two days: introduction (with teacher), complete the KQL form (independently or in pairs), reading with KQL form (independently or in pairs), discussion (with teacher), an unrelated task, and SSR (independently).

- Guided reading selection
    - Introduction
        - Read the title
        - Talk about the pictures
        - Review difficult words
    - Work in pairs:
        - Fill out first two columns of KQL form
        - Read

- Fill out third column
  - Discuss KQL form ideas
- Day 6: Assessment: Students complete a KQL form for a picture book that the teacher will read aloud. They need to list at least four things total for prior knowledge and questions (the idea being that if they have a lot of prior knowledge, they may have fewer questions and vice versa). Read the book aloud (multiple times if needed). Students will list at least two things they learned. A total of nine items (a combination of prior knowledge and things they learned) constitutes a high score.

Tier 2

- Daily plan
  - Activities below
  - Play Wheel of Fortune (p. 68), if time
  - Celebrations (self or others) and reminder for home practice
- Day 1
  - Introduce types of questions using Little Red Riding Hood as an example
    - Fact = What animal did LRRH meet? Where was LRRH going?
    - Vocabulary = woodsman
    - Inference = Why might LRRH's mom have asked her to take the basket? Why might LRRH have wandered off the path in the woods?
    - Evaluative = Do you think LRRH's mother should have sent her out into the woods alone?
  - Conduct a picture book read-aloud. Finish by asking questions from all types; model how to respond in complete sentences but DON'T insist.
- Day 2
  - Review question types

- I recommend using stories from the text *Days with Frog and Toad* (by Arnold Lobel); it is a commonly found text—and all references here are to stories from that collection—but another collection of short stories can be substituted. Read "Tomorrow," using assisted reading (p. 67).
- Ask the following questions:
  - Fact = What is wrong with Toad's house? (multiple answers) What did Toad do at the end of the story?
  - Vocabulary = take life easy (5), cupboard (11), in the dumps (14)
  - Inference = Why do you think Toad pulled the covers over his head?
  - Evaluation = Do you think Toad made good decisions? Why or why not?

◆ Day 3: Read "The Kite" using assisted reading; the teacher asks questions.
◆ Day 4: Children read "Shivers" with a partner; in the discussion that follows, the teacher again asks the questions.
◆ Day 5: Children read "The Hat" with a partner; partners write one question of each type; in the follow-up discussion, students ask and answer questions.
◆ Day 6: Children read "Alone" independently and write answers to the following questions (or provide the answers in a one-on-one conference with the teacher):

- Why did Frog go out?
- How did Toad get across the water to see Frog?
- What is an *island*?
- What does *spoiled* mean in this story?
- Why did Frog want to be alone when he was happy?
- Do you think Toad should have gone after Frog? Why or why not?

◆ Day 7: Review and present certificates

Tier 3
See Tables 7.1 and 7.2.

TABLE 7.1 Structures for Answering Questions

Define/describe	Providing an answer to a question about a text; levels include literal, vocabulary, inferential, and higher level.
Why important to be a better reader	If we understand what we've read, we should be able to answer most questions about the text.
Model	(same text as in Tier 2 is intentionally used here) What animal did LRRH meet? What is a woodsman? Why do you think LRRH didn't recognize the wolf at her grandma's house? Do you think the mother should have sent LRRH to her grandma's alone? Why or why not? If you don't remember the answer to a factual or vocabulary question, scan for the answer.
Activate prior experience	Have you been asked different types of questions before? Tell about it.
S does with explicit T direction step-by-step	Begin with reading single sentences; then expand to two to three sentences, a paragraph, a page, sections/chapters.
S does with initial hints from T	Hints: Kind of question? L/V (literal or vocabulary): remember or look back; I/H (inferential or higher level): think.
When to use/not use	Use: When asked.
How to know if it's effective	You are able to remember or find quickly the answers to F/V and figure out the answers to I/H.
How to transfer to class/home	Bookmark with hints.
Independent practice and debrief	The child reads a self-selected text and responds to one of each type of question provided by the teacher.

TABLE 7.2 Structures for Asking Questions

Define/describe	Coming up with a question(s) about what you want to know or what you think someone else should know.
Why important to be a better reader	Asking questions gives us a reason to read and to stay focused: in order to find the answers to our questions.
Model	I am going to read a book about pandas. I want to know: Where do pandas live? What is their body like? What do they eat? What are their babies like? What other interesting information does the book tell me about pandas?
Activate prior experience	Have you ever thought of questions before you read? Tell about it.
S does with explicit T direction step-by-step	Read the title and cover picture for _____. What questions do you think the book will answer? Sentence frame: I want to know _____.
S does with initial hints from T	Hints: Title & picture. Think. Write questions.
When to use/not use	Use: Especially before you begin reading or if what you read makes you think of a question that might be answered later in the book or in another book.
How to know if it's effective	Many of your questions are answered in the book.
How to transfer to class/home	Bookmark with hints.
Independent practice and debrief	The child reads a self-selected text and generates at least one of each type of question.

Informational Text Standard RI 2.5: *Know and use various text features (e.g., captions, bold print, subheadings, glossaries, indexes, electronic menus, icons) to locate key facts or information in a text efficiently.*

Note: An article that may prove helpful is Kelley and Clausen-Grace (2010).

Tier 1

- Day 1: Introduction and interactive read-aloud: Remind students that the main point of reading information texts is to gain knowledge about a given topic. They will certainly learn information from the words in such a text, but they will gain additional information from the visuals. Provide a range of information texts for students to peruse and discuss the visuals they see in partners. Ask students to name any types of visuals/text features (you will use the terms interchangeably) they found in these texts; they may be likely to list drawings and photographs, but might also mention maps, charts, etc. Tell them you will be reading aloud a book in which there are a lot of text features and that, whenever they see one, they should raise their hands; tell them that they can do this even if they don't know what the visual is called. Read the book aloud, stopping when prompted by students and whenever there is a text feature they don't mention. For each, discuss what information the visual provides and why it might be more effective and/or efficient than writing it out in words. Exit slip (p. 66–67): *Name one text feature you noticed in today's read aloud. What information did it give you?*
- Day 2: Reading Workshop: Review with students the visuals they saw in the previous day's read-aloud. Each student needs an information text self-selected book that contains some visuals—most likely a picture book. As they read (20+ minutes), they mark text features with Post-its. Discuss which visuals they found and what information they got from those features, first with a partner and then in the whole group. Exit slip: *Name one feature you or your partner found in your book today. Try to make it a different one than you noted on yesterday's exit slip. What information did it give you?*

- Day 3: Shared reading: Select an information text with many visuals for which you have multiple copies. Use shared reading to go through the text. Students should interrupt the reading when they note text features; discuss the roles of these features. Use the following protocol to conduct a close reading activity. For each of several text features:
    - Ask students to explain feelings and thoughts the visual brings up for them, referring directly to the visual as they explain.
    - Ask students to talk about particular words and phrases associated with the visuals and what seems important about them.
    - Ask students to make connections between two text features and explain how they are connected.
    - Ask students to connect a visual to a similar visual in the Day 1 read-aloud or their self-selected reading book from Day 2.
    - Ask for any other ideas.
- Days 4–5: Guided reading: Students are divided into three groups. There are six "time slots" in the guided reading process which extends over two days: introduction (with teacher), list all the text features in the selection (independently or in pairs), reading with the text features list (independently or in pairs), discussion (with teacher), an unrelated task, and self-select reading (independently).
    - Introduction
        - Read the title
        - Talk about the pictures
        - Review difficult words
    - Work in partners:
        - List all the visuals in the text
        - Read, noting the information each visual provided on the list
    - Discuss information gained from visuals

♦ Day 6: Assessment: Read aloud a short information picture book with many visuals (multiple times if needed). As you read, students are to list one text feature in each section of a piece of paper folded in quarters and what information they gained from that feature. Scoring: one point each for the visual and two points each for information bits. A total of 11 points constitutes a high score.

Tier 2

This Tier 2 unit is based on having students produce their own visuals with captions—one visual for each day of class—including as many of the following as you wish: map, chart, timeline, graph, diagram, glossary. Each day opens with a question, such as what would you draw if:

♦ You wanted to help a new friend get to your house?
♦ You wanted to show what fruits you ate each day this week?
♦ You wanted to show the most important things that have happened in your life so far?
♦ You wanted to show how many minutes of exercise you got each day this week?
♦ You wanted to show what the inside of your backpack looks like?
♦ You wanted to explain the meanings of important words?, and so on.

For each day, discuss the text feature that is the best answer to the question. Give students time and materials to craft the features, providing individual support as needed. Ask them to write a caption for the day's feature that explains the main point the visual is intended to convey (e.g., This is how you get from your house to my house). End the class with students sharing their text features and captions with the group.

Tier 3
See Table 7.3.

TABLE 7.3 Structures for Using Text Features
This example focuses on maps, but the same structure can be used for other text features.

Define/describe	Using visuals in a text to gain information in a way that is simpler and clearer than reading words.
Why important to be a better reader	If we don't understand the information that is provided in text features, we are unlikely to understand a lot of what the author is trying to help us learn.
Model	This is a map. The purpose of a map is to show the location of certain places and how to get from one place to another. Describe what information you get from the map.
Activate prior experience	Have you seen a map before? What do you remember about it?
S does with explicit T direction step-by-step	Please find a map in this book. Tell me what you see. What information does the author want you to get from the map?
S does with initial hints from T	Hints: Find a map. What do you see? What information do you get?
When to use/not use	Use: Whenever you see a text feature in something you are reading.
How to know if it's effective	You learn something from the map that you wouldn't know without it.
How to transfer to class/home	Bookmark with hints.
Independent practice and debrief	The child reads a self-selected text, finds a text feature, and describes what information is gained from it.

Foundational Skills Standard 2.4c: *Use context to confirm or self-correct word recognition and understanding, re-reading as necessary.*

Tier 1

- Day 1: Introduction and interactive read-aloud: Select a picture book and list five to six sentences from it on the board, substituting a blank for one word in each sentence; ideally, the sentences will offer clues before or after the blank, in a picture, or that knowing what the word is not crucial (e.g., an adjective). Ask students to raise their hands if they have ever been reading and noticed that the text didn't seem to make sense. Ask them to describe what they did. They may say that they slowed down, looked at a picture, kept on reading to the end of the sentence, went back and re-read, or just kept on reading if they generally understood. Read the book aloud. When you get to one of the sentences on the board, read it as it is written there rather than how it is written in the book. Discuss words that might make sense in the blank. Exit slip (p. 66–67): *Name one thing you can do if you are reading and something doesn't seem to make sense?*
- Day 2: Reading Workshop: Review what students learned the previous day and list ideas on the board. Each student needs a self-selected book. As they read (20+ minutes), they will place Post-its in their book when they run into something that doesn't make sense to them; they will write on the Post-it what they did as a result: RA = read ahead, RR = re-read, P = used a picture, S = skipped it but still understood. Debrief, first with a partner and then share out in the large group. Exit slip: *Is it ever OK to skip a word and keep reading? When?*
- Day 3: Shared reading: Provide multiple copies of a text that has been altered by putting spaces in place of a number of words. When the group gets to one of the spaces, ask students to describe what strategies they used to figure out what might go in the space.
- Days 4–5: Guided reading: Students are divided into three groups. There are six "time slots" in the guided reading process which extends over two days: introduction (with teacher), reading with a text that has a number of words

covered with Post-it-like tape (independently or in pairs), re-reading the text with words filled in (independently or in pairs), discussion (with teacher), an unrelated task, and self-selected reading (independently).

- Introduction
  - Read the title
  - Talk about the pictures
  - Review only VERY difficult words (since they are working on using context to figure out most of them)
- Work in partners:
  - Read, stopping to discuss places where blanks are
  - Re-read with fluency and expression
- Discuss the use of context, process, and text as a whole.

♦ Day 6: Assessment: This is a maze assessment. Students receive a typed text in which three options are given for each of eight to ten words. Multiple texts may be needed if students read at a range of levels. They are to circle the word that makes sense for each place where options are given. In the margin, they are to write the code to state what strategy or strategies they used to figure it out: RA (read ahead) or RR (re-read). 90% correct is a high and 80% correct is an acceptable score.

Tier 2

♦ Progress monitoring assessment: Percentage of miscues from the Informal Reading Inventory assessment that maintain meaning and/or are self-corrected
♦ Daily plan (most days)

- Wheel of Fortune Game (p. 68) that serves both as practice in the use of context to figure out the message and a review of the previous day's content
- New strategy for the day

- Independent reading, emphasizing the use of context; debrief at the end, sharing examples of the day's strategy
- Celebrations (own or others) and reminder for home practice

◆ Day 1: Noticing errors

- Give out enrollment slips (Appendix D, p. 217)
- Review letter to go home (Appendix D, p. 218)
- Lesson set: What does it mean when I say that I don't *know* a word? (emphasize understanding as well as pronunciation) Have you ever been reading and realized that what you read didn't make sense? What did you do? Emphasize use of context (explain term: using the words and/or sentences surrounding an unknown word to figure it out).
- Read aloud "Henry Possum" (Appendix D, p. 219), approximately one sentence at a time, having students tell you what words (miscues) don't make sense; students do *not* have copies of the selection. Explain that a reader must be able to *notice* that something doesn't make sense before being able to *do* anything about it.
- Independent reading: look for times when something doesn't seem to make sense; "I noticed ____ didn't make sense."

◆ Day 2: How do I know and explain what's wrong?

- Introduce the Wheel of Fortune game to review the previous day's focus, using the sentence: *It is important to stop reading if the sentence doesn't make sense.* Point out how students make use of other words as they figure out the message:
- Lesson set: How do you know when something you are reading doesn't make sense? Introduce the idea of clue words: words that give hints about the meaning of the word.

- Read aloud "The Wolves" (Appendix D, p. 220); students do *not* have copies of the selection. What do they notice?
- Hand out copies of the story, with the footnotes cut off the bottom, and discuss how we use clue words to help us notice that *fork* is not a place and *sip* is not something you can smell.
- Call on two volunteers to read aloud for fluency.
- Independent reading: look for clue words; "I noticed that _____ didn't make sense when I saw the clue word(s) _____."

♦ Day 3: Before and after clues

- Wheel of Fortune: There are clue words that tell us when something doesn't make sense.
- Lesson set: Where might clue words be located? In addition to immediately before or after the unknown word, they might be in the title or some other location relatively remote from the unknown word.
- Present sentences in which clue words come both before and after the unknown word (e.g., I ran to the _____. _____ tastes good.); brainstorm possible solutions.
- Hand out copies of "A Plant for Mama" (Appendix D, p. 221) and read the story aloud, saying the word *blank* whenever there is a space in the text.
- Discuss which words serve as clues to the unknown word (e.g., Donny is likely to find his wallet after he wakes up, so *bed* fits in the first blank). Don't talk about what goes in the blank yet—just what the clue words are.
- Ask students to fill in as many blanks as they can in partners or independently.
- Review and discuss their choices.
- Call on two volunteers to read aloud for fluency.
- Independent reading: Look for clue words both before and after a difficult word; "I found the clue word(s) _____ after/before the word that didn't make sense."

- Day 4: Confirm with the initial sound

  - Wheel of Fortune: Clue words can come before or after the unknown word.
  - Lesson set: How can we figure out what the unknown word is if several words make sense in the sentence? Review the two sentences used in Lesson 3; this time add the initial sound(s) to each blank—*p* for both blanks; discuss how this narrows the possibilities.
  - Hand out copies of the beginning of *The Magic Finger* (Appendix D, p. 222) and read the story aloud, saying *blank* whenever there is a space in the text; have students complete the blanks as best they can, using the initial sound to help them; discuss their answers.
  - Call on two volunteers to read aloud for fluency.
  - Independent reading: Apply initial sound to figure out unknown word; "I used the beginning sound ____ to help me figure out the word I didn't know."

- Day 5: When can I just go on?

  - Wheel of Fortune: We should use the beginning sound to confirm our word guess.
  - Hand out copies of "Nothing to Do" (Appendix D, p. 223) and read it aloud, saying nothing when there are spaces; ask students what they notice (that it still makes sense even without the missing words; explain that this is an extreme example but that sometimes they will be able to skip unknown words and still understand).
  - Introduce the following process for dealing with unknown words:

    - FIGURE IT OUT from the context and initial sound(s).
    - If you can't, try to SKIP it.
    - If you can't understand the sentence, GET HELP.

- Independent reading: Apply the above process; "When I ran into an unknown word, the steps I used were _____."

♦ Day 6: Writing exchange

- Wheel of Fortune: We can skip over unknown words once in a while if we can still understand the sentence.
- Have each student write a story, leaving blanks in the story every now and then with just the first letter showing. Exchange with a partner to try to fill in blanks.
- Independent reading, if time.

♦ Day 7: Wrap-up

- Wheel of Fortune: We have learned a lot about using context clues to help us read.
- Have students read in a book of their own choosing; it needs to be relatively challenging, so they may need to select a different book than the one they've been reading so far.
- During independent reading, have students mark words that give them trouble with a small Post-it coded with an "F" if they figured it out, an "S" if they couldn't figure it out but could skip it and still understand, or an "H" if skipping it didn't work, and they needed help.
- As students read, move around the room, and note words which students have marked; choose a few that will be good for teaching purposes and jot down the phrase or sentence from the book. Write these on the board and, after some reading time has passed, go over them with the students.
- What did you learn in this unit? When/where can you use what you learned?
- Present certificates

Tier 3
See Table 7.4.

TABLE 7.4 Structures for Comprehension Monitoring

Define/describe	Figuring out what to do when there is a word or idea you don't understand.
Why important to be a better reader	Readers need to know what to do when they don't understand so they can comprehend the text.
Model	Word example: The man combed the *goatee* on his chin. Idea example: *The dogs at Leo's house had always belonged more to his father than anyone else. He fed them and took them for walks and they sat at his feet as he read in the evening.*
Activate prior experience	Have you ever been reading and noticed that you didn't understand? What did you do?
S does with explicit T direction step-by-step	Read the title and cover picture for _____. I notice that I don't understand _____.
S does with initial hints from T	Hints: Read. Notice not understanding. Word or idea? Try fix-ups: Read ahead. Re-read. Skip and try to understand. Source (like a dictionary) or ask for help.
When to use/not use	Use: When you are reading a difficult text or text about a topic you aren't familiar with. Don't use: When everything seems clear.
How to know if it's effective	If you feel you understand what is going on.
How to transfer to class/home	Bookmark with hints.
Independent practice and debrief	The child reads a self-selected text, notes words and/or ideas that are confusing, and explains what steps they took to deal with the difficulty.

Grade 4

Informational Text Standard RI 4.2: *Determine the main idea of a text and explain how it is supported by key details; summarize the text.*

Tier 1

- ♦ Day 1: Introduction and interactive read-aloud

    - Introduce the concepts of general and specific. Ask all students wearing shorts (or some other item of clothing) to come up to the front of the room. Note that "students wearing shorts" is the *general* idea and that each student wearing shorts is a *specific* example of the general idea. Repeat with a couple more examples. Then do the reverse: call the names of all the students who have something in common (e.g., wearing glasses, went to Chinese Club, have names beginning with the same letter). Explain that these students are specific examples of a general idea; see if students can figure out what the general idea is.
    - Explain that, in reading, the terms we normally use for general and specific are main idea and details. Relate to the activity above. Sometimes when we read, the main ideas are clearly stated (usually the first sentence in a paragraph) but other times we have to figure them out.
    - Explain that you will read some pages from a text with the main ideas stated at the beginning of some paragraphs. It is their job to listen for the main idea and also remember as much as they can about what they hear. After each page, ask them to provide the things they remember; write them on the board. If one of the things is the main idea, explain how it relates to ALL of the other statements. If they didn't remember the main idea, read it again, and then link it to the other statements.

- Explain that you will read some other pages whose main idea is NOT stated but must be figured out. Go through the same process as above. This will probably be more challenging.
- Exit Slip (p. 66–67): Write these words on your paper: snake, reptile, lizard, turtle, crocodile. Circle the *general* word.

◆ Day 2: Reading Workshop

- Minilesson: Return to the previous day's work, discussing what they learned about the location of main ideas.
- Independent reading: Students need to read an information text. As they read, they are to write down several important things they noticed; it may be beneficial to stop them at several points in their reading and have them do this.
- Debrief: Model a conversation about the main idea/details: Share a statement you wrote down and have the class help you determine if it is a main idea or a detail. Have students share a statement with a partner and go through the same process. Then have some students share with the whole group.
- Exit slip: Look at the sentences on the board. Write the main idea on your paper:
  - Mercury is covered with round holes called craters.
  - Venus is wrapped in swirling clouds.
  - We know a lot about the planets.
  - Mars is nicknamed the Red Planet because of its red-orange color.
  - Jupiter is the largest planet.

◆ Day 3: Shared reading

- Explain that you will be reading another information text. The reading will be divided into sections, and you will work together to determine the main

idea of each section. After reading each section using assisted reading (p. 67), ask students to brainstorm some ideas they remember; write them on the board. Talk together to figure out the main idea, either stated or inferred.
- Explain to students what the topic of the whole text is (e.g., rabbits) and what the main idea is (e.g., Rabbits are interesting animals.).
- Read the text, using the shared reading process.
- Close reading—Follow the close reading protocol (p. 67). For this selection use the last paragraph in the article. Ask for a volunteer to read the paragraph aloud. Repeat one more time with another student. Divide students into groups of four to five. Ask them to discuss the first bullet; then have each group share out one idea. Continue this way through the other bullets.
- Exit Slip: Read the details on the board. Write a main idea to go with them.
  - Snakes can be poisonous.
  - Insects can bite and leave itchy bumps on your skin.
  - Cats can scratch you.

♦ Day 4: Summarizing from shared reading

- Give out copies of a partially filled-out outline for the text from the previous day. As a group, finish filling out about half of the outline, referring back to the text, as needed. Have students work in pairs to complete the rest of the outline. Review what they've done.
- Model how to write a summary for about the first half of the outline, one paragraph per section with the main idea in the first sentence. Have students work in partners to complete the rest of the summary. Review what they've done.
- Independent reading, if time.

- Days 5–7: Guided reading
  - This is a three-day process and has six activities: introduction, reading and main idea sheet, discussion, independent reading, writing a summary, and proofreading the summary. On day 3, students will draft their own summary using the outline developed during the reading of the text and discussed/revised during discussion; then they'll use a proofreading checklist to polish it.
  - Introduction for all guided reading selections: read title, picture walk, list prior knowledge, list questions that might be answered, introduce vocabulary, set purpose: write down three main ideas (often the first sentence in a paragraph). Review challenging vocabulary.
- Day 8: Re-teach as needed, based on results of summaries.
- Day 9: Assessment: Students are to read "Exploring Caves" (Appendix D, p. 224–225). Then they fill out the outline sheet (Appendix D, p. 226). Finally, they write the summary paragraph. An assessment protocol can be found in Appendix D, p. 227.

Tier 2

- Progress monitoring assessment: Pre-assessment: inadequate score on classroom written summary. Post-assessment: use a brief information text with a relatively clear structure. Read, fill out the information text structure form, and write a retell.
- Daily plan:
  - Wheel of Fortune (p. 68); on the first day, the sentence is: *We will be reading a text called* _____ (for which you have multiple copies). After the first day, select a sentence from the chapter(s) read during the previous session.

- Read aloud as students follow along in the text. Stop regularly to fill in an article structure outline.
- Celebrations (self and others) and reminder for home practice.

♦ Third-to-last session

- Wheel of Fortune: *We will work together to retell* _____ (name of text from the previous day).
- Using the article structure outline for the text, have students dictate a summary of the first 2/3 or so of the book and you record this on chart paper; help them revise as needed.
- Have students work in partners to finish writing the summary.

♦ Second-to-last session

- Wheel of Fortune: You will prepare for writing your own summary today.
- Students read a brief, well-structured article independently or in pairs, filling out an article structure form.

♦ Final session

- Students use the article structure form to support them as they write the summary (independently or in pairs).
- Wheel of Fortune: You wrote your own summary today.
- What did you learn in this unit? When/where can you use what you learned?
- Present certificates

Tier 3
See Table 7.5.

TABLE 7.5 Structures for Determining Main Idea

Define/describe	Stating in a few words (topic) or a sentence or two (main idea) what the text is basically about; general/specific lesson: select the general term from a list, generate specific terms for a general term, generate a general term from specific terms.
Why important to be a better reader	If we really understand what we've read, we should be able to tell what it was about in very few words.
Model	Read aloud a chapter or so of an information text. State the topic (e.g., planets) and the main idea (e.g., Some planets are more similar to Earth than others).
Activate prior experience	Has anyone ever asked you, "What is that book about?" Tell about it.
S does with explicit T direction step-by-step	Read a segment of _____. What is the main information the segment presents? Sentence frames: This text talks about _____ (topic). The main thing it says about _____ (topic) is _____ (main idea).
S does with initial hints from T	Hints: Read. Stop. What's general? Check each sentence.
When to use/not use	Use: when you get to the end of a section of the text.
How to know if it's effective	If you re-read the section and find that (nearly) every sentence relates to the topic/main idea.
How to transfer to class/home	Bookmark with hints.
Independent practice and debrief	The child reads a self-selected text, noticing what the topic and main idea are.

Foundational Skills Standard RF4.4b: *Read grade-level prose and poetry orally with accuracy, appropriate rate, and expression on successive readings.*

Tier 1

♦ Day 1: Introduction and Reading Workshop: Ask students what they think is the most important goal of reading. Tell them that the most important thing about reading is understanding what you've read, but sometimes reading fluently helps you to understand.

- Minilesson: Re-read a paragraph or two of a book you have been reading aloud to the class several times, each time demonstrating a different fluency problem; explain what each problem is:
    - Making many errors without correcting them
    - Ignoring some punctuation and putting in others
    - Accurate reading, but word-by-word
    - Chunked into phrases, but choppy
    - Smooth but without expression
    - Fluent but too soft
    - Fluent but too fast
    - Ideal
- Practice time: Introduce my fluency chart (fluency rating form (Appendix D, p. 228)). Students read self-select books that are not too challenging for them. After stopping, students should read the next one to two paragraphs (that they have NOT yet read) for a partner three times. Partners discuss the reading and agree on a rating after each reading. Two times is fine if the reader receives the highest rating on the second reading. Then the other partner reads.
- Debrief: What did you notice about your reading?
- Exit Slips (p. 66–67): What is the most important thing you noticed about your reading aloud today?
- Homework: Practice reading a couple of paragraphs, rating yourself on the form.

♦ Day 2: Reading Workshop: Rate variation

- Minilesson: Good readers don't read at the same rate all the time. If I am reading the sports page of the newspaper and you want to know the score of last night's game, I quickly scan until I find two numbers with a dash in between. If I read a story several days ago and someone asks me to tell what happened in the story and I don't remember, I might skim by reading the first sentence of each paragraph with five or more lines. If I am having difficulty or I am studying for a test, I often slow down to understand better. As you read today, put Post-its in your book when you notice that you are speeding up or slowing down. As a group, set a goal for how many Post-its the class can put in.
- Practice time.
- Debrief: Share times when they sped up or slowed down and why.
- Exit slip: Two reasons to change my reading rate are _____.

♦ Day 3: Shared reading: A selection from a class text: Read the selection and discuss.

♦ Day 4 (two to three days after Day 3)

- To practice skimming, have them read the first sentence in each paragraph of the Day 3 text with five or more lines. Do a round-robin retell of the story. Talk about how skimming helped them remember what the selection was about after several days.
- To practice scanning, ask specific questions, tell them the page number the answer is on, have them look quickly for the answer, and put their finger on it before raising their hands.
- Close reading: Follow the close reading protocol (p. 67) as a class or in small groups.

- Days 5–6: Guided reading:
  - Day 1
    - Before reading
      - Predict from title and picture
      - Personal experience connection to the title and picture
      - Introduce difficult words
      - Set a purpose for reading
    - Students read independently
    - Writing assignment
  - Day 2
    - Practice skimming (read the first sentence of each paragraph with five or more lines) to prepare for retelling.
    - Round-robin retell.
    - Practice scanning: Ask specific questions and tell the page the answer is on; have students read quickly to find the answer, put a finger on it, and then raise their hands.
    - Discussion, including the writing assignment, making pictures in your mind, and connections.
- Days 7–8: Guided reading in groups using other selections, emphasizing skimming and scanning.
- In lieu of an assessment for this unit, pair up with a 1st-grade classroom. Have each 4th-grade student select a text to practice in preparation for reading to the younger children. This might be the beginning of a regular buddy reading time, with 1st graders sometimes reading to 4th graders.

Tier 2

- ♦ Progress monitoring assessment:
  - Acknowledge the child's strength in meaning-making
  - Explain that there is some evidence that they could learn to read more fluently
  - Have them read a few paragraphs from the Informal Reading Inventory text immediately below their instructional level, instructing them to read accurately, smoothly, and with expressions
  - Time the first three minutes in a way that is not noticeable to the child
  - Collaboratively mark the fluency chart (Appendix D, p. 228)
  - Use the same passage for pre- and post-assessment

- ♦ Daily plan (after the first session)
  - Read aloud *Rotten Island* with fluency discussion (and a brief discussion of the story)
  - Echo read a short text (such as a selection from Arnold Lobel's *Fables*), sentence by sentence; in echo reading, the teacher reads a sentence aloud and then the students re-read that sentence
  - Minilesson
  - Partner read: Students choose a paragraph from a self-select book to read aloud three times and discuss fluency with a partner
  - Celebration (self or others) and reminder for home practice

- ♦ Day 1
  - Give out enrollment slips (Appendix D, p. 229) stating that, while they are good at understanding what they read, they are enrolled because of low accuracy, rate, expression, and/or their own expressed interest; have each child set a fluency-related goal.
  - Review letter to go home (Appendix D, p. 130).

Additional Curriculum Units ◆ 127

- Read aloud from a picture book text, such as *Rotten Island*, stopping after each page to talk about fluency.

◆ Day 2
  - Punctuation minilesson
    - Write on the board and ask students to read the following: The man went to the party we will go. Who's going to the party? (depends if the period is placed after *went* or after *party*).
    - Read aloud from another text (which will also be used on Days 3–6) while students follow along in their own copies of the text; they knock where periods belong.

◆ Day 3
  - Accuracy minilesson
    - Read aloud from the text, making errors that don't affect the meaning; what do they notice? (probably nothing).
    - Then make errors that alter the meaning; what do they notice this time?
    - Read aloud with accuracy but word-by-word; ask students what problem they notice.

◆ Day 4
  - Chunking minilesson
    - Read aloud from the text, accurately but word-by-word, like last time; what's the problem?
    - Read aloud chunking: What's better? What problem remains?

◆ Day 5
  - Smoothness minilesson
    - Read aloud from the text, chunking like last time; what problem remains?

- Read aloud smoothly, but in a monotone: What's better? What problem remains?

◆ Day 6

- Expression minilesson
    - Read aloud from the text, smoothly like last time; what problem remains?
    - Read aloud with overly exaggerated expression; what's the problem now?
    - Read aloud with appropriate expression; what good things do you notice about this reading?

◆ Day 7

- Students write own brief fables (individually or with a partner), practice reading them aloud, and share with the group.
- What did you learn in this unit? When/where can you use what you learned?
- Present certificates.

Tier 3

Fluency instruction at Tier 3 will look similar to Tier 2. The instructor should be sure that the student understands why fluent reading is important (so that meaning is more easily accessed) and that speed, in and of itself, is not the goal. All texts should be self-selected by the student.

Writing Standard W4.1A, B, & D: *Introduce a topic or text clearly, state an opinion, and create an organizational structure in which related ideas are grouped to support the writer's purpose. Provide reasons that are supported by facts and details. Provide a concluding statement or section related to the opinion presented.*

Tier 1

◆ Day 1

- Argument game
    - This game will introduce you to crafting an argument: thinking of something you believe and providing reasons for it.

- Intro to the problem: convincing the rest of your classmates that your small group should receive a batch of cookies
- Form self-selected groups of four to five
- Write and/or draw to make others believe your group should get the cookies; designate a spokesperson
- Presentations (two to three minutes each)
- Evaluations of the arguments: what did various groups do?
- Vote (anonymous) with reason: can't vote for own group; all get cookies!

- Vocabulary introduction: discuss the following terms:
  - Issue: what you are talking or writing about (e.g., getting cookies)
  - Argument: what you believe or want others to believe (e.g., WE should get the cookies)—contrast *argument* with *fight*
  - Reasons: why you believe what you believe (e.g., why your group should get the cookies)
  - Details/evidence: facts that fit with your reasons
  - Convince/persuade: to get others to believe what you believe
  - Audience: who you are trying to persuade AND who can do something about your argument (e.g., classmates)
  - Review vocabulary and play Finger Flash (for several days)

◆ Day 2
- Finger Flash (p. 68) for issue, argument, reasons, convince/persuade, audience
- Use assisted reading (p. 67) to read a persuasive text selection. Discuss:
  - Issue
  - Audience (the reader)

- Pro argument
- Reasons
- Con argument
- Reasons
- Make a continuum line on the board with one extreme view on one end and the other extreme view on the other end. Talk about what the midpoint might mean. Give each student a small Post-it. They write their names on the Post-its and place it on the continuum. Discuss.
- If possible, show students how to access www.thisibelieve.org and have them select their own mentor text.

♦ Day 3

- Repeat Finger Flash for above terms.
- Have students share mentor texts if they were able to access them.
- Sometimes when we write or speak, whether anyone listens to us has to do with what groups we belong to. For example, sometimes adults don't listen to arguments children make because they think they are too young. Sometimes teenagers don't listen to arguments adults make because they think adults don't remember what it was like to be a teenager.

♦ Day 4

- Fill out (as a group, step-by-step) How Much Would People Listen to Me? form (list of arguments [e.g., Getting along with siblings is challenging]; rating self on a 1–5 scale about how much they think others would listen to them and why) (Appendix D, p. 231).
- Read aloud about a girl named Erica who fought the construction of a power plant: name issue, argument, audience, reasons provided (Appendix D, p. 232).
- Give out the Persuasive Issues List (Appendix D, p. 233). Have students complete the list and ask several volunteers to read their lists aloud.

- Add to the list; record their ideas on chart paper.

◆ Day 5

- Accept nominations for an issue the class will write about; narrow down to two.
- Review the Persuasive Letter Issue Plan form (Appendix D, p. 234) and the Persuasive Letter Plan form (Appendix D, p. 235).
- Fill out the Persuasive Letter Plan Form on chart paper for the two issues under consideration for shared writing.
- Students fill out their copies of the Persuasive Letter Issue Form and then the Persuasive Letter Plan Form.
- Note: If possible, have students do research on their issue.

◆ Day 6

- As a group, draft group issue introduction, attending to objectives on revision checklist throughout.
- Students draft their individual introductions.
- Some students will finish each segment before others; they may work on other writing.

◆ Day 7

- Continue shared writing: first body paragraph.
- Continue individual writing: first body paragraph.
- Continue shared writing: second body paragraph.
- Continue individual writing: second body paragraph.

◆ Day 8

- Continue shared writing: third body paragraph.
- Continue individual writing: third body paragraph.
- Continue shared writing: conclusion.
- Continue individual writing: conclusion.

◆ Day 9

- Introduce the Persuasive Letter Revision form (Appendix D, pp. 236–237).

- Go through the form on the document camera as a group for the shared writing (have students discuss in small groups and then call on a random student to come up to do the underlining, etc.).

♦ Day 10

- Lead students step-by-step as they go through the revision form.
- Introduce the Persuasive Letter Peer Conference Form (Appendix D, p. 238).

♦ Day 11

- Students have peer conferences.
- When complete, they turn in their draft with the conference form attached and work on other writing.

♦ Day 12 and on

- When the first letter is returned to a student who is ready to proofread, introduce the Persuasive Letter Proofreading Form (Appendix D, p. 239).
- Students proofread and submit their drafts with the proofreading form attached.
- Once proofreading is complete, students make the final draft.
- Students research the address of the audience, address it, and mail it.
- Note: If possible, consider what actions (other than sending letters) students might take in support of their issues (may require more research).

Tier 2

Because the students attending this group struggled with persuasive writing in their classrooms, it might be tempting to switch to part-to-whole instruction. But it is important to base the Tier 2 work on students' own writing. This can occur by having students work in pairs to craft a persuasive letter, beginning by discussing any aspects of their school that bother them. Students agree about a school problem that they care about and that a particular person (e.g., principal) has control over.

The Tier 2 teacher asks students to work in pairs to plan for and write a persuasive letter, following the general process used at Tier 1. There are minilessons each day to reinforce the aspects they need to focus on, including editing.

The teacher also sends a note home to parents/guardians asking them to have a discussion with their child about a family challenge. This letter describes the process for the conversation: again, reflecting the steps from Tier 1. The group discusses these family interactions. The teacher then assists students in planning for, drafting, and editing a persuasive letter to their parents, advocating for a change related to the family challenge.

Tier 3

It is possible that, even after the experience of Tier 2 instruction, some students may not demonstrate mastery of the addressed standard. So, the Tier 3 level of instruction begins where Tier 2 left off, with the teacher retracing their steps to plan for a letter on the family issue. At the end of each day's session, the student and teacher will set a very specific goal for the following session so that the student can see clear progress.

If the student struggles with getting ideas down on paper, the teacher may take dictation. If not, the teacher will work on their own persuasive letter on a topic of interest—including some "mistakes" common to persuasive texts (e.g., failing to clearly state the argument) and mechanical errors—while the student composes theirs. When it is time for the editing process, they will work together to revise and proofread their texts.

Finally, the student and teacher select another issue of interest to the student and complete the planning form together. Then the child drafts their narrative independently. When it comes to the revision and proofreading checklist, the teacher sits with the student as they go step-by-step through the checklist but does not help them with it.

In reading this book so far, you might have the impression that all standards are taught in isolation from each other. But the most interesting—and often effective—units are those that integrate several literacy standards. They may also incorporate information from other content areas. We'll look at this possibility in Chapter 7.

Bibliography

Kelley, M.J., & Clausen-Grace, N. (2010). Guiding students through expository text with feature walks. *The Reading Teacher, 64* (3), 191–195. doi: 10.1598/RT.64.3.4

8

Integrated Units

In many cases, it will be most effective to teach units focusing on a single standard. Sometimes, however, it may be more efficient to combine multiple standards in a single unit. Doing so also conveys to students that knowledge and skills are most meaningful when integrated.

In this chapter, I will present examples of integrated units. In Chapters 4–6, I intentionally addressed different standards in the 2nd and 4th grades so as to cover examples of as many standards as possible. In this chapter, however, I will offer units at the two grade levels that address very similar standards. In doing so, the contrasts between what work looks like at the two levels will be more evident. I will begin with the 4th-grade unit, so it will be easy to see how expectations for second graders have been adjusted appropriately.

Fourth-Grade Unit for Research Project and Oral Report

Tier 1
- ♦ CCSS:
  - RI 1. *Refer to details and examples in a text when explaining what the text says explicitly and when drawing inferences from the text.*

- RI 7. *Interpret information presented visually, orally, or quantitatively.*
- RI 9. *Integrate information from two texts on the same topic in order to write or speak about the subject knowledgeably.*
- W 7. *Conduct a research project by investigating different aspects of a topic.*
- W 8. *Recall relevant information from experiences or gather information from print and digital sources; take notes, categorize information, and provide a list of sources.*
- SL 2. *Paraphrase information presented in diverse media and formats, including visually and orally.*
- SL 4. *Report on a topic in an organized manner, using facts to support main ideas; speak clearly and at an understandable pace.*
- SL 5. *Add visual displays to presentations.*
- SL 6 & L 3. *Differentiate between contexts that call for formal and informal English; use formal English when appropriate.*

Note: The timing of these minilessons can't be predicted. When at least one child in the class is ready for a given minilesson, it should be taught to the whole class. You will be conducting research on your topic—modeling the process—as the students work on theirs.

- ◆ Topics minilesson: Decide on three possible topics that you are considering. Collect at least four sources each (books, web pages, etc.) about two topics and less than this for the other. Use the document camera to show how you list your topics on the Research Project Plan Form (Appendix D, pp. 240–242). Explain how you are eliminating the topic with little available information and tell how you are choosing between the other two. After this minilesson, students go through the same process by generating three topics, visiting the library/searching the Internet, and selecting a final topic.

- Prior knowledge, asking questions, and taking notes minilesson: Remind students that it helps to think about what they already know and ask questions before reading. On the document camera, model how you list prior knowledge about your topic, ask students for additional information, and then come up with three general questions. Write bibliographic information for your first source on the Research Bibliography Form (Appendix D, p. 243). Write each question at the top of a piece of paper and write Other Information at the top of a fourth piece. Model how you find information in one of your sources, using the contents and index to do so (show on the document camera). Model how you write as few words as possible as notes; it might be easier for them to understand if you write a full sentence and then show how many words you can cross out while still maintaining the meaning. Number the bits of information and skip lines. Circle one or two interesting vocabulary words. Find information for another of your questions in the same source and record it on the correct piece of paper. Find an interesting piece of information unrelated to your questions and model recording that on the Other Information page. After this minilesson, students take notes about their own topic on their Research Project Plan Form; remind students to have you circle the bullet for each step as they complete it (after a while, students who are further along can perform this function). At the end of each work session, form small groups and allow each student to share an interesting piece of information they learned that day with others.
- Selecting information minilesson: On the document camera, model the process of going through each page of your notes, highlighting the three facts you want to share related to each question. Fill out the Oral Report Notes Form (Appendix D, p. 244). As students finish notetaking, they go through this selection process themselves.

- Making/finding an illustration minilesson: Demonstrate how you draw or find on the Internet an illustration (picture, chart, graph, map, etc.) to include in your oral report. As students complete the Oral Report Notes Form, they find/make an illustration.
- Oral report practice minilesson: Talk with students about what they have learned about making oral presentations (e.g., book reports). Put a copy of the Oral Report Rubric (Appendix D, p. 245) on the document camera. Model giving your report. Be sure to make one or two significant errors (e.g., bringing in an unrelated illustration, not defining challenging words, talking too fast); ask the class to evaluate your report on each aspect. Explain what you will do to remedy these problems. As students finish their illustration, they practice with a partner; the partner is required to mark "Work on This" for at least one area.
- Once students have practiced with a partner, they make whatever changes are necessary and then practice with another partner. Once the "Did Well" column is checked for all areas, they are in a position to do their final presentation. They may choose whether to present to the whole class or to a small group; if they present to a small group, it should be comprised of students who are far along in the process so that students who are moving more slowly aren't delayed. Listeners are expected to offer compliments and ask questions; presenters should know that it is acceptable to answer a question by saying, "I don't know." The Oral Report Rubric can be used, if desired.
- Note: This work can serve as a foundation for a written report unit.

Tier 2 and Tier 3 Units

The 2nd-grade unit below can serve as the foundation for a Tier 2 unit for 4th graders. A Tier 3 unit would simply be more individualized.

Second-Grade Unit for Research Project and Oral Report

Tier 1 Unit
- ♦ CCSS:
    - RI 1. *Ask and answer such questions as who, what, where, when, why, and how to demonstrate understanding of key details in a text.*
    - RI 7. *Explain how specific images (e.g., a diagram showing how a machine works) contribute to and clarify a text.*
    - RI 9. *Compare and contrast the most important points presented by two texts on the same topic.*
    - W 7. *Participate in shared research and writing projects (e.g., read a number of books on a single topic to produce a report; record science observations).*
    - W 8. *Recall information from experiences or gather information from provided sources to answer a question.*
    - SL 2. *Recount or describe key ideas or details from a text read aloud or information presented orally or through other media.*
    - SL 4. *Tell a story or recount an experience with appropriate facts and relevant, descriptive details, speaking audibly in coherent sentences.*
    - SL 5. *Add drawings or other visual displays to stories or recounts of experiences when appropriate to clarify ideas, thoughts, and feelings.*
    - SL 6. *Produce complete sentences when appropriate to the task and situation in order to provide requested detail or clarification.*

Note: The timing of these minilessons can't be predicted. When at least one child in the class is ready for a given minilesson, it should be taught to the whole class. You will be conducting research on your topic—modeling the process—as the students work on theirs.

- Topics minilesson: Decide on two possible animals that you are considering studying. Collect at least two sources (books, web pages, etc.) for each. Use the document camera to show how you list your topics on the Research Project Plan Form (Appendix D, p. 246–247). Explain how you are choosing between the two. Students will work in pairs for this project; it may be helpful to pair stronger with weaker readers to support the research process. After this minilesson, partners generate two animals of interest. Then the class visits the library to look for books on their topics. Students make a final decision based on, among other things, the availability of resources. The teacher brings in other sources (e.g., from the Internet) as needed.
- Prior knowledge, asking questions, and taking notes minilesson: Remind students that it helps to think about what they already know and to ask questions before reading. On the document camera, model how you list prior knowledge about your topic, ask students for additional information, and then come up with two general questions: choosing from among *who, what, where, when, why,* and *how* (*what, why,* and *how* are often the most interesting). Write each question at the top of a piece of paper and write Other Information at the top of a third piece. Model how you find information in one of your sources: skimming headings, the table of contents, and the index to do so (show on the document camera). Model how you write as few words as possible in the notes you take; it might be easier for them to understand if you write a full sentence and then show how many words you can cross out and still maintain the meaning. Number the bits of information and skip lines. Circle one or two interesting vocabulary words. Find information for another of your questions in the same source and record it on the correct piece of paper. Find an interesting piece of information unrelated to your questions and model recording that on the Other Information page. After this minilesson, students will take notes for their own topic on their Research Project Plan Form; remind students

to have you circle the bullet for each step as they complete it (after a while, students who are further along can perform this function). At the end of each work session, form small groups and allow each student to share an interesting piece of information they learned that day.

♦ Selecting information minilesson: On the document camera, model the process of going through each page of your notes, highlighting the two to three facts you want to share related to each question. Fill out the Oral Report Notes Form (Appendix D, p. 248). As students finish notetaking, they go through this selection process themselves.

♦ Making/finding an illustration minilesson: Demonstrate how you draw—or find on the Internet—an illustration (picture, chart, graph, map, etc.) to include in your oral report. As students complete the Oral Report Notes Form, they find/make an illustration.

♦ Oral report practice minilesson: Talk with students about what they know about making oral presentations (e.g., book reports). Put a copy of the checklist on the document camera. Model giving your report. Be sure to make one or two significant errors (e.g., bringing in an unrelated illustration, not defining words, talking too fast); ask the class to evaluate your report on each aspect. Explain what you will do to remedy these problems. As partners finish their illustration, they practice with another set of partners.

♦ Partners may choose whether to present to the whole class or to a small group; if they present to a small group, it should be comprised of students who are far along in the process so that students who are moving more slowly aren't delayed. Listeners are expected to offer compliments and ask questions; presenters should know that it is acceptable to answer a question by saying, "I don't know." Listeners may also make a limited number of suggestions, if the presenting partners ask them to do so.

♦ Note: This work can serve as a foundation for a written report unit.

There are several ways in which the 4th-grade integrated unit has been altered to make it more appropriate for younger children. Second graders will:

- Generate two possible topics rather than three, and those topics will be selected from the over-arching topic of animals to avoid the potential paralysis of unlimited choice.
- Conduct all work in partners for ongoing support.
- Be expected to draw from two rather than three sources.
- Benefit from the support of the teacher in accessing sources, especially those from the Internet.
- Experience less focus on polishing their oral report since this may be a relatively new experience; when they present, they will receive compliments and questions—suggestions only if they explicitly ask for them.

Tier 2 and 3 Units

At Tier 2 and Tier 3, students simply benefit from the more intense support available in a small group or tutorial.

There are times when standards are best addressed in isolation—if they are particularly challenging or just appear to be largely unrelated to any other standards. However, if standards can be integrated within a single unit this may be far more efficient and also convey to students the idea that knowledge is rarely learned and understood in discrete bits.

Ideally, Tier 2 and Tier 3 instruction would always emerge out of Tier 1 instruction. But there are times when readers have gaps in their skills and knowledge related to standards from previous grade levels. In this case, it may be beneficial for them to receive this instruction in small groups and individual tutoring. Chapter 9 examines this phenomenon.

9
Tier 2 and Tier 3 Units Based on Informal Reading and Writing Assessments

Up to this point in this book, the focus has been on developing a strong classroom curriculum (Tier 1), as well as supportive small group (Tier 2) and individual interventions (Tier 3) based on needs demonstrated via the unit assessments given to all students in Tier 1. This is the foundation of work toward mastery of grade-level sophisticated standards within the multi-tiered support system (MTSS) framework. Nevertheless, for some students, Tier 2 and Tier 3 support for mastery of standards at lower grade levels—or areas of literacy which most lists of advanced standards fail to cover—may be beneficial in their overall literacy trajectory.

It has been my experience that Tier 2 and Tier 3 classes running in parallel to those described earlier in the book prove fruitful for many children who are categorized as "struggling" readers. Enrollment in these classes can be determined through administration of informal assessments: generally speaking, an Informal Reading Inventory (IRI) and a writing sample.

Informal Reading Inventories (IRIs)

Describing the details of IRI administration is beyond the scope of this text. However, a brief review is warranted here. IRIs consist of a series of passages at a range of difficulties. The administrator selects a passage to begin the assessment, often by having the child read lists of words of increasing levels of challenge and selecting the level at which the child's word-reading accuracy is approximately 70%. The child reads the passage aloud and the administrator records all miscues (errors) on another copy of the text. After completing the reading, the child is asked to provide an oral retelling and/or answer a series of questions. If the text is determined to be at the child's frustration level (this differs from one IRI to the next, but approximately below 92% accuracy and/or below 70% comprehension), they read the passage that is a bit easier; this process continues until the child reads a passage at their instructional level (92+% accuracy and 70+% comprehension). If the first passage is at the child's independent level (98% accuracy and 90% comprehension) or instructional level, they continue to read more difficult passages until they reach the frustration level.

There are a range of beliefs about the use of IRIs. The predominant concern about these instruments—initially expressed more than 40 years ago (McKenna, 1983) and studied thoroughly for about 20 years after that (Spector, 2005)—has been the inadequacy of reliability data. In the most recently published critique addressing this point, Nilsson (2013) claims that the issue has not been resolved. Additional concerns have included inattention to the interest level of passages, type and passage dependency of questions, accuracy criteria, and the generally accepted practice of having the child read aloud at sight (Applegate et al., 2002; McKenna, 1983).

Nevertheless, we have known for at least 45 years that children demonstrate patterns in their reading and that those patterns are relatively consistent over initial readings vs. re-readings, and between instructional and frustration levels (Gonzales & Elijah, 1978). As a result, IRIs offer a wealth of information about tailoring instruction to the specific needs of individual children. Researchers have demonstrated that children who struggle with reading do so for a variety of reasons, and most of these children have reading strengths as well as challenges (Buly & Valencia, 2002)—strengths and challenges that are regularly evidenced in IRI data.

The child's instructional and independent levels, as estimated by the IRI, are helpful in selecting teaching materials and guiding the child toward texts for independent reading. For the purpose of grouping children to receive Tier 2 or Tier 3 support, however, the most important information gained is from an analysis of miscues and of retellings and/or responses to questions. Two children reading at the same level may require vastly different instructional support, whereas children whose reading levels are quite different may share the same strengths and weaknesses and benefit from similar instruction. Whether or not they are included in an IRI protocol, we can add additional prompts to probe the child's facility with metacognitive strategies, such as predicting and visualizing, and request that they provide a personal response verbally or in writing (Manzo & Manzo, 2013); we may offer classes to address those aspects of reading and writing as well. We might do well to heed Estes and Vaughan's (1973) recommendation that we "accept the philosophy of the IRI as being a strategy, not a test, for studying the behavior of the reader in depth" (p. 152).

Informal Emergent Literacy Inventory (IELI)

For children who are not yet reading on their own, I developed the IELI (Appendix E, p. 280–281). It addresses meaning, print, and sound skills.

- ♦ The child is first asked to make a prediction about what might happen in a story based on the title alone. Then they are shown an initial picture from the story and asked to revise or extend their prediction. The adult then reads to the climax of the story and the child is asked to predict how the story might end. Predictions are rated by the extent to which they are logically derived from the

information given and by the child's willingness to revise them based on new information.
- ◆ At the completion of the story, the child is asked to provide a retelling. The retell is evaluated based on its accuracy, completeness, logical sequence, emphasis on significant rather than extraneous detail, and awareness of audience (i.e., if the child begins the retell with pronouns for which the referent is unclear, this would be a negative).
- ◆ The adult takes the child back into the story and asks them to point to the words as the adult reads aloud on two separate pages. The child's ability to point accurately demonstrates the strength of their concept of word boundaries, an essential skill for beginning readers. The child is then asked to match a word card to the same word in the story, point to a word in a line of text which has just been read to them, and read a word in a line of text which has just been read. The ability to perform these tasks demonstrates a more advanced level of print awareness.
- ◆ The remainder of the screening tool is not connected to the story read earlier. First, the adult reads a sentence from which a word has been omitted (e.g., My favorite color is _____. The child is asked to complete the sentence with a word that maintains the meaning of the sentence. This is the kind of "guessing" activity we engage in constantly as we read.
- ◆ Next, phonemic awareness is checked. This is the ability to isolate sounds within words and is a clear and important prerequisite for phonics instruction and invented spelling. There are four increasingly difficult tasks involved in this part of the assessment. The child is asked to provide a word which rhymes with a given word. Then, they are asked to clap syllables in a word. Next, when the adult pronounces several isolated sounds (e.g., /k/ /a/ /t/), the child is asked to blend them into a word (e.g., "cat"). Finally, given a word (e.g., "go" or "past"), the child is asked to segment that word into sounds (e.g., /g/ /o/ or /p/ /a/ /s/ /t/).

- Knowledge of several consonant sounds is also checked.
- The child is asked to read a limited number of sight words. Because the child is not yet considered to be a "reader," the point of this assessment is not so much to assess sight word knowledge as to check for risk-taking and strategic behavior.
- Finally, a writing sample is collected. The child is asked to read what they have written. This sample is not analyzed formally, but such attributes as fluency, content, level of invented spelling use, spacing, etc. are noted.

Use of Informal Data for Developing and Teaching Tier 2 and Tier 3 Units

The IELI assessment takes minimal time to administer and is appropriate for many children in the second half of kindergarten through the first half of first grade (and beyond, as needed). IRI administration, however, can be a time-consuming process. Therefore, it may be wise to use a screening measure—results from a group test—to narrow down the number of children who will benefit from one-on-one IRI testing. In the past, I have used scores from the state standards test to play this role. Because I am not fully confident in the predictive power of this test, I administer an IRI to all children who score in the fifth stanine or below, plus any children new to the class.

I vary typical IRI administration and data analysis in two significant ways. In addition to a retelling—followed by literal, inferential, and higher-level follow-up questions—I add other prompts such as a prediction or request for prior knowledge based on the title, and requests to visualize a part of the selection and to make personal connections. Most researchers describing miscue analysis (e.g., Provost et al., 2010) recommend focusing on the reader's use of graphic, syntactic, and semantic cues. But I have found categorizing miscues according to aspects of reading—sight words, basic phonics, use of context, multi-syllable decoding, and vocabulary—links more directly to instruction.

Appendix E provides several exemplar IRI passages and a chart for recording miscues for analysis (pp. 282–287).

Tier 2   Units Based on IELI and Writing Analysis

I developed a range of Tier 2 units that reflect student needs noted in the IELI. These units are appropriate for use at grade 1 primarily. The standard addressed, daily routine, plans, and last day are described below.

- Emergent meaning unit
  - **CCSS**
    - RL K-1st 2. *Retell familiar stories, including key details.*
    - RL K-1st 7. *Describe the relationship between illustrations and the story in which they appear.*
    - L K 4. *Determine or clarify the meaning of unknown and multiple-meaning words and phrases.*
    - W K 3. *Use a combination of drawing, dictating, and writing to narrate a single event or several loosely linked events.*
  - **Daily routine**
    - Send home enrollment form for the class (Appendix D, p. 249).
    - Follow the plan below to do a picture book read-aloud; for some of the elements (e.g., predictions and wonderings), have students talk with a partner before sharing out with the whole group.
    - Use letter tiles to make words or sing songs from the auditory unit (see below).
    - Celebrations (self or others) and reminder for home practice.

- **Picture book read-aloud plan**
    - Read the title, discuss the cover picture, and introduce the main point of the story.
    - Have students tell you what they know about the topic of the book. "I know …"
    - Do a Picture Walk, flipping through the pages and having them tell what they notice in the pictures. "I notice …"
    - Ask them to make predictions and give reasons for them. "I think … because …"
    - Ask them what they are wondering about.
    - Read the story aloud to them, stopping at points to have students retell each section and make new predictions. Ask for an overall retell at the end.
    - Do oral cloze: Re-read several sentences leaving out a word (usually at the end); ask them to come up with words that would make sense in the sentence. They don't need to come up with the actual word, but one that is logical. They are not looking at the book while they do this.
    - Re-read a few sentences with challenging words. See if they can figure out the approximate meaning of each word (e.g., they may not know that *porridge* is oatmeal, but they should be able to figure out that it is something you eat).
- **Then** … After you've read aloud enough picture books, so students are quite confident with all elements, have the group dictate a story to you one day, and allow them to each write a story the next day. They should draw a picture for their story either before or after writing.
- **Last day**—Present certificates.

♦ Emergent print unit
  - **CCSS**

- RF K 1a. *Follow words from left to right, top to bottom, page by page.*
- RF K 1b. *Recognize that spoken words are represented in written language by specific sequences of letters.*
- RF K 1c. *Understand that words are separated by spaces in print.*
- RF K1d. *Recognize and name all upper- and lower-case letters of the alphabet.*

- **Daily routine**
    - Send home enrollment form for the class (Appendix D, p. 250).
    - Read aloud.
    - Core practice (see below).
    - Celebrations (self and others) and reminder for home practice.
    - Note: Initial lessons should include letter recognition, Names Project, and self-selected words; if, for example, letter recognition and Names Project are covered in one session, begin with self-select words the following day. Continue as long as needed. When all alphabet letters have been covered, drop that part. When all students' names have been covered, drop that part and add Big Books and Word Wall.
- **Letter recognition**: on-going work with sandpaper letters, etc., on an as-needed basis.
- **Names project**
    - Write each child's name on a tag board strip.
    - Each day, pull one student's name at random.
    - Interview that student—about family, what they are good at, likes and dislikes, etc.—while other students listen.
    - As a group, count the number of letters in the name, name the letters, and chant the spelling.
    - Re-write the name on another piece of tagboard, cut it apart into separate letters, and, as a group, rebuild the name.

- Discuss physical attributes of the child (e.g., hair color, eye color, glasses or not, etc.).
- Each child copies the name on a piece of paper and draws a picture of the child who is the focus of the day.
- Each day, compare the new name to previous names (e.g., length, similar letters, etc.).

- **Self-select words**
  - Each day, each child chooses a word they would like to read.
  - Write the word on a 3 × 5 card using a crayon.
  - The child traces the crayon letters with their finger and reads the word.
  - Occasionally, ask children to revisit the words, practicing with a partner.

- **Big books**: use two Big Books to teach the remaining print concepts.
  - Discussion related to the topic of the book.
  - Predict from the title and cover picture.
  - Picture Walk: make sure to point out words which tell what the picture is.
  - Reading:
    1. 1st reading: teacher reads and points to the words.
    2. 2nd: teacher and students read as the teacher points to the words; then, model how to find and read individual words.
    3. 3rd: divide pages among students; each child comes up, reads the page, and points to the words (may request that teacher reads along); then, the teacher names a word on the page and asks the child to point to it and finally the teacher points to a word on the page and asks the child to read it.

- **Word wall**
  - Introduce a few words from the current Big Book or the first column of the early sight words list (Appendix D, p. 252); write them on 3 × 5 cards and place them on the Word Wall.
  - Clap and chant the spelling of a word.
  - Each child writes the word in crayon on a 3 × 5 card.
  - After five words are on the Word Wall, play "Read My Mind": Give clues to the word you are thinking of: it's on the Word Wall, it has (number) letters, it begins with ... (sound or letter), it rhymes with ..., it completes the following sentence ..., etc.
- **Last day**—present certificates.

◆ Emergent auditory unit
  - CCSS
    - RF K 2a. *Recognize and produce rhyming words.*
    - RF K 2b. *Count, pronounce, blend, and segment syllables in spoken words.*
    - RF K 2c. *Blend and segment onsets and rimes of single-syllable spoken words.*
    - RF K 2d. *Isolate and pronounce the initial, medial vowel, and final sounds in three-phoneme words.*
    - RF K 2e. *Add or substitute individual sounds in simple, one-syllable words to make new words.*
    - RF 1 2b. *Orally produce single-syllable words by blending sounds, including consonant blends.*
    - RF 1 2d. *Segment spoken single-syllable words into their complete sequence of individual sounds.*
    - W K 3. *Use a combination of drawing, dictating, and writing to narrate a single event or several loosely linked events.*
  - **Daily routine**
    - Send home enrollment form for the class (Appendix D, p. 251).

- Read aloud and discuss a picture book (to maintain a focus on meaning during this sound-based unit).
- Core practice (see below).
- Celebrations (self and others) and reminder for home practice.

- **Rhymes and syllables**
  - Day 1: Introduce the concept of rhyme: words that sound the same in the middle and end but have different initial sounds.
  - Day 1 & 2.
    1. Choose a word that has several rhymes (e.g., park) and provide examples of words that rhyme with it (orally, rather than writing them).
    2. Say the word (e.g., park) and ask students to think of a word which rhymes with it, but means the sound a dog makes, or what it's like when the lights are turned off at night, etc.
    3. Repeat with several words.
    4. Beginning with two-syllable words, demonstrate and practice how to clap syllables (orally); move up to words with more syllables as students are ready.
  - Day 3: Read a heavily rhymed book (e.g., *The Cat in the Hat*). If a stanza has an ABAB rhyme pattern, read the first three lines intact, read the last line up to the rhyme, and ask kids to provide the last word.

- **Isolating, blending, and substituting sounds (Days 4–6)**: Note—The following activities are taken from Yopp (1992).
  - Isolating sounds: sung to the tune of "Old MacDonald Had a Farm": "What's the sound that starts these words? *Turtle, time,* and *teeth*? /t/ is the sound that starts these words. *Turtle, time,* and *teeth.* With a /t/, /t/ here ..." (p. 700).

- Blending sounds: sung to the tune of "If You're Happy and You Know It, Clap Your Hands": "If you think you know this word, shout it out! If you think you know this word, shout it out! If you think you know this word, then tell me what you heard. If you think you know this word, shout it out! /k/-/a/-/t/" (pp. 700–701).
- Substituting sounds: sung to the tune of "The Birthday Song": "Bappy Birthday bo boo ..." (p. 701).
- Writing, if time (see Days 10–11).

- **Segmenting sounds (Days 7–9)**

  - Sung to the tune of "Twinkle, Twinkle, Little Star": "Listen, listen, to my word. Then tell me all the sounds you heard: *race*. (slowly) /r/ is one sound, /ai/ is two, /s/ is last in *race* it's true" (p. 702).
  - Work with Elkonin boxes (https://www.readingrockets.org/classroom/classroom-strategies/elkonin-boxes). Each child gets a "placemat" with two (later three) boxes on it and a circle below each box. Use small objects, such as beans; children put one object in the first box when you say the first sound and one in the second box when you say the second sound. Start with two-sound words beginning with a consonant (e.g., go, shoe).
  - Writing, if time (see Days 10–11).

- **Writing (Days 10–11)**: Provide time for students to write; they can ask for help by listening to you "stretch" the word to separate the sounds (accuracy not expected).
- **Consonant sounds unit (as many days as needed)**

  - Say several words beginning with the target consonant sound and ask students what sound (NOT letter) each word begins with (e.g., "buh" for B).

- Say a pair of words which either begin with the same sound or different sounds. Students each have a card with S (= same) on one side and D (= different) on the other, and when you say, "Go," they are to hold up the correct side of the card. Repeat with as many pairs as it takes for most children to be accurate.
- Write the upper- and lower-case letters that usually represent that sound on the board.
- Ask students to think of all the words they know which begin with that sound/letter; list them on the board.
- Figure out which of the words are "drawable"; each child chooses one of these words.
- Give each child a 3 × 5 card and an envelope with their name on it for keeping the cards. On the card, they should write the word, underline the initial letter, and draw a picture of the word.
- After several consonant sounds have been covered, give students time to practice; the goal is for them to be able to say the sound and/or name the picture on the card (without looking) when told what the beginning letter is.
- **Last day**—Present certificates.

◆ Emergent writing unit:
- CCSS:
    - RF1a. *Follow words from left to right, top to bottom, and page by page.*
    - RF1b. *Recognize that spoken words are represented in written language by specific sequences of letters.*
    - RF1c. *Understand that words are separated by spaces in print.*
    - W K 3. *Use a combination of drawing, dictating, and writing to narrate a single event or several loosely linked events.*

- Teaching practices for this unit are straightforward.
  - Interactive writing: The group decides on an idea for a story or a topic for an information text. One child suggests a beginning to the text and the teacher writes it on a piece of chart paper, demonstrating how to figure out the spelling for each word, maintaining spaces between words, using capitals and end punctuation. Beginning with the second sentence, children take turns "sharing the pen": individuals come up to the chart paper to write a part of the text, using the same practices modeled by the teacher.
  - Independent writing: Children have time to write on a topic of their choosing. The teacher circulates to help them with spacing, to sound their way through words phonetically (NOT emphasizing accurate but rather logical spelling), etc.

Tier 2   Units Based on IRI and Writing

I developed a range of Tier 2 units that reflect student needs noted in miscue, comprehension, and writing analysis. These units are appropriate for use at a range of elementary grade levels. The standard addressed, progress monitoring assessment, daily routine, plans, and the last day are described below.

- ◆ Sight words unit
  - **CCSS**
    - RF K 3c. *Read common, high-frequency words by sight.*
    - RF 1 3g and RF 2 3f. *Recognize and read grade-appropriate irregularly spelled words.*
  - **Progress monitoring assessment**: Top 50 Most Frequent Words from Children's Literature list for children not yet reading at the pre-primer level (Appendix D, p. 252) and a sub-set of a longer list of sight words for those who are.

- **Daily routine**
  - Give the child enrollment form to students and have them set goals (Appendix D, p. 253).
  - Send home enrollment form for the class (Appendix D, p. 254).
  - Independent writing time with a focus on spelling of sight words they've mastered.
  - Poetry for Sight Words activity.
  - Celebrations (self and others) and reminder for home practice.
- **Poetry for sight word development (Appendix D, p. 255)**
  - Needed: a collection of short poems, a word card for each word in the poem, and a record sheet (with the name of each poem followed by four check-off boxes).
  - Begin by introducing the first poem. Read the poem aloud to the students. Read the poem again, this time with students pointing to the words as you read. Draw attention to phrasing, punctuation marks, and other expressive reading indicators.
  - Then have them join in, reading the poem aloud with you and continuing to point to the words.
  - When most students seem to be able to read the poem quite well, tell them it is their job to practice their poem until they can read it accurately.
  - When a child can read the poem without assistance, pointing to the words as they read, mark their chart for that poem in the first column and provide the word cards for that poem.
  - Now they are to use the cards to "build" the poem on a desk while looking at the poem and matching the words visually. When they have done this, they need to be checked by you, and you will mark their chart in the second column.

- Then they are to once again build the poem, but this time they are to keep the poem face down unless they get stuck; this is a visual-to-auditory match. You check and mark their chart under the third column.
- Finally, students are to practice the word cards in random order (as flash cards) until they know all the words. They should initially make two piles of cards: words they know at sight and words they do not know. Then they can go back to the poem to match the unknown word to that same word in the context of the poem to figure it out, rather than asking you. Once they can read all the cards in isolation, you mark their chart under the last column and they advance to the next poem.
- You may choose to begin each day's session by reading together all poems that anyone is working on. Once all children have completed the first poem, drop it from those you continue to read together. As soon as one child is ready to move to a new poem, introduce it to the whole group.
- **Last day**—present certificates.

◆ Simple decoding unit

- **CCSS**
    - RF 1 3a. *Know the spelling-sound correspondences for common consonant digraphs.*
    - RF 1 3b. *Decode regularly spelled one-syllable words.*
    - RF 1 3c. *Know final –e and common vowel team conventions for representing long vowel sounds.*
- **Progress monitoring assessment (Appendix D, p. 256)**
    - Assessment 1: Check to see which of the eight consonant sounds are known. If the child misses more than 1, check all remaining consonant sounds and

then stop. This places the child at the Individual Consonant Sound level.
- Assessment 2: If the child knows the sound for at least seven of the consonants, ask them to read the five nonsense words that fit the consonant/vowel/consonant (CVC) pattern. If the child misses more than one, stop. This places the child at the Simple Blending level.
- Assessment 3: If the child can read at least four of the CVC words, ask them to read the 12 single-syllable words with blends and digraphs. If the child misses more than three, stop. This places the child at the Diverse Blending level.
- Assessment 4: If the child can read at least nine of the blend/digraph words, ask them to read the four long vowel words. If the child misses more than one, stop. This places the child at the Long Vowel level.
- Assessment 5: If the child can read at least three of the long vowel words, they may need help with structural analysis but will probably not benefit from further basic phonics instruction.
- Note: This assessment will be repeated at the end of each unit section. Begin by working with just the Individual Sound level students using the curriculum noted below. When they have progressed significantly, add the Simple Blending students to the group and teach the lessons related to this sub-unit, and so on.

- **Daily routine**
  - Send home enrollment form for the class (Appendix D, p. 257).
  - Read aloud a chapter from a short novel or a picture book (to maintain the focus on meaning-making).
  - Routines described below.
  - Celebrations (self and others) and reminder for home practice.

- **Dealing with unknown words: Introductory lesson (repeat at the beginning of each sub-unit)**
  - **Word-reading strategies**: Elicit from students strategies they use for figuring out words they don't know at sight. Then establish a basic list:
    - Check to see if it is a name
    - Sound out and check for understanding
    - Break the word into parts
    - Read ahead, looking for clues farther ahead in the sentence
    - Re-read, looking for clues earlier in the sentence
    - Use a picture clue (less helpful in chapter books)
    - Skip the word (if the text still makes sense)
    - Substitute another word that makes sense
    - Get help
  - Explain that in this unit they will be working on using letter sounds and breaking words into parts.
- *Individual consonant sound level*
  - **Teaching a phonics element**: Use the multi-step lesson below, followed by the Wheel of Fortune game (p. 68), to introduce consonant sounds not known.
    - Choose the consonant sound you wish to teach.
    - Say several words which begin with the consonant sound (e.g., sun, saw, sock for /s/). Ask students if they can tell you how all the words are alike.
    - Give each child a card with *S* on one side and *D* on the other. Choose a key word which includes the element (e.g., sun). Give examples of other words, some of which include the element and some of which do not. Say the

pair of words (e.g., sun/saw). When you say "Go," students are to immediately hold up the S side of the card if the two words have the same element or the D side if they have different elements.
- Now have students brainstorm a list of as many words as they can think of that share this element. Write them on the board. Decide which words would make good pictures. Give each child a 3 × 5 card. On the blank side, have each child choose one of the "picturable" words. They should write the word on the card, underline the element (e.g., sun), and draw a picture to go with it.
- Say aloud some sentences which include a word with the target element in it. Students are to listen for the target word. Then have them make up their own sentences for others to guess.
- Put the element (e.g., s-) on the board. In another column, list possible phonograms which could be blended with that element to form real words (e.g., -un, -aw, -ock). Call on students to pick a phonogram and blend the target element onto it. On the board, this would look something like this:

    s-   1. -un (Child would say /s/ /un/ /sun/)
              2. -aw
              3. -ock
              4. -it

- **Wheel of Fortune**: Play the game using a sentence with as many words as possible which include the target element.

- *Simple blending level*

  - **Teaching a phonics element**: Use the multi-step lesson below, followed by the Wheel of Fortune game, to introduce the most common short vowel CVC phonograms: -at, -ell, -ill, -ot, -ug. If students struggle with these five phonograms, continue to work with others: -ip, -am, -ag, -ack, -ick, ing, -ap,-op, -in, -an, -ed.

- Choose the phonogram you wish to teach.
- Say several words which end with the phonogram you wish to teach (e.g., bat, cat, and rat for -at). Ask students if they can tell you how all the words are alike.
- Give each child a card with *S* on one side and *D* on the other. Choose a key word which includes the phonogram (e.g., bat). Give examples of other words, some of which include the phonogram and some of which do not. Say a pair of words (e.g., bat/cat or bat/kit). When you say "Go," students are to immediately hold up the *S* side of the card if the two words have the same element or the *D* side if they have different elements.
- Now have students brainstorm a list of as many words as they can which share this phonogram. Write them on the board. Decide which words would make good pictures. Give each child a 3 × 5 card. On the blank side, have each child choose one of the "picturable" words. They should write the word on the card, underline the phonogram (e.g., b<u>at</u>) and draw a picture to go with it.
- Say aloud some sentences which include a word with the target phonogram in it. Students are to listen for the target word. Then have them make up their own sentences for others to guess.
- Put the phonogram (e.g., -at) on the board. In another column, list possible initial letters which could be blended with that element to

form real words (e.g., b, c, f). Call on students to pick an initial sound and blend it onto the phonogram. On the board, this would look something like this:

1. b-   at   (This would be /b/ /at/ /bat/)
2. c-
3. f-
4. h-

- **Wheel of Fortune**: Play the game using a sentence with as many words as possible which include the target phonogram.
- **Word Sort**: Once you have covered at least two of these phonograms, you can also begin to do Word Sorts. Let's say you have taught -ill and -ip. Each child needs a set of all the -ill words and all the -ip cards you have worked on.
    - For a Closed Word Sort, tell the students that they are to put the word FILL at the top of column one and RIP at the top of column two, and then sort the words into two columns.
    - For an Open Word Sort, give the students their cards and ask them to separate them into two columns without telling them the key word for each column. They may come up with alternative ways of sorting (even into three or more columns) so long as they are able to explain the unifying concept for each column.
- *Diverse blending level*
    - **Teaching a phonics element**: Use the multi-step lesson below, followed by the Wheel of Fortune game, to introduce consonant blends and digraphs with which students have struggled.
        - Choose the blend/digraph you wish to teach. If working with a native Spanish-speaking population, it may be a good idea to include

blends which do not appear in Spanish (e.g., st, sp, sm, sl, sn, sw, tw).
- Say several words which begin with the blend/digraph you wish to teach (e.g., slip, slide, slope). Ask students if they can tell you how all the words are alike.
- Give each child a card with *S* on one side and *D* on the other. Choose a key word which includes the element (e.g., slip). Give examples of other words, some of which include the element and some of which do not. Say the pair of words (e.g., slip/slide or slip/side). When you say "Go," students are to immediately hold up the *S* side of the card if the two words have the same element or the *D* side if they have different elements.
- Now have students brainstorm a list of as many words as they can which share this element. Write them on the board. Decide which words would make good pictures. Give each child a 3 × 5 card. On the blank side, have each child choose one of the "picturable" words. They should write the word on the card, underline the element (e.g., sl̲im), and draw a picture to go with it.
- Say aloud some sentences which include a word with the target element in it. Students are to listen for the target word. Then have them make up their own sentences for others to guess.
- Put the element (e.g., sl-) on the board. In another column, list possible phonograms which could be blended with that element to form real words (e.g., -ant, -ick). Call on students to pick a phonogram and blend the target element onto it. On the board, this would look something like this:

sl- 1. -ip (Child would say /sl/ /ip/ /slip/)
2. -ab
3. -id
4. -ot

- **Wheel of Fortune**: Play the game using a sentence with as many words as possible which include the target element.
- **Making Words**: Making Words is another technique which is appropriate for this level. Children manipulate letter cards to form longer and longer words. A full description of this activity is found in Cunningham and Cunningham (1992).

- *Long vowel level*: Follow the curriculum for the Simple Blending level except using long vowel phonograms (e.g., -ate, -oat).
- Present certificates.

♦ Multi-syllable decoding unit

- **CCSS**
    - RF 3 3c. Decode multi-syllable words.
- **Progress monitoring assessment**
    - Acknowledge the child's strength in meaning-making by showing them miscues they made that made sense in context or ones that they self-corrected.
    - Explain that there is some evidence that they find long words challenging; again, show miscue evidence.
    - Conduct the Names Test, using the first four names plus the 16 names that have four or more syllables (20 names in total); repeat for post-assessment. A full description of this assessment is found in Cunningham, P. (1990). The Names Test: A

quick assessment of decoding ability. *The Reading Teacher, 44* (2), 124–129.

- **Daily routine (most days)**
  - Send home enrollment form for the class (Appendix D, p. 260).
  - Read aloud a few pages from *Sylvester and the Magic Pebble* or another picture book that has many multi-syllable words for which you have multiple copies. The teacher reads all short words, and children may raise their hands if they would like to read one of the longer words. At the end of reading, discuss the story. Also, record some of the longer words from the text on the board, draw in dividing lines between syllables, and call on students to read them.
  - Making Big Words in pairs (sets # 40, 16, and 134): A full description of this activity is found in the Cunningham article on Making Words referenced above.
  - Independent reading, putting Post-its in their books to note challenging words.
  - Share out words from their book: "A word I had trouble with was …" (the child may read it if they were able to figure it out or spell it, if not).
  - Celebrations (own or others) and reminder for home practice.
- 1st session
  - Give out enrollment slips (Appendix D, p. 258-259) stating that they are enrolled because of IRI results, results from the Names Test, and/or expressed interest; have them set a goal.
  - Independent reading, putting Post-its in the book to note challenging words and share out words.
- 2nd–6th sessions—as per daily plan.
- 7th session

- Have students brainstorm a list of words with three or more syllables; record them on the board.
- Students write, using as many of those words (or other longer words) as possible.
- Students read aloud their writing for the group.
- What did you learn in this unit? When/where can you use what you learned?
- Present certificates.

◆ Metacognition unit
- CCSS: none (The CCSS do not specifically address the need for readers to reflect on their thinking as they process text. Nevertheless, it has been my experience that lessons designed to address metacognitive strategies are beneficial for all readers and especially for those who struggle.)
    - **Daily plan**: The curriculum is listed by topic rather than by day. Don't rush things and just begin where you left off the previous day. Complete each session by celebrating successes (self and others) and a reminder for home practice. Note: Picture books are recommended but others may be substituted. Send home enrollment form for the class (Appendix D, p. 261).
- Topic 1: Know/Predict/Wonder/Revise
    - Introduction and interactive read-aloud for Know/Predict/Wonder/Revise:
        1. Remind them about metacognitive thinking: "Sometimes when we are reading, we think about how the reading is going; the big term for this is *metacognitive thinking*. We might make a prediction or form a picture in our mind or think about how the book is like our own life. In the next few days, we'll practice metacognitive strategies: Know/Predict/Wonder/Revise, visualizing, and making connections.

Today I'm going to read aloud a book called *Sam Johnson and the Blue-Ribbon Quilt*. Given the title and the cover picture, what's one thing you KNOW about this story?" List on the board/chart paper the ideas students suggest. "What's something that you PREDICT will happen in the story, but you are not sure? Give a reason for your prediction." Share out and list. "Now what's a question you are WONDERING about?" Share out and list. "As I read, raise your hand if you have something to say about what's happening in the book."
2. Read the book, stopping to discuss (e.g., make new predictions, revise old ones, etc.)

- Independent reading (at least 15 minutes): Take time to help them find books they will really enjoy and encourage them to stick with a book through the unit. They are to list one thing each that they know, predict, and wonder, and then read.
- Discuss their readings as a group and allow students who wish to read aloud a section of what they've read.
- Topic 2: Visualization
  - Introduction and interactive read-aloud for visualization:
    1. "I'm going to read aloud a book called *The Map Book*. On each page the author has drawn some sort of map. I'll tell you what the map is about before showing you the picture and I'd like you to try to imagine what the drawings on the page are like."
    2. Read aloud, stopping to discuss what they imagine: "I imagine this map …"
  - Independent reading (at least 15 minutes): They are to stop at one or more points to sketch something from the book.

- Discuss their readings as a group and allow students who wish to read aloud a section of what they've read.
- Topic 3: Connections
  - Introduction and interactive read-aloud for connections:
    1. "I'm going to read aloud a book called *My Very Own Room*. As I read, we'll stop to talk about things in the book that remind you (or are unlike) your own life."
    2. Read aloud, stopping to discuss connections: "My connection is …"
  - Independent reading (at least 15 minutes): Ask students to mark with Post-its spots that remind them of (or are unlike) their own life.
  - Discuss their readings as a group and allow students who wish to read aloud a section of what they've read.
- Review:
  - Select a picture book to read aloud, stopping to discuss all of the metacognitive strategies you've taught. Then do the same with their independent reading time and discuss.
  - What did you learn in this unit? When/where can you use what you learned?
  - Present certificates.

◆ Comprehension monitoring and fix-ups unit
  - CCSS—none (The CCSS do not specifically address the need for readers to monitor their comprehension as they process text. Nevertheless, it has been my experience that lessons designed to address comprehension monitoring and fix-up strategies are beneficial for all readers and especially for those who struggle.)

- Day 1: Introduction and interactive read-aloud.
  - Send home the enrollment form for the class (Appendix D, p. 262).
  - "Remember when we talked about metacognitive thinking? One of the things we talked about was noticing when you didn't understand as you were reading. This can be caused by not understanding the meaning of a word or by not understanding an idea." List on the board the following ways of dealing with difficulty and add others they come up with:
    1. Slow down
    2. Read ahead a little
    3. Re-read
    4. Think about your own life
    5. Look at a picture or form a picture in your mind
    6. Get help
  - Read aloud a picture book that is vague or confusing in some ways. Ask students to stop you if and when they are confused.
- Day 2: Reading Workshop
  - Wheel of Fortune puzzle (p. 68): Both words and ideas can cause confusion.
  - Minilesson: Remind students that everyone gets confused sometimes when they read and why it's important to notice when they are confused; review the fix-ups from the previous day. "I'm going to tell you about my thinking as I read _____ (the book from the previous day)." Go through the book and explain all the points of confusion noted on the Post-its and what you did to try to resolve the confusion.
  - Practice time: They need to have a relatively challenging independent reading book. Explain the three-column monitor chart (Appendix D, p. 263).

Have them fill out the chart as they read: listing the page number where they got confused, whether it was a word-based or an idea-based confusion, and the number of the strategy or strategies they used.
- Debrief: Have students share one example with a partner prior to sharing with the full group.

- Day 3: Shared reading:
  - Wheel of Fortune (p. 68): What are some strategies to use if you get confused?
  - Select a short story (possibly from the textbook if classroom teachers aren't using it). It needs to be confusing in some way or another. Discuss points of confusion as you read.
  - Close reading (p. 67): Select a confusing paragraph. Ask for a volunteer to read the paragraphs aloud. Repeat one more time with another student. Divide students into groups of four or five. Ask them to discuss their experience.
- Days 4: Guided reading with selected text
  - Introduction
    1. Prior knowledge/experience connection.
    2. Read the title.
    3. Look at the pictures throughout. Are any of them confusing? What should we do?
    4. Introduce Points of Confusion chart (Appendix D, p. 264).
    5. Describe what they do while reading: keep track of confusion on the chart.
    6. Describe writing assignment: Make a Venn diagram showing commonalities and differences between two events/concepts from the text.
  - **Independent work time**: reading and writing assignment
  - **Discussion**

1. Skim to remember information
2. Round-robin-retell
3. Discuss any times they were confused and what they did
4. Talk about their Venn diagrams
   - Last day
     - What did you learn in this unit? When/where can you use what you learned?
     - Present certificates
- Inference unit
  - **CCSS**
    - RL 4.1. *Refer to details and examples in a text when explaining what the text says explicitly and when drawing inferences from the text.*
  - Send home the enrollment form for the class (Appendix D, p. 263)
  - Use the interactive read-aloud, Reading Workshop, shared reading, and guided reading plan as per the monitoring comprehension unit above. Each reading selection should offer a range of inferences, and the discussion should focus on questions such as:
    - What do we know about Character A?—e.g., what they are thinking and feeling (inference) How do we know this? (providing evidence).
    - What do we notice about character A?—e.g., they are crying, they are running away (evidence) What does this behavior tell us about the character? (drawing an inference).
- Oral retell unit
  - **CCSS**
    - RL 2 2 & 3 2. *Recount stories, including fables.*
  - Note: It is beneficial to use fables from the book *Fables* (by Arnold Lobel) for this unit.

- **Progress monitoring assessment**: Pre-test: They read (aloud or silently—their choice) "The Ducks and the Fox" (Appendix D, p. 260–267). They retell and I audiotape the retelling. Post-test: The same process using "Poor Old Dog" (Appendix D, p. 268).
- **Daily plan (most days)**:
  - Give child enrollment forms to students and have them set goals (Appendix, D, p. 265).
  - Send home the enrollment form for the class (Appendix D, p. 264).
  - Wheel of Fortune using sentence from previous day's fable (p. 68).
  - Lesson.
  - SSR with retell and collaborative rating on scale (Appendix D, p. 269); note: students should select a not-too-difficult book for independent reading that they can return to each day.
  - Celebration (self and others) and reminder for home practice.
- Day 1: "The Crocodile in the Bedroom"
  - What do you need to keep in mind as you retell a story? (characters, problem/solution, outcome, not every detail).
  - Teacher reads aloud as they follow along silently in a Xeroxed copy.
  - Teacher tells them what sentences to highlight and then retells, focusing on the highlighted sentences.
  - Each child retells to the group.
- Day 2: "The Hen and the Apple Tree"
  - Wheel of Fortune using a sentence from "The Ducks and the Fox."
  - Teacher reads aloud as they follow along in a Xeroxed copy.
  - Teacher tells them what sentences to highlight.

- Each child retells to a partner, focusing on the highlighted sentences.
- Day 3: "The Baboon's Umbrella"
  - Wheel of Fortune using a sentence from "The Hen and the Apple Tree."
  - Teacher reads aloud as they follow along in a Xeroxed copy.
  - Students highlight what they believe to be the key sentences.
  - Each child retells to a partner, focusing on the highlighted sentences.
- Day 4: "The Camel Dances"
  - Wheel of Fortune using a sentence from "The Baboon's Umbrella."
  - Students read the fable silently.
  - They highlight key sentences.
  - Each child retells to a partner.
- Day 5
  - Wheel of Fortune using a sentence from "The Camel Dances."
  - Each child is assigned his own fable (King Lion and the Beetle, The Bear and the Crow, or The Bad Kangaroo) and they read silently.
  - They highlight key sentences.
  - Each child retells to a partner who has not read that fable. Partners provide feedback about how well they were able to understand the story based on the retelling.
  - What did you learn in this unit? When/where can you use what you learned?
  - Present certificates.

◆ Paragraph writing unit
  - **CCSS**

- W3.4. *With guidance and support from adults, produce writing in which the development and organization are appropriate to task and purpose.*
- W3.5. *With guidance and support from peers and adults, develop and strengthen writing as needed by planning, revising, and editing.*
- L4.2a. *Use correct capitalization.*
- L4.2d. *Spell grade-appropriate words correctly, consulting references as needed.*

- Pre-assessment: Ask students to write a paragraph about something they like to do. Give no further directions. Any student who writes a "perfect paragraph"—a statement of what they like to do with examples, correct paragraph form, and few editing errors—would not be enrolled in this unit.
- Day 1
  - Tell students that we will be focusing on paragraph writing since they'll use paragraphs for all other prose writing.
  - Ask students what they think a paragraph is.
  - Define: Several sentences that are closely related. The first line is indented, and one sentence follows right after the other. For our purposes, the main idea of a paragraph will be stated in the topic sentence, which comes first in the paragraph, followed by supporting sentences.
  - Introduce the dictation activity:
    1. The whole paragraph will be read aloud once, all the way through without stopping so that students can understand what it is about.
    2. Then the paragraph will be read again, a few words at a time. Students will write down each part. Each segment will be read a second time, but no more. Students will be told when a sentence ends, but not told what kind of punctuation goes there. After the paragraph

dictation is complete, it will be read again, all the way through.
3. Next, students will be given a correct copy of the paragraph. Students use a pen, colored pencil, or fine-point marker to correct any errors they made. If they forgot to indent, they should use the paragraph mark to show that.
4. The teacher reviews the corrected version and returns the paragraphs to the students. They use the Dictation Graph (Appendix D, p. 270) to record whether they remembered correct paragraph form and how many errors remained uncorrected.

- Do dictation: Narrative paragraph # 1 (Appendix D, p. 271).
- Exit slips (p. 66–67): *What is a paragraph?*

- Day 2

    - Conduct any necessary reteaching based on Exit Slip responses.
    - Finger Flash vocabulary activity (p. 68): *prose, paragraph, indent, topic sentence, supporting sentences.*
    - Which words go together? worksheet (Appendix D, p. 272).
    - Second dictation: Narrative paragraph # 2 (Appendix D, p. 271).
    - Exit slips: *What is the difference between topic sentences and supporting sentences?*

- Day 3

    - Conduct any necessary reteaching based on Exit Slip responses.
    - Third dictation: Narrative paragraph # 3 (Appendix D, p. 272).

- Day 4

    - Read aloud the book *Little Nino's Pizzeria*.

- On the document camera, place the three paragraphs relating to *Little Nino's* that need topic sentences; what are some options? (Appendix D, p. 273–274).
- Fourth dictation: Narrative paragraph # 4 (Appendix D, p. 271).

• Day 5

- On the document camera, place the three paragraphs relating to *Little Nino's* that need supporting sentences; what are some options? (Appendix D, p. 274–275).
- Fifth dictation: Narrative paragraph # 5 (Appendix D, p. 271).

• Day 6

- Introduce the Paragraph Editing Checklist (Appendix D, p. 276).
- Go step-by-step through the paragraph on cooking (Appendix D, p. 277).
- Sixth dictation: Expository paragraph # 1 (Appendix D, p. 278).

• Day 7

- Have students work in partners with the checklist for the paragraph on bats (Appendix D, p. 279).
- Review as a group.
- Seventh dictation: Expository paragraph # 2 (Appendix D, p. 278).

• Day 8

- Draft a paragraph about something you like to do on chart paper/document camera (not indenting, including irrelevant sentences, committing errors).
- They select their topic and write their paragraph; they may write on the same topic as they used for their pre-assessment or a different one.

- Eighth dictation: Expository paragraph # 3 (Appendix D, p. 279).
- Day 9
  - Edit your paragraph using the editing checklist.
  - They edit their own paragraphs, staple checklist to the paragraph, and turn their work in.
  - Ninth dictation for those who finish in time: Expository paragraph # 4 (Appendix D, p. 279).
- Before Day 10: The teacher reviews the paragraphs and provides feedback (e.g., you need to indent, this word is misspelled).
- Day 10
  - Students complete any additional editing needed and turn it in.
  - The teacher writes PUBLISH on papers that are correct. Then they make a final copy, clip it to their other papers, and turn it in.
  - Expect PERFECTION in their recopying so they get this down prior to.

Tier 3   Units Based on IELI/IRI and Writing Analysis

Whatever the strengths of these Tier 2 units, it is likely that one or two children will continue to struggle with a given aspect of reading or writing and will need individualized instruction. In many cases, the plan for instruction will simply be an individualized version of the work in Tier 2. In other cases, the plan may be quite different. Tier 3 units that will be essentially the same as Tier 2 are: emergent skills, sight words, simple decoding, multi-syllable decoding, and paragraph writing. Because they are quite a bit different at Tier 3, specific plans are provided for the following units: metacognition, comprehension monitoring and fix-ups, inference, and oral retelling.

◆ Metacognition: For focusing on metacognition at the Tier 3 level, the four aspects—prior knowledge, prediction, visualization, and making connections—have been separated into individual sub-units.

- Prior Knowledge Sub-unit (Table 9.1).

TABLE 9.1 Structures for Assessing Prior Knowledge

Define/describe	Things you know about and experiences you have had before you begin to read.
Why important to be a better reader	If we have some knowledge ahead of time, the new information we get will be easier to understand and remember.
Model	If I have cooked before, reading a recipe will be easier because I will understand cooking words (e.g., stir, bring to a boil) and I will be familiar with the way recipes are written (e.g., ingredients written first, short sentences, in chronological order). *Sometimes* we have misinformation that must be discarded.
Activate prior experience	Have you ever read something on a topic you already knew something about? Have you ever read something about an experience you have already had?
S does with explicit T direction step-by-step	General: What do you already know about _____? (the topic of the information text the child will be reading) Specific: What about _____? What about _____? Read to prove/disprove and learn. Sentence frame: I know some things about _____.
S does with hints from T	Know? Read. Prove/disprove. Learn.

(*Continued*)

TABLE 9.1 (Continued)

When to use/not use	This strategy may not work well if you know very little about the topic of the text.
How to know if it's effective	If much of your prior knowledge is confirmed.
How to transfer to class/home	Bookmark: see hints above.
Independent practice and debrief	The child generates a list of prior knowledge about the topic of a self-selected information text and reads to confirm or disconfirm.

- Prediction Sub-unit (Table 9.2).

TABLE 9.2 Structures for Making Predictions

Define/describe	A guess about what will happen based on what you already know; a good prediction is one for which you can give a reason—not just ones that end up being correct.
Why important to be a better reader	Predicting gives us a reason to read and to stay focused: to find out if our prediction is correct.
Model (and, maybe, non-model)	It is December. Wild guess: It will be sunny and 85°. Reason? None. Prediction: It will be cool and rainy. Reason? Time of year, recent days' weather, forecast.
Activate prior experience	Have you ever made a prediction before? Tell about it.
S does with explicit T direction step-by-step	Read the title and cover picture for _____ (a narrative text). Think about what will happen and why you think so. Make a prediction. Give a reason. Read to find out. Check your prediction. Hold on to your prediction if it's correct; let it go if it is not. Sentence frame: I predict _____ because _____.

(Continued)

TABLE 9.2 (Continued)

S does with initial hints from T	Think. Predict. Give reason. Read. Check. Hold on or let go.
When to use/not use	Use: Especially before beginning to read and until you get "into" the story. If you begin to lose interest. Not use: When you are fully engaged in the reading.
How to know if it's effective	Most of your predictions are correct and/or you are letting go if not.
How to transfer to class/home	Use bookmark: see hints above.
Independent practice and debrief	The child generates a prediction about a self-selected narrative text and reads to confirm or disconfirm.

- **Visualization Sub-unit (Table 9.3)**

Define/describe	To make pictures or movies in your head about what is going on in the book you are reading.
Why important to be a better reader	Visualizing helps us to imagine what is going on and better understand the book.
Model (and, maybe, non-model)	Describe an item in the room and see if the student can figure out what it is. Describe something you might do in the room (e.g., walking around slowly, etc.) and see if the student can repeat it.
Activate prior experience	Have you ever made a picture or movie in your head while reading? Tell about it.
S does with explicit T direction step-by-step	Imagine a TV screen in your mind. When I read aloud a paragraph or two, make a picture or movie on the screen. Sentence frames: The picture I made in my mind is _____. The movie I made in my mind is _____.

(*Continued*)

(Continued)

S does with initial hints from T	TV. Picture or movie.
When to use/not use	Use: Especially when you begin to read. If you begin to lose interest. Not use: When you are fully engaged in the reading.
How to know if it's effective	You can make pictures and/or movies and it helps you understand.
How to transfer to class/home	Use bookmark: see hints above.
Independent practice and debrief	The child reads from a self-selected narrative text without pictures. At some point, they stop to describe—or even draw—what they see in their mind.

- Making Connections Sub-Unit (Table 9.4).

TABLE 9.4 Structures for Making Connections

Define/describe	Finding something in the text that is similar to something in the reader's life.
Why important to be a better reader	If you can make a connection to your own life, you are better able to understand what the character does or feels.
Model	When Little Red Riding Hood's mom sends her off to her grandmother's, it reminds me of when I've had to decide how much responsibility to give my own children.
Activate prior experience	Have you ever made a link between what was happening in a book and your own life?
S does with explicit T direction step-by-step	Read the title and cover picture for _____ (a narrative text). Sentence frame: When _____, I felt a link to my own life because _____.

(*Continued*)

TABLE 9.4 (Continued)

S does with initial hints from T	Hints: Read. Think about own life. Link.
When to use/not use	Use: when the book is about something that you don't immediately feel a connection with. No real need to use when the book is very similar to your life.
How to know if it's effective	If you feel you understand the story or character better.
How to transfer to class/home	Bookmark: with hints.
Independent practice and debrief	The child reads from a self-selected narrative text. At some point, they stop to make a connection to what is happening in the story.

♦ Comprehension monitoring and fix-ups (Table 9.5).

TABLE 9.5 Structures for Comprehension Monitoring and Fix-Ups

Define/describe	Figuring out what to do when there is a word or idea you don't understand.
Why important to be a better reader	Readers need to know what to do when they don't understand so they can fix their comprehension.
Model	Word example: The man combed the *goatee* on his chin. Idea example: The dogs at Leo's house had always belonged more to his father than anyone else. He fed them and took them for walks and they sat at his feet as he read in the evening.
Activate prior experience	Have you ever been reading and noticed that you didn't understand? What did you do?
S does with explicit T direction step-by-step	Read the title and cover picture for _____ (a narrative or information text). I notice that I don't understand _____.

(*Continued*)

TABLE 9.5 (Continued)

S does with initial hints from T	Hints: Read. Notice not understanding. Word or idea? Try fix-ups: Read ahead. Re-read. Skip and try to understand. Source or ask for help.
When to use/not use	Use: When you are reading a difficult text or text about a topic you aren't familiar with. Don't use: When everything seems clear.
How to know if it's effective	If you feel you understand what is going on.
How to transfer to class/home	Bookmark: with hints.
Independent practice and debrief	The child reads from a self-selected narrative text. They stop when a word or idea doesn't make sense to them and use the fix-up strategies.

♦ Inference (Table 9.6).

TABLE 9.6 Structures for Inferring

Define/describe	Ideas that are not stated in the text.
Why important to be a better reader	In order to understand a text, readers need to figure out ideas that the author has in mind but doesn't state directly.
Model	A character has his head down with tears streaming down his face. How does he feel?
Activate prior experience	Have you ever been able to figure something out without being told directly?
S does with explicit T direction step-by-step	Read the title and cover picture for _____ (a narrative text). Since _____, I can infer that _____.
S does with initial hints from T	Hints: Read. Important event. Infer. Prove.
When to use/not use	Use: When you are trying to understand a character or an important event. Don't use: When everything seems clear.

(Continued)

TABLE 9.6 (Continued)

How to know if it's effective	If you feel you understand what is going on and what the characters are like.
How to transfer to class/home	Bookmark: with hints.
Independent practice and debrief	The child reads from a self-selected narrative text. They stop when they notice they have figured out something that wasn't explicitly stated. Note: This may be challenging for students. The teacher may need to read along in the same text and interrupt the reading to point to what might be an inference.

♦ Oral retelling (Table 9.7).

TABLE 9.7 Structures for Oral Retelling

Define/describe	Tell the main events of a story in the order in which they happened.
Why important to be a better reader	If we really understand what we've read, we should be able to tell what happened, including the important events.
Model	Retell Little Red Riding Hood. Retell what happened, noting how to include character names and leave out unimportant details. Do the same with a short story _____.
Activate prior experience	Has anyone ever asked you, "What is that book about?" Tell about it.
S does with explicit T direction step-by-step	Read a segment of _____ (a narrative text). What main events have happened so far?
S does with initial hints from T	Hints: Read. Stop. Main things.
When to use/not use	Use: When you get to the end of a section of the text.
How to know if it's effective	If you can retell a story so another person can understand what happened.
How to transfer to class/home	Bookmark with hints.
Independent practice and debrief	The child reads from a self-selected narrative text. They stop now and then to tell what's happened so far.

For even the small number of students in a given grade level who need off-level support at the Tier 2 and Tier 3 levels, an effectively run program will ensure that they complete these units within a semester, a year at most. This will ensure that they miss as little class time as possible moving forward.

Bibliography

Applegate, M.D., Quinn, K.B., & Applegate, A.J. (2002). Levels of thinking required by comprehension questions in informal reading inventories. *The Reading Teacher, 56* (2), 174–180.

Buly, M.R., & Valencia, S.W. (2002). Below the bar: Profiles of students who fail state reading assessments. *Education Evaluation and Policy Analysis, 24* (3), 219–239. doi: 10.3102/01623737024003219

Cunningham, P.M., & Cunningham, J.W. (1992). Making words: Enhancing the invented spelling-decoding connection. *The Reading Teacher, 46* (2), 106–115.

Estes, T.H., & Vaughan, Jr., J.L. (1973). Reading interest and comprehension: Implications. *The Reading Teacher, 27* (2), 149–153.

Gonzales, P., & Elijah, D. (1978). Stability of error patterns on the informal reading inventory. *Reading Improvement, 15* (4), 279–288.

Manzo, A.V., & Manzo, U. (2013). The informal reading-thinking inventory: Twenty-first century assessment formats for discovering reading and writing needs—And strengths. *Reading and Writing Quarterly, 29* (3), 231–251. doi: 10.1080/10573569.2013.789783

McKenna, M.C. (1983). Informal reading inventories: A review of the issues. *The Reading Teacher, 36* (7), 670–679.

Nilsson, N.L. (2013). The reliability of informal reading inventories: What has changed? *Reading and Writing Quarterly, 29* (3), 208–230. doi: 10.1080/10573569.2013.789779

Provost, M.C., Lambert, M.A., & Babkie, A.M. (2010). Informal reading inventories: Creating teacher-designed literature-based assessments. *Intervention in School and Clinic, 45* (4), 211–220. doi: 10.1177/1053451209353444

Spector, J.E. (2005). How reliable are informal reading inventories? *Psychology in the Schools, 42* (6), 593–603. doi: 10.1002/pits.20104

Yopp, H.K. (1992). Developing phonemic awareness in young children. *The Reading Teacher, 45* (9), 696–703.

10
Conclusion

As I have argued over the course of this book, I believe our tendency to "silo" various aspects of education is problematic. Specifically, when we advocate for, plan for, and enact sophisticated standards such as the Common Core State Standards (CCSS) and their variants without considering the needs of students who struggle, these students are unlikely to reach their full potential. The outcome is similar when we advocate for, plan for, and enact structured supports for struggling learners but fail to focus these supports on intellectually demanding content over and above basic skills. In the former situation, the perspective seems to be that if we provide excellent classroom instruction, everyone will learn. In the latter situation, the perspective seems to be that children who struggle are incapable of thinking about and producing work related to sophisticated content because they may not have fully mastered lower-level skills and strategies. Neither of these things are true.

A second argument I have made is that the curriculum and instructional structures we employ in school contexts that serve a range of students must be of higher quality than what can typically be found in purchased materials. The related argument is that the time and energy teachers and administrators will require to adapt these materials to meet the needs of all students is greater than what it takes to develop curriculum themselves. This text provides the skeleton of such a curriculum—as well as examples of instructional units—substantive enough, I believe, for school and/or district personnel to develop the curriculum needed to teach sophisticated standards across the multi-tiered support system (MTSS) levels of Tier 1 classroom instruction, Tier 2 small group lessons, and Tier 3 tutorials—as well as what I've termed Tier 0: students who have clearly mastered grade-level content prior to instruction.

Although the research studies provided in Appendices F and G are not quantitative in nature with a control group and refined statistical analysis, these studies suggest that a curriculum that integrates the best of what we know about the CCSS (and their offshoots) and MTSS instructional supports increases achievement. When we view these initiatives as closely-linked partners—rather than isolated silos—all children will benefit.

Appendix A
Reading Workshop Minilessons

- Comprehension monitoring: Talk about times when they've had difficulty understanding what they've read and why ("whys" should include difficulty with particular words, convoluted sentence structure, keeping speakers straight in conversation, need for more background information, dialect, etc.). Tell students that their focus for the lesson will be on noticing when they are having difficulty understanding as they read. Students keep track of places where they became confused in the books they read. Note: They need to be reading a relatively challenging book.
- Visualization: Talk about what happens in their brains when they read, the formation of visual images, or even "movies" being one. Many good readers do this as a way of keeping track of what is going on in the story as they read. One option for a read-aloud includes the p. 1 description of Anastasia in *Anastasia Krupnik* and the p. 23 description of her packing to leave. Ask students to draw or describe orally what they imagine. Ask students to find a section from a book read during independent reading to draw or describe.
- Story structure: Discuss with students how buildings are constructed, emphasizing that a skeleton structure is built first and only later is siding, etc. added. Explain that this is true for authors writing stories as well. Tell them that if they pay attention to the structure of the story, it will help them to know what is likely to come next (e.g., if they know the main characters and the setting, the problem

is likely to come up next). Introduce the most common story structure in Western cultures:

- Characters
- Setting (place and time)
- Problem/goal
- Events
- Ending

You may wish to tell students that this form is *not* common in other cultures, especially those in Asia and Africa. Read aloud a story which follows this structure (i.e., with a single problem), stopping at various points to fill in the Story Plan described above. Ask students to do the same with a book they are reading. Obviously, depending on how much of the book they have completed, they may not have enough information to complete the plan, so you may choose to use a shared story instead.

♦ Retelling: This lesson is based on the previous one. Explain that another use for a Story Plan is to help them retell what they have read, either orally or in writing. Show them how you can retell the read-aloud story from yesterday using only the Story Plan you made together. Now ask them to do the same with a partner using their Story Plans.

♦ Characterization: Explain that we are much more likely to get involved in a story if we can relate to the main character. Students complete a characterization worksheet to describe themselves. With reference to their own characteristics, talk about how we get the same kind of information about book characters. You may wish to read descriptions of the physical attributes, feelings, and actions of various characters for further practice. For example, from the book *Anastasia Krupnik*, pp. 1–2: physical description, pp. 3–4: likes, pp. 5–7: dislikes, pp. 20–21: feelings. Students look for character description in their independent reading books.

Higher-Level Thinking

♦ Character relationships: Mention to students that the relationship among characters in a story is a large part of what holds the reader's interest. Select a story to read aloud in which character relationships are significant, such as *Too Many Tamales*. Make a tree diagram with the name of the main character in an oval in the middle and other characters in ovals surrounding them. Connect the characters with lines, noting on the lines how the main character feels about each of the other characters and vice versa. Students construct similar charts for characters in books they are reading independently.

♦ Wondering: Tell students some things you wonder about (e.g., whether it will be sunny on the weekend, how long the staff meeting will last, why you've been feeling tired lately). Ask them to talk about what they wonder about. Explain that good readers are constantly wondering before, during, and after their reading. Select a read-aloud text that encourages wondering. Tell what you wonder about as you read. Ask students to make a list of wonderings they have as they read.

♦ Predicting and altering predictions as needed: Connect this lesson to the one on preparing to read, if you have previously taught it. Remind students that there will be times when the predictions that they make will have to be revised as new information comes to light; this does not mean the prediction was a poor one, but only that it didn't happen to be true for this story. If the reader is not flexible in their thinking, the remainder of the story/article may prove confusing. Read aloud the title of a story which might lead students to predictions significantly different from the actual content of the story. As you then read the story, stop at various points to revise their predictions. Ask students to predict what may come next in their independent reading books and

see if they need to alter their predictions to fit new facts as they emerge.
- ♦ Inferences: Remind students that not everything they understand about a story is stated directly in the text. Read aloud from a book with clear inferences to be drawn, stopping to ask questions about events, feelings, etc. for which there are quite clear answers, but these answers are not stated per say. Note: There is a difference here between inference and prediction, the latter being more open-ended. Ask students to find text in the books they are reading from which other students might be able to draw an inference.
- ♦ Making connections: Explain to students that another way to keep themselves engaged in a book they are reading is to think about ways their own life experiences connect to those of a character, how a book they are currently reading connects to one they have previously read, or how that book connects with some knowledge they have about the world. Read aloud a story to which they may be able to make connections. Some of these connections should be more subtle, as in a story in which the main character is an older person. Students will note connections between the books they are reading independently and their own experiences.
- ♦ Sensitivity to language: Tell students that they are to imagine that they could save only six words from the English language and they are to pick the words that sounded the most wonderful. Which six would they save and why? Remind them that many authors use words not only to tell a story, but also to sound beautiful. Then read some examples of particularly interesting uses of language. Talk about the way in which authors use such language to make their writing effective. Give a "boring paraphrase" example from each book and have students find the comparable, interesting sentence in the book. Note: I find that most words/phrases that kids notice in these books are examples of rhyme, alliteration,

onomatopoeia, simile, metaphor, and other descriptive language. It often makes much better sense to divide the lesson into two to four sub-lessons so as not to overdo on any one day. Students look for interesting language in their independent reading books.
♦ Point of view: Ask students to pretend that a fight has broken out on the playground and discuss ways in which various people might view it differently. Read aloud to students an example of a book in which the point of view of the narrator is significant. Discuss how the story is altered when viewed from the perspective of a different character. Ask students to describe a part of the story they have recently read, explain whose point of view it was written from, and how the story might be different if seen through the eyes of another character.

Decoding

♦ Word parts mini-lesson: Show students a piece of modern art which may be quite abstract overall, but which has some recognizable feature(s). Tell them that this is likely to be true of long words they encounter as they read. Teach them the following technique using a word such as *misunderstanding*:

1. Take off the -ing.
2. Take off the mis-.
3. Notice -under-.
4. Notice -stand-.
5. Put -under- and -stand- together to get -understand-.
6. Add -ing to get -understanding.
7. Add mis- to get misunderstanding.

Ask students to note long words in their books as they read. Later, go through the above steps as a group.

- Dealing with unknown words: Elicit from students strategies they use for figuring out words they don't immediately recognize; then, establish a basic list: check to see if it is a name, slow down/sound out/cross-check, break words into parts, read ahead, re-read, use a picture clue, skip/substitute, get help. Practice these using a story on the overhead. Make bookmarks with the strategies listed on them. Students keep a list of difficult words and their predictions from their independent reading books. Note: They need to be reading a relatively challenging book.

Fluency

- Punctuation and syntax: Offer an example of a situation in which punctuation and the way sentences flow together can make a difference in meaning (e.g., I was happy at first when we went to the store I lost my ring = either, I was happy at first. When we went to the store, I lost my ring. -or- I was happy at first when we went to the store. I lost my ring.) Note: The next four lessons build upon each other.
- Accuracy: Give students a copy of a piece of text that you will read aloud to them. Ask them to note any problems you have as you read. As you read the text the first time, make a number of errors which do not affect the meaning (e.g., *a* for *the*, *woods* for *forest*, etc.). If students point out that you made several mistakes, elicit from them that the types of mistakes were superficial. Then read the selection again, making errors which significantly affect meaning (e.g., *a* for *and*, *fork* for *forest*, etc.). Discuss the difference. Ask students to practice reading a half page or so. Then they should meet with a partner and read aloud, focusing on meaning-based accuracy.
- "Chunked" phrases: Choose another selection. This time read the piece with complete accuracy but in a very one-word-at-a-time way (e.g., I—would—not—eat—them—

with—a—fox). Again, ask for their feedback. Now read the piece again, this time grouping words into phrases (e.g., I—would not—eat them—with a fox); the reading should still be choppy, but at least now it is grouped into meaning units. Ask students to practice reading a half page or so. Then they should meet with a partner and read aloud, focusing on meaning-based accuracy.
- Smoothness: As above, but this time smooth the chunked phrases together. The reading should be done in a monotone.
- With expression: As above, but with expression.
- Varied rates of reading: Discuss the fact that people sometimes move slowly and sometimes quickly and the possible consequences of not varying speed as needed. Elicit any awareness they might have of the need to vary rate in reading. Introduce four basic reading rates: scanning—extremely fast (looking for details), skimming—fast (looking for main idea[s]), moderate—general rate for narrative reading, and slower—for difficult passages and study reading.

  - (slowing down; scanning) Have students read a selection silently, monitoring any changes in their rate of reading (especially when they slow down to deal with difficulty). Then practice using a scanning rate to find details. Students practice this by scanning for names, descriptive words, etc. in their independent reading books.
  - (skimming) The next day, ask students to retell the story from the day before. They will probably have difficulty. Talk about ways they could remind themselves of what happened. Introduce and practice reading the first sentence in each paragraph of five or more lines as a tool for remembering. Then do a "round robin" oral plot summary with each student contributing a part. Students meet in partners to practice this technique with a section of text read the previous day.

Appendix B
Literature Circles Supplement

Frequently Asked Questions

Q1: What do I do if a child chooses a book which I believe to be too difficult or too easy?

A: I try, as much as possible, to honor the choices children make. Because there will be other stronger readers in the group, I often suggest (either to the child who has chosen a difficult book or to all the students) that anyone may choose to read with a partner if they wish. Stronger readers can learn a lot from reading an easier book and being an aide to others. If "poor" selection choice seems to be a pattern for a particular child, try to guide the selection process more carefully (teaching the students that, on a given page, there should be no more than five unknown words, for example) or limit the child's choice to two or three of the more appropriate books.

Q2: What does the teacher do as students are reading?

A: You'll want to do different things at different times. Sometimes you'll want to be sitting with groups as they read, helping them to note possible points of emphasis or misunderstanding. Other times you'll want to be listening to particular students; this is a great time to keep in touch with their growth as readers. You may use this time to look at students' assignments. Eventually, you'll be involved in discussions.

Q3: How often do discussions occur?

A: Traditionally, the first discussion does not occur until after the reading has been completed. Depending on the length of the book, this still may be the way to go. Many teachers like to schedule discussions more frequently: generally, one to two during the course of the reading and one to two more after the book has been completed. If there are two discussions after students have finished the book, the first tends to be a sort of free-roaming response time and the second a more focused discussion after students have returned to the text to search for evidence relevant to topics raised initially. It is crucial that, prior to a discussion, students have read a large enough section and/or are at a particularly exciting part, both of which add to the richness of the discussion.

Q4: How do I schedule the discussions?

A: This is bound to be a bit tricky. You'll tentatively schedule the first discussion based on the group's estimate of the time it will take them to read (I usually ask groups to make these estimates after they have read for a day or two). Plan for about a half hour per group. You'll hit a glitch now and then when estimates and reality don't connect. Students may sometimes need to use this time for other assignments or silent reading in a self-selected book until you can get back on schedule.

Q5: When I ask a group for a response to the book, I'm greeted by a stony silence. What do I do?

A: I find this happens far less than I expected, but if it does, first WAIT. The research on teacher wait time is amazing: we think we are waiting for an eternity, when in fact it's usually a second or two! Give students time to be thoughtful in their responses. Encourage them to look back at the text. If this gets nowhere, you might simply say, "Well, I noticed that…Did anyone else?" This usually gets the ball rolling.

Q6: How do I tell if my students are engaged in meaningful discussions?

A: Dr. Katherine Schlick Noe suggests that there are several signs that children are "making deeper connections to literature"; they begin to:

- ♦ Ask questions of each other
- ♦ Refer to the text to support their opinions

- Talk about authors and other books
- Make connections between the text and their own experiences
- Use specific language from the story as they discuss it
- Return to the story to re-think what has gone on

Assignments While Reading

- Retell and response form: I regularly ask students to work together as a group to write a summary of the section they've recently read and then, individually, write a response to what's happened.
- Character diary: Write about the story from the point of view of a character, including main events and character's feelings.
- Letter to a character: Write a letter to a character, offering encouragement, advice, etc.
- Illustration: Choose a scene from the story which is carefully described by the author. Imagine you are an illustrator. Draw a picture of the scene which is true to the author's description.
- Timeline: Create a timeline of key events.
- Key sentence: Choose what you believe to be the most important sentence from the section of text you have just read. Explain why you feel this is the most significant sentence.
- Character knowledge: As you read, keep a running list of things the main character says or does which seem important to you. When you finish the book, see what your list tells you about what kind of person the character is.
- Cooperative point of view: Place slips with the names of the book's characters—as many slips as there are students—in a hat. Students choose a slip at random. They meet with other students who have the same character to discuss how the character might feel about a significant event which has recently happened in the book. Then students work independently to write a statement

from the point of view of that character, telling how they believe the character feels. Finally, students meet with classmates who are representing other characters to compare responses.
- Pick-a-spot: Stop reading at a "cliff-hanger" point in the book. With their group, students make a list of several possible options for what might happen next or what the character should do next. Different spots in the room will be assigned different options and, as individuals, students go to the place in the room which reflects their opinion. Students talk with the others who are there (or think alone if they are the only one) and plan a statement which the group will make to the other groups defending their idea. After all the statements have been made, students move to a new place in the room if they have changed their mind. Discuss as a whole group what caused people to change their opinions.
- Calm-to-exciting scale: Rate the sections of the story according to level of excitement. It sometimes works best to save this assignment to the end of the book because perspective seems to improve.
- Mood chart: Evaluate a character's mood and name their feelings throughout the book.
- Word drama: Assign to pairs of students a word from the text; alternatively, partners can choose a word from the text which they think some students will understand and some may not. The goal is to make sure they understand the meaning of the word *as it is used in this book*. All words will be listed on the board. Finally, partners act out the meaning of their word and other students try to guess what word it is.

Culminating Projects

It's often a good idea for groups to work together to choose a culminating activity that best represents the book to others who have not read it. The trick here is to keep a balance between the creative and industrious act of making a project and the ever-pressing need to move on to more reading. Unless students are doing a project which has recently been modeled for them, it may be wise to ask them to come up with a detailed plan in advance. Going through the process of planning helps them to think carefully about what it is they really want to accomplish and how best to do so. I explain to students that I see a project as successful if it meets the following criteria:

- Students have to look more closely at the book or re-read the text in order to complete the project.
- The project gives the rest of the class a good idea of what the book is about.
- Students learn what it takes to plan, complete, and present a project.

While I prefer to allow groups to generate their own project ideas, here are some of my favorites:

- Cooperative visualization: With a partner, select two characters from the book. Decide on a symbolic visual representation of the relationship between the two characters. Pay careful attention to the use of color.
- Create-a-game: Think about the characteristics of board games (e.g., "go ahead" and "go back" spaces, lose or get an extra turn, etc.). Design a board game that reflects the plot of the book. Include all the major events.
- Book review: Students select a partner, preferably one whose opinion of the book differs in some way from their own. Then they rehearse a pair review of the book and present it to the class.
- Readers theater or skit: Students rewrite part of their book as a Readers Theater script, practice, and perform it. Alternatively, they may act or mime a scene from the book.
- Picture book rewrite: Students rewrite their book as a picture book. Include all the main events but write it for a younger child. Take special care with the illustrations.

- Puppet show: Make puppets and act out a scene from the story.
- Hot seat: You will need as many students as there are main characters, plus other students to ask questions. One student represents each character from the book. Other students ask questions of that student, and they respond from the character's point of view.
- ABC book: Focus on key events, characters, and information.
- Commemorative stamp: Develop a stamp which commemorates a character, scene, or theme.
- Jackdaw: Collect and display artifacts representing the book. Label each to explain its connection to the book.
- Map: Make a map of the setting of the book.

Assessment

- You should keep track of student behaviors during discussion. List names of all students. Then use the following key for record keeping: T=topic/question introduced, C=comment made on that topic, R=repetitious comment, O=comment off topic, I=interruption, N=chats to neighbor, P=offers proof from text, F=forgets when called on; a circle around T or C = exceptionally thoughtful response, //=end of topic (see form on p. 204).
- Discussion evaluation: Students should choose from the strengths, weaknesses, and goals list below:
  - Not interrupting
  - Being clear
  - Staying on topic
  - Disagreeing politely
  - Raising good topics
  - Offering thoughtful responses
  - Finding proof in the text
  - Talking more (or less)
  - Listening well

- Connecting one idea to another
- Using good volume
- Speaking at a moderate rate

♦ Group self-evaluation: I am increasingly committed to the value of self-evaluation. This evaluation can focus on both products and group process. I often ask my students to do reflective writing about the interaction of their groups: what went well, what needs work, etc. For any real impact to be felt, reflective activities like this need to be followed, at least some of the time, by discussion (see form on p. 205).

Special Situations

♦ Working with emerging readers: Christy Clausen describes the way in which she uses Literature Circles with her first graders. In the fall, this approach makes up about 10% of her language arts program and by spring the percentage has increased to about 25%. Here's an overview of her basic schedule:

- Friday: Introducing and Selecting Books: Four books are introduced, children make their requests, and groups are formed. Books are placed in a zip-lock bag along with some blank Post-it notes. Parents are asked to read the book with their child several times during the weekend and talk together about the book. They help their child to place a Post-it or two somewhere in the text at a part which the child wishes to share.
- Monday and Tuesday: Discussion Days: Christy meets with two groups each day while the other children read independently or do other assignments. The discussion usually begins with an open-ended question like, "What did you think of this book?" Discussions generally last about 10–15 minutes. Christy has

noticed three patterns which have emerged as she listens to first graders in discussion:

- Discussions most often involve ideas related to personal experience.
- Discussions sometimes involve relationships among characters.
- Discussions may address emotions and the author's craft.

- Wednesday: Journal writing: Christy models ideas for writing about process and product in a short minilesson. This may include a prompt such as "That reminds me of…" or "I think…" Then children write in their response journals. She reads their writing later and responds to each one.
- Thursday: Literature response: Christy demonstrates a new way to respond to literature, such as reading another book by the same author, writing a letter to the author, painting a mural, dramatizing events, etc.

♦ Working with students who need more structure: Sometimes a class you are working with proves to be less self-directed and more teacher-dependent than is typical. Here are two structures determined by teacher Kari Brown to be beneficial:

- Book selection: Initially, you may want to use a read-aloud as material and then an all-class novel with discussion occurring in the Literature Circle format. Only then did she offer two related choices and finally a larger range of choices.
- Scheduling: Begin by meeting with only one group at a time rather than having all students in groups simultaneously and floating among them. Groups can then meet less often, but they are more focused when they do meet.

Literature Circles Discussion Record

Text: _____   Date _____

T = brought up a topic
T! = very interesting topic
C = made a comment
C! = very interesting comment
O = off-topic comment
R = repeated something already said
I = interrupted
N = chatted with a neighbor

Names:

_____
_____
_____
_____
_____
_____
_____
_____
_____
_____

Topics:

1. _____
2. _____
3. _____
4. _____
5. _____
6. _____

Lit Circles: Group Evaluation Form   Date _____

Book _____

Group Members:

- How well did we get along with each other today?

- How well did we stick to our work today?

- How well did we do at making sure everyone participated?

- How good were our ideas today?

- The next time we work in literature circles, we will …

Appendix C
Writing Workshop Supplement

Writing Workshop Glossary

1. Argument: what you believe should happen
2. Audience: the person/people you are trying to get to believe your argument
3. Caret (^): the mark used to insert ideas into a draft
4. Conclusion: the ending of a story or the last paragraph of an essay
5. Convince/persuade: to get a person or people to believe what you believe
6. Details/evidence: the facts you use to support your reasons
7. Dialogue: when characters are talking
8. Draft: a piece of writing while it's being written
9. Editing: revision and proofreading
10. Expository writing: something written in a way that presents information rather than telling a story
11. Final draft: a piece of writing in its final, complete form
12. Genre: a type of writing (e.g., short story, report, etc.)
13. Hot spot: the most interesting/exciting part of a story
14. Indent: going in about 1 inch from the margin to start a new paragraph
15. Introduction: the first paragraph of an essay
16. Issue: the topic of your argument
17. Lead: the first sentence or two of a piece of writing
18. Line: the amount of a poem which is on one line
19. Line break: the end of a line
20. Minilesson: a short lesson, the purpose of which is to teach you how to do something better in your writing
21. Narrative writing: something written in a way that tells a story, either true or make-believe
22. Paragraph: several sentences which are closely related

23. Peer conference: a meeting with another student when you want help with your writing
24. Personal narrative: a story about something that happened to you
25. Persuasive writing: a piece of writing whose purpose is to convince someone else of what you believe
26. Poem: a piece of writing written in lines and stanzas
27. Pre-write: an activity for getting ready to write (e.g., webbing, sketching, story map, rehearsal)
28. Proofreading: fixing spelling, punctuation, usage, etc.
29. Prose: all writing which is not poetry or play
30. Publish: to put your writing out to the world in a final draft, tape recording, poster, read aloud, etc.)
31. Punctuation: periods, question marks, exclamation points, commas, etc.
32. Quotation marks: show where characters are talking (e.g., "How are you?")
33. Reasons: why you believe what you believe
34. Rehearsal: a pre-write in which you tell someone else what you plan to write about
35. Report: a piece of writing the intent of which is to provide information on a topic
36. Responder: a person who listens to and comments on a writer's work
37. Response to literature: a piece of writing which tells the author's opinions about something they have read as well as evidence for these opinions
38. Revision: changing the meaning of a piece of writing
39. Rhyme: words that sound the same at the end (e.g., tent, rent, spent) are sometimes used at the end of a line in poetry
40. Rhythm: the way words sound together
41. Setting: the time and place in which a story occurs
42. Short story: a short, make-believe narrative with a few characters and one major problem
43. Sketching: a pre-write in which you make quick drawings of what you plan to write about

44. Stanza: a section of a poem (sort of like a paragraph in prose)
45. Supporting sentences: the sentences in a paragraph that provide details relating to the topic sentence
46. Theme: the writer's message
47. Thesaurus: a book that provides ideas for different words to use
48. Thought shot: a place in a story where a character lets us know how they are feeling, by showing or telling us
49. Title: the name a writer gives to a piece of writing
50. Topic: an idea for something you might write about
51. Topic sentence: the sentence in a paragraph (usually the first) that tells what the paragraph is about
52. Usage: the use of words (e.g., we say "I *go* to the store." not "I *goes* to the store.")
53. Voice: your own special way of saying what you have to say
54. Webbing: a pre-write in which you put your topic in the middle of the paper and then connect other related words to it
55. Working title: the title the writer uses while writing a piece; it may be changed later

Writing Workshop Expectations

1. Find topics and purposes for your writing that matter to you.
2. Write as well and as much as you can; work hard.
3. Understand that writing is thinking. Do nothing to distract other writers. Find your own private, silent writing place, lock the door, and listen to your voice.
4. Save everything; you never know what you might want to come back to later.
5. Date and label everything (e.g., Notes, Pre-Write, Draft #1, etc.).
6. Write in sentences as much as you can (lines and stanzas for poetry).
7. Don't expect your first draft to be perfect; you WILL change it before it reaches final draft.
8. When you're stuck or uncertain, use the resources you have available: dictionary, thesaurus, etc.
9. When you confer with me or a peer, whisper.
10. When you need to confer with peers, use a conference area and record responses on a Peer Conference Form. Conferences should last about five to ten minutes.
11. Listen to, ask questions about, and comment on others' work in ways that help them move forward in their writing.
12. Recognize that, in order for your writing to be fully appreciated, your final drafts need to use accurate spelling, punctuation, and English language usage.
13. Sometime during this year produce a finished piece of writing in each of the following genres: poem, personal narrative, persuasive essay, research report, short story, and response to literature.

Writing Workshop Steps

1. Decode what **GENRE** you want to do (poem, story, etc.)
2. Decide what you want to write about. Look at your **TOPICS** list if you can't think of anything.
3. Write your **DRAFT**. Skip lines and write on only one side of the page.
4. Fill out your **PEER CONFERENCE** form and ask someone to be your partner.
5. Sit near the outside of the room and **TALK QUIETLY** with your partner.
6. Make any **CHANGES** you agreed to.
7. Fill out the **PROOFREADING CHECKLIST**. Edit as carefully as you can using a pen or thin marker.
8. **STAPLE** together your draft, the Peer Conference form, and the Proofreading checklist before turning it in.
9. Work on **ANOTHER PIECE** of writing.
10. If I return your draft to you and it does not say publish on it, this means you need to **EDIT MORE CAREFULLY**. Here are the symbols I use to help you know what you still need to fix:

    ? = this part is confusing
    C = needs a capital letter
    Ꞓ = Does NOT need a capital letter
    P = needs punctuation
    P̶ = does NOT need punctuation
    S = spelling mistake

    After you make further improvements turn it in again.
11. When you get your piece back with the words **PUBLISH** on it, write or type a good copy.
12. **CLIP** the good copy to the rest of the papers and turn it in.

Appendix D
Supporting Materials for Curriculum Units

Active	Passive
Brave	Afraid
Calm	Frantic
Cool	Uninteresting
Effective	Helpless
Friendly	Unfriendly
Grown-up	Childish
Happy	Unhappy
Hard-working	Lazy
Helpful	Unwilling to help
Kind	Mean
Knowledgeable	Lacking in knowledge
Loyal	Not Loyal
Observant	Not observant
Patient	Impatient
Persistent	Gives up easily
Respectful	Disrespectful
Strong	Weak
Thoughtful	Thoughtless

Traits and Evidence Form

Character Traits and Evidence for _____

Trait	Evidence

Character Pre-Assessment

Directions: Think about the main character in the read aloud you just listened to. On the lines below, write a paragraph about the character you chose.

    I understand what kind of character _____ is. I know he is _____ because _____ _____.

I know he is _____ because _____ _____.

I know he is _____ because _____ _____.

Personal Narrative Plan Form

- *Where* does my story take place?

- *When* does my story take place?

- Events in my story (at least three):
  1. _____

  2. _____

  3. _____

- Two thoughts and/or feelings I had were:
  1.

  2.

Personal Narrative Revision and Proofreading Checklist

1. Did you use first person point of view (e.g., I, me, my, mine, we us, our, ours)?   ___ yes   ___ no

2. Write the first sentence or two of your story here. _____

3. Does it make your reader want to keep reading? If no, change it in your story with pen.

4. Did you put in all main events?   ___ yes   ___ no

5. Are they in the correct order?   ___ yes   ___ no

6. Make any changes with a pen.

7. Did you tell what you thought or felt? If no, add to your story with pen.

8. Did I wrap up my story? If no, add that.

9. Make sure your sentences start with capital letters. Fix with a pen.

10. Make sure your sentences end with .? or ! Fix with a pen.

11. Circle any words that might be spelled wrong with a pen.

12. Staple this to your draft and give it to your teacher.

Copyright material from Elizabeth L. Jaeger (2026), *Integrating Sophisticated Standards and Systems of Support for Elementary Readers*, Routledge

Know/Question/Learned Form

What I Think I Know	Questions I Have	What I Learned
1.	1.	1.
2.	2.	2.
3.	3.	3.
4.	4.	4.
5.	5.	5.

Date _____

Hi _____,

You are enrolled in my class on using context to figure out words because:

- ☐ You had difficulty self-correcting when you read with me
- ☐ You said that self-correcting was a challenge for you on the survey you filled out at the beginning of the year

On your most recent reading assessment, ____% of the words you misread made sense in the sentence or you corrected them.

Check the box below that tells how well you think you remember to self-correct as you are reading:

- ☐ This is something I am very good at.
- ☐ This is something that is hard for me, but I notice that I am getting better.
- ☐ This is something that is really hard for me.

My goal for this class is to have ____% of my miscues make sense in the sentence (or to correct them)

Date _____

At the end of class, ____% of your miscues made sense or you corrected them.

Check the box below that tells how well you think you remember to self-correct as you are reading:

- ☐ This is something I am very good at.
- ☐ This is something that is hard for me, but I notice that I am getting better.
- ☐ This is something that is really hard for me and I need more help.

Date _____

Enrollment Form for Parent

Dear Parent/Guardian,

My name is _____ and I am the reading specialist at _____ School. I am recommending that your child _____ attend a class that will help them use context clues to figure out the pronunciation and meaning of unknown words.

Over the course of the next several weeks, I'd like to recommend a home reading activity. Have your child select a relatively challenging book. Spend a few minutes—each day, if possible—reading in the following way:

- Have your child read a page silently.
- Ask your child if there were any words they struggled with (difficult to pronounce or to understand). Look at the words that were hard and talk about the words before and after them and what clues they might provide. For example, if the sentence says "The man ordered a pastrami sandwich" you can point out that the word *sandwich* gives us a clue that *pastrami* is something you put on a sandwich.
- For this practice, avoid talking about letter sounds in order to focus your child's attention on context clues.

Sincerely,

Henry Possum

One day a mother possum took her five children off **here**[1] back. She **linned**[2] them up in front of her.

"It is time you learn to play dead," she said. She rolled over and lay **every**[3] still on the ground.

"Now you try," she said. And **on by on**[4] all of her children rolled over and played dead. All, that is, **expect**[5] Henry. He was **huming**[6] and watching butterflies.

"Henry," said his mother, "come here." And she laid him on the **grand**[7] and tried to make him lie still. But it was no use. Henry kept on **huming**.

"You" never fool anyone," she **scalded**.[8] "What will you do if a bear comes after you? Or a fox? Or a bobcat?"

"I never **through**[9] of that," said Henry.

---

[1] her
[2] lined
[3] very
[4] one by one
[5] except
[6] humming
[7] ground
[8] scolded
[9] thought

The Wolves

One day, a sheep and a goat went into the **fork**[10] to look for food. On the way, they found a wolf's **hide.**[11] The goat picked it up and put it in his **sick.**[12] They walked on and soon it began to get dark. Then they saw a fire in the forest. "Let's go and **slip**[13] by that fire," said the sheep.

"We'll get some food there, too," said the goat. "I smell **sip.**[14]"

They went up to the fire, but what did they see? Three wolves! Three wolves making soup at the fire. The sheep and the goat were **fighting.**[15] They wanted to run away, but the wolves had seen them and would run after them.

---

[10] forest
[11] head
[12] sack
[13] sleep
[14] soup
[15] frightened

Copyright material from Elizabeth L. Jaeger (2026), *Integrating Sophisticated Standards and Systems of Support for Elementary Readers*, Routledge

A Plant for Mama

Donny saw his wallet right where he had put it before he went to _____, on the chair on top of his clean _____, and he remembered what day it was. It was his _____ birthday. Donny went in the bathroom and splashed _____
on his face and wiped it with a _____.

He had something important to do. He hoped nobody had bought the _____. The big one with the waxy, green _____ and the little flowers that hung down like bells, pink as _____ ice cream. Mr. Haynes had promised to _____ it to him for a dollar, if nobody bought it by _____. Donny smiled to himself, thinking about how surprised his mother was going to be when he brought it home.

The Magic Finger

The farm next to ours is owned by Mr. and Mrs. Gregg. The Greggs have two ch_____, both of them b_____.
Their names are Philip and William. Sometimes I go over to their farm to p_____ with them. I am a g_____ and I am eight y_____ old.

   Last w_____ something very funny happened to the Gregg family. I am going to tell you about it as best I can.

   Now the one thing Mr. Gregg and his two boys love to do more than anything was to go h_____. Every Sa_____ morning they would take their guns and go off into the w_____ to look for animals and birds to sh_____.

Nothing to Do

After the wedding, everyone felt let down, the way they always felt the day after Christmas _____[16] _____[17]. Nothing seemed interesting after so much excitement.

"Girls, please stop moping around," said Mrs. Jones

"We can't _____[18] _____[19] find anything to do," said Bea.

Ann was _____[20] silent. If she complained, her mother would tell her to clean out her _____[21] closet.

"Read a book," said Mrs. Jones. "Read a _____,[22] _____[23] book."

---

[16] only
[17] worse
[18] seem
[19] to
[20] completely
[21] messy
[22] nice
[23] long

Exploring Caves

Caves are dark, hidden worlds that some people like to explore. These people are called cavers. Cavers have fun crawling, climbing, and sliding through rocky spaces—some tiny and some huge—to learn about these interesting places.

How Are Caves Formed?

Scientists have different ideas about how caves are formed. Most think caves are created by water. When rain falls, it mixes with an invisible gas in the air. When the water reaches the ground, it seeps into the earth. The water continues going deeper into the earth until it touches rock. Very slowly, the water eats away at the rock and causes tiny cracks to develop. The cracks in the rock grow wider with time. Then the water flows out and leaves behind a cave.

Safety First

Cavers love adventure, but they have to be smart and careful. One rule they follow is never to explore alone. There must be at least three people in a group. That way, if there's an accident, someone can go get help. Cavers follow another rule—be prepared! It can get very cold inside a cave, so cavers wear warm clothing. They also wear helmets to protect their heads from falling rocks. Sturdy hiking boots help them walk along bumpy or slippery paths. It's very dark inside a cave, but instead of carrying flashlights, many cavers wear helmets with lights attached to them. That way their hands are free to hold on as they climb on rocks.

Cave Animals and Plants

A variety of different animals live in caves. Most people think of bats when they think of caves. Cave bats sleep in caves during the day and fly out at night to search for food. Some other animals live their entire lives inside caves. Most of these unusual animals cannot see, but their other senses—such as smell, hearing, touch—become very strong.

Plants need sunlight to survive, so no plants can grow deep inside a cave. Mosses and ferns often grow in the rich, wet soil near cave entrances, but as cavers move into a cave, they do not find any plant life.

Cave Forms

Amazing forms grow inside many caves. Some shapes hang from cavern ceilings and look like icicles. These forms are called stalactites [stuh LAK tyts]. These beautiful shapes are created when water drips from the ceiling. A tiny bit of material is left behind and forms the shape of a ring. With each drop, another ring is formed. It takes many, many years for stalactites to grow. Other shapes grow up from the cave floor. They are called stalagmites [stuh LAG myts]. The water that drops from the ceiling lands on the cave floor. Each drop makes the stalagmite grow taller and taller. Most stalactites and stalagmites grow very slowly.

Exploring Caves Summary

Read the article titled "Exploring Caves." Then fill in the information below.

- ♦ What will be the first sentence in your summary paragraph (the sentence that tells what the whole article is about)?

  _____

- ♦ What is the main idea in the introduction paragraph that starts "Caves are …"?

  _____

- ♦ What is the main idea in the section called "How Are Caves Formed?"

  _____

- ♦ What is the main idea in the section called "Safety First"?

  _____

- ♦ What is the main idea in the section called "Cave Animals and Plants"?

  _____

- ♦ What is the main idea in the section called "Cave Forms"?

  _____

Take the sentences you have written above and turn them into a summary paragraph on lined paper. Your paragraph should have about six sentences (one for each line above). Make sure to use correct paragraph form. When you are done, use a colored pencil, pen, or marker to: (1) circle any words that might be misspelled, (2) add capital letters at the beginning of sentences, and (3) add periods at the end of sentences.

Copyright material from Elizabeth L. Jaeger (2026), *Integrating Sophisticated Standards and Systems of Support for Elementary Readers*, Routledge

Main Idea and Summary Assessment for _____

- ♦ Main idea of the whole article (2) _____
- ♦ Main ideas of article segments (5) _____
- ♦ Topic sentence for the paragraph (2) _____
- ♦ Included all the rest of the main points (3) _____
- ♦ Correct paragraph form (2) _____
- ♦ Misspelled words circled, as needed (2) _____
- ♦ Periods (2) _____
- ♦ Capital letters (2) _____
- ♦ TOTAL (20) _____

My Fluency Chart

Name _____ Date _____

Reading # 1:   <u>1</u>   2   3   4   5   6

Reading # 2:   <u>1</u>   2   3   4   5   6

Reading # 3:   <u>1</u>   2   3   4   5   6

1 = I had trouble reading many words.
2 = I read almost all the words correctly, but I read pretty much one word at a time.
3 = I chunked words together into phrases, but my reading was not smooth.
4 = My reading was smooth, but my voice did not go "up and down" with expression as it should.
5 = I read smoothly and with expression.
6 = I also wasn't too loud or soft and I wasn't too fast or slow.

Date _____

Hi _____,

You are enrolled in my class on reading more fluently because:

- ☐ You had difficulty reading smoothly and with expression when you read with me.
- ☐ You said that reading fluently was a challenge for you on the survey you filled out at the beginning of the year.

On the fluency chart, you rated yourself at Level _____ _____.

Check the box below that tells how you think of yourself as a fluent reader:

- ☐ This is something I am very good at.
- ☐ This is something that is hard for me, but I notice that I am getting better.
- ☐ This is something that is really hard for me.

My goal for this class is to get to Level _____ on the fluency chart.

Date _____

At the end of class, you reached Level _____ on the fluency chart.

Check the box below that tells how you think of yourself as a fluent reader:

- ☐ This is something I am very good at.
- ☐ This is something that is hard for me, but I notice that I am getting better.
- ☐ This is something that is really hard for me and I need more help.

Date _____

Dear Parent/Guardian,

My name is _____ and I am the reading specialist at _____ School. I am recommending that your child _____ attend a class on reading fluency because they demonstrated difficulty with reading smoothly and with expression on the fall reading assessment.

Over the course of the next several weeks, I'd like to recommend a home reading activity. Have your child select a relatively easy book. Select a page that they have not read before. Have them read the page. Then discuss the reading, using the fluency chart as a guide. Then the child reads the same page again and marks the chart based on your feedback. Repeat a third time. Then mark the questions at the bottom.

Sincerely,

Name _____ Date _____

How Much Would People Listen to Me?

Directions: Under "How many will listen? Write a number from one to five to tell how many people you think would listen to you:

1 = no one   2 = very few people   3 = some people
4 = many people   5 = most people

Under "Group that Helps," write a group you belong to that would help you be listened to. If you gave yourself a 1, tell why no one would be likely to listen to you.

Argument	How many will listen?	Group that Helps
• Middle-aged women should get more exercise.		
• Education in English and Spanish is a good idea.		
• It is important for kids to learn keyboarding skills.		
• Soccer is a terrific sport.		
• You have to work hard to get along with siblings.		

Erica Fernandez cares about the environment. She was 16 years old when she heard that a natural gas plant would be built near her hometown. Erica learned that the plant would pollute the air. It would bring harmful chemicals to nearby towns.

    Erica decided to do something about it. She organized groups to protest the plant. They spoke out publicly. They wrote letters to the government. Eventually, the state agreed to cancel the plans for the plant. Thanks to Erica, the local environment was saved.

Copyright material from Elizabeth L. Jaeger (2026), *Integrating Sophisticated Standards and Systems of Support for Elementary Readers*, Routledge

Persuasive Issues List

School	Family and Community	World
• school equipment (furniture, books, computers, etc.) • school fights • school rules • teachers yelling at kids • school safety/security • more recess time • after-school program • school activities • people's feelings being hurt • field trips • class size • length of school day • number of days in the school year • school lunches • teacher aides • bullying • science experiments • number of bathrooms • homework	• divorcing parents • family communication • parenting • improved streets • smoking • recreation facilities, like parks, swimming pools, etc. • help for families • jobs • housing • support for poor people • shelters for unhoused people • animal abuse • jobs with less hours • more nature areas • police • drugs/alcohol • litter • texting while driving	• war • the environment • violence • hunger • gun control • gas prices • border issues

Name _____ Date _____

Persuasive Letter Issue Plan

♦ One issue I am interested in is _____

  • People might listen to me because _____

  • _____

  • (circle one) I think some many most people would listen

♦ Another issue I am interested in is _____

  • People might listen to me because _____

  • _____

  • (circle one) I think some many most people would listen

♦ The issue I am going to write about is _____

Name _____

Persuasive Letter Plan

- ♦ The issue I am going to write about is _____
- ♦ Argument: I believe _____
  _____
- ♦ My reasons are:
  - • _____
  - • _____
  - • _____
- ♦ Audience: Who would listen to you AND could do something about what

  you want? _____

Name _____   Date _____

Persuasive Letter Revision

Directions: As you revise your persuasive letter, use a PEN to mark your letter. Then check off each blank on the left. When your teacher looks over your letter, they will check the blank on the right.

- ♦ Introduction

  _____ 1. My letter starts with a greeting to my audience. _____

  _____ 2. I have an attention-grabbing lead related to my issue. _____
  (Draw a wavy line under your lead)

  _____ 3. I have clearly stated my argument on the issue. _____
  (Make a box around your argument)

  _____ 4. My argument does not include the word *because*. _____

  _____ 5. I have said, I think you will listen to me because … _____

- ♦ Body Paragraphs (note: you may have three body paragraphs)

  _____ 6. The first sentence of the first body paragraph tells my first reason.
  (Circle the reason) _____

  _____ 7. The other sentences in the paragraph offer details to support that reason.
  (Underline the details) _____

  _____ 8. The first sentence of the second body paragraph tells my second reason.
  (Circle the reason) _____

_____ 9. The other sentences in the paragraph offer details to support that reason. (Underline the details) _____

♦ Conclusion

_____ 10. I have re-stated my argument. (Make a box around your argument) _____
_____ 11. I have re-stated my reasons. (Circle your reasons) _____
(Put a wavy line under the call to action)
_____ 12. I have stated what I intend to do or what I want my audience to do. _____
(Put a wavy line under the call to action)

♦ Overall

_____ 13. I have re-read my letter. All my writing makes sense. _____

♦ Fill out a Persuasive Letter Peer Conference Form and have a peer conference.

Writer's Name _____

Helper's Name _____

Persuasive Letter Peer Conference

- Read your persuasive letter to yourself. Change anything that doesn't make sense with your PEN.
- Check the boxes below to tell how you feel; at least one check must be in the "I Want Help" column.

Part of Story	I Like It	I Want Help
Attention-grabbing lead		
Stating the argument		
Explaining why the audience will listen		
Reasons		
Details		
Conclusion		

- Read your letter to your partner. Ask your partner to stop you if something doesn't make sense. Make any changes you need to your report with your PEN.
- Ask your partner to help you with the things you checked as "I Want Help." Read your story to your partner again. Make changes with your PEN.
- Staple this sheet to your letter.

Name _____ Date _____

Persuasive Letter Proofreading

Directions: Wait to do this proofreading section until after your teacher has OK'd your revisions. Use a PEN to make corrections. You check the blank on the left. Staple it to your draft and turn it in.

_____ I have used correct paragraph form. _____

_____ None of my sentences begin with *because, and, so, like, or that*. _____

_____ I've put capital letters at the beginning of sentences. _____

_____ I've put proper punctuation at the ends of sentences (.!?). _____

_____ My writing sounds like formal English. _____

_____ I have circled all words that might be misspelled and fixed them, if I knew how. _____

_____ I've put capital letters on proper nouns (names of people or places). _____

Research Project Plan Form for _____

Have your teacher circle the black dot next to each task as you finish it.

- ♦ List three topics you are interested in researching
    - • _____
    - • _____
    - • _____

- ♦ Look for sources in the library and on the Internet; put a check mark next to all the topics for which you think you can find a large amount of information (at least three sources)

- ♦ The topic I am going to research is _____

- ♦ In the space below, list at least five things you already know about your topic:
    - • _____
    - • _____
    - • _____
    - • _____
    - • _____
    - • _____
    - • _____

- ♦ In the space below, list at least two things your classmates know about your topic:
    - • _____

Copyright material from Elizabeth L. Jaeger (2026), *Integrating Sophisticated Standards and Systems of Support for Elementary Readers*, Routledge

- • _____
- • _____

♦ List three questions you want to find answers to. These questions need to be general questions (for example, How do koala bears care for their babies?) not specific questions (How many babies do koala bears have?):

- • _____
- • _____
- • _____

♦ Get four pieces of lined paper. Write one of your questions at the top of each piece of paper. Write **Other Information** at the top of the other piece.

♦ Start your Bibliography Form by filling in the information for your first source. Use your first source to get information. Use the Contents and Index to help you. Write information on the correct paper. For example, if information helps to answer your Question 1, it goes on that page; if it is interesting, but doesn't connect to any of your questions, it goes on the **Other Information** page. If you run into some interesting vocabulary, circle it. SKIP LINES AS YOU WRITE!!!

♦ Do the same with your second source.

♦ Do the same with your third source.

♦ Read through the notes for your first question. Use a highlighter to show the three facts you want to share. Do the same with your second and third question and **Other Information**.

♦ Fill out the Oral Report Notes form

- Find or draw an illustration to go with your report

- Give your oral report to a partner. Ask them to check off either "Did Well" or "Work on This" for each. There needs to be at least one check in the "Work on This" side

Did Well		Work on This
	Topic was clear	
	Facts were interesting	
	Illustration was related	
	Speaker was clear	
	Speaker was not too soft and not too loud	
	Speaker was not too fast and not too slow	
	Speaker defined at least two words	
	Speaker said the most interesting thing he or she learned and why	
	Speaker told something he or she still wants to know	

- Improve anything marked "Work on This"

- Give your oral report to another partner

- Give your oral report to the whole class or a small group

Name _____

Research Bibliography Form

This is how you record the information about the sources you use.

- ♦ Book: Cole, J. (1987). *The magic school bus inside the earth.* Scholastic.
- ♦ Web site: Jaeger, E.L. (2014, March). How to do a science report. Retrieved from http://www.sciencereports.com

Source 1

_____

_____

_____

Source 2

_____

_____

_____

Source 3

_____

_____

_____

Source 4

_____

_____

_____

Name _____ Topic _____

Oral Report Notes Form

- ♦ Question 1: _____
  - Fact 1: _____
  - Fact 2: _____
  - Fact 3: _____
- ♦ Question 2: _____
  - Fact 1: _____
  - Fact 2: _____
  - Fact 3: _____
- ♦ Question 3: _____
  - Fact 1: _____
  - Fact 2: _____
  - Fact 3: _____
- ♦ Other Interesting Information
  - Fact 1: _____
  - Fact 2: _____
  - Fact 3: _____
- ♦ Words I Learned
  - _____ means _____
  - _____ means _____
- ♦ The most interesting thing I learned was _____ _____. It was the most interesting because_____
- ♦ I still want to know_____ _____

Oral Report Rubric

Name _____

	1	2	3
Amount of Information	Little	Some	Lots
Use of Notes	Read	Looked a lot	Glanced
Volume	Too loud/ too soft	Mostly OK	Very good
Clarity	Vague	Mostly OK	Very clear
Expression	Little	Some	A lot
Audience Connection	No attempt	Some	A lot
Overall	Not acceptable	Acceptable	Excellent

Research Project Plan Form for _____

_____

Have your teacher circle the black dot next to each task as you finish it.

- ♦ List two animals you are interested in

    - • _____
    - • _____

- ♦ Visit the library. Talk with a partner about which animal you will choose. Talk with your teacher about which animal you will choose.

- ♦ The animal I am going to research is _____ _____

- ♦ In the space below, list at least three things you already know about your animal:

    - • _____
    - • _____
    - • _____
    - • _____

- ♦ In the space below, list at least two things your classmates know about your topic:

    - • _____
    - • _____
    - • _____

Copyright material from Elizabeth L. Jaeger (2026), *Integrating Sophisticated Standards and Systems of Support for Elementary Readers*, Routledge

- List two questions you want to find answers to. These questions need to be general questions (How do koala bears care for their babies?) not specific questions (How many babies do koala bears have?):

  - _____
  - _____

- Get three pieces of lined paper. Write one of your questions at the top of each piece of paper. Write **Other Information** at the top of the other piece.

- Use your first source to get information. Write information on the correct paper. If it is interesting, but doesn't connect to any of your questions, it goes on the **Other Information** page. If you run into some interesting words, circle them. SKIP LINES AS YOU WRITE!!!

- Do the same with your second source.

- Read through the notes for your first question. Use a highlighter to show the three facts you want to share. Do the same with your second question and **Other Information**.

- Fill out the Oral Report Notes form.

- Find or draw an illustration to go with your report.

- Give your oral report to a partner.

- Give your oral report to the whole class or a small group.

Name _____ Animal _____

Oral Report Notes Form

- ♦ Question 1: _____
  - Fact 1: _____
  - Fact 2: _____
  - Fact 3: _____
- ♦ Question 2: _____
  - Fact 1: _____
  - Fact 2: _____
  - Fact 3: _____
- ♦ Question 3: _____
  - Fact 1: _____
  - Fact 2: _____
  - Fact 3: _____
- ♦ Other Interesting Information
  - Fact 1: _____
  - Fact 2: _____
  - Fact 3: _____
- ♦ The most interesting thing I learned was _____
  _____
- ♦ I still want to know _____
  _____

Date _____

Dear Parent/Guardian,

My name is _____ and I am the reading specialist at _____ School.

    I am recommending that your child _____ attend a class that will help students to better understand and think about what they read.

Over the course of the next several weeks, I'd like to recommend a home reading activity: Before you read aloud a picture book to your child, do a Picture Walk—looking through the book to notice the pictures, make predictions, and think what she/he is wondering about. As you read, stop now and then and ask your child to tell you what is happening.

    Your child will receive a certificate of participation upon completion of the class.

Sincerely,

Date _____

Dear Parent/Guardian,

My name is _____ and I am the reading specialist at _____ School. I am recommending that your child _____ attend a class that will help students to better handle printed words as they begin to read.

Over the course of the next several weeks, I'd like to recommend a home reading activity: When you read aloud to your child, occasionally select a book with relatively large print. Hold the book where they can see it and, every five pages or so, have your child point to the words as you read that page.

Your child will receive a certificate of participation upon completion of the class.

Sincerely,

Date _____

Dear Parent/Guardian,

My name is _____ and I am the reading specialist at _____ School. I am recommending that your child _____ attend a class that will help them more effectively use letter sounds in reading and writing.

Over the course of the next several weeks, I'd like to recommend some home reading activities:

- Practice thinking of rhyming words (e.g., what's a word that rhymes with *star*?)
- Clap syllables (say a long-ish word like pajamas and clap the syllables—pa/jam/as)
- Blend sounds (e.g., say buh/a/duh and ask your child to make a word from the sounds—*bad*)
- Segment sounds (e.g., do the opposite from blending: say *bad* and see if your child can say buh/a/duh)

Your child will receive a certificate of participation upon completion of the class.

Sincerely,

Name _____ Date _____

Most Frequent 50 Words from Children's Literature

the	they	out
and	my	up
a	of	are
I	on	will
to	me	look
said	all	some
you	be	day
he	go	at
it	can	have
in	with	your
was	one	mother
she	her	come
for	what	not
that	we	like
is	him	then
his	no	get
but	so	

Copyright material from Elizabeth L. Jaeger (2026), *Integrating Sophisticated Standards and Systems of Support for Elementary Readers*, Routledge

Date _____

Hi _____,

You are enrolled in my class on reading short words because:

☐ You had difficulty with these words when you read with me.
☐ You had difficulty with these words on the sight word test.

Of the 50 words on the Sight Words Test, you pronounced _____ correctly.

Check the box below that tells how you think of yourself as a reader of short words:

☐ This is something I am very good at.
☐ This is something that is hard for me, but I notice that I am getting better.
☐ This is something that is really hard for me.

My goal for this class is to read _____ of the 50 words correctly.

Date _____

At the end of class, you read _____ of the 50 words correctly.

Check the box below that tells how you think of yourself as a reader of long words:

☐ This is something I am very good at.
☐ This is something that is hard for me, but I notice that I am getting better.
☐ This is something that is really hard for me and I need more help.

Copyright material from Elizabeth L. Jaeger (2026), *Integrating Sophisticated Standards and Systems of Support for Elementary Readers*, Routledge

Date _____

Dear Parent/Guardian,

My name is _____ and I am the reading specialist at _____ School. I am recommending that your child _____ attend a class that will help them more effectively read short words that should be known quickly at sight. On a sight word assessment, they read _____ of 54 words correctly. Before the class begins, your child will set a goal for improvement. We will assess their progress after the class is over.

Over the course of the next several weeks, I'd like to recommend a home reading activity. Have your child go on a "sight word hunt." They can look through books, magazines, etc. for sight words. I've included a list for you in case it's not clear what kind of words we're talking about.

    Your child will receive a certificate of participation upon completion of the class.

Sincerely,

Poems for the Poetry for Sight Words Activity

Shorter Poems	Longer Poems
My Mother Said	What a Day
My mother said,	What a day,
"Don't jump in bed!"	Oh, what a day.
And so I don't.	My little brother ran away,
I hop instead.	And now my tuba will not play.
Batty	I'm eight years old and turning gray
The baby bat	What a day,
Screamed out in fright,	Oh, what a day.
"Turn on the dark.	Why Is It?
I'm afraid of the light!"	Why is it some mornings
Animals	Your clothes just don't fit?
Always be kind to animals.	Your pants are too short
Morning, noon, and night.	To bend over or sit.
For animals have feelings, too,	Your sleeves are too long
And furthermore they BITE!	And your hat is too tight—
	Why is it some mornings
	Your clothes don't feel right?

Copyright material from Elizabeth L. Jaeger (2026), *Integrating Sophisticated Standards and Systems of Support for Elementary Readers*, Routledge

Phonics Assessment

Name _____ Date _____

♦ **Part 1: Consonant Sounds**

B	F	J	M
P	S	T	W

♦ **Part 2: Simple Blending**

dat	fep	pim
tob	nug	

♦ **Part 3: Diverse Blending**

blick	stip	trut	sman
slad	spon	swit	twep
flot	cham	shap	thim

♦ **Part 4: Long Vowels**

wode	hime	coap	pait

Date _____

Dear Parent/Guardian,

My name is _____ and I am the reading specialist at _____ School. I am recommending that your child _____ attend a class that will help them more effectively use letter sounds to read new words. On a phonics assessment with four levels, they scored ____ at level ____. I will assess their progress after the class is over.

Over the course of the next several weeks, I'd like to recommend a home reading activity. Have your child select a relatively difficult book on a topic of interest. Spend a few minutes—each day, if possible—reading the book aloud to your child. Stop occasionally at short but uncommon words and ask your child to read them. Talk about the word meanings, too, if needed.

Your child will receive a certificate of participation upon completion of the class.

Sincerely,

Date _____

Hi _____,

You are enrolled in my class on using word parts to figure out longer words because:

- ☐ You had difficulty with these words on the Names Test
- ☐ You said that reading these words was a challenge for you on the survey you filled out at the beginning of the year

Of the 78 word parts on the Names Test, you pronounced _____ correctly.

Check the box below that tells how you think of yourself as a reader of long words:

- ☐ This is something I am very good at.
- ☐ This is something that is hard for me, but I notice that I am getting better.
- ☐ This is something that is really hard for me.

My goal for this class is to pronounce _____ of the 78 syllables correctly.

Date _____

At the end of class, you pronounced _____ of the 78 syllables correctly.

Check the box below that tells how you think of yourself as a reader of long words:

- ☐ This is something I am very good at.
- ☐ This is something that is hard for me, but I notice that I am getting better.
- ☐ This is something that is really hard for me and I need more help.

Date _____

Dear Parent/Guardian,

My name is _____ and I am the reading specialist at _____ School. I am recommending that your child _____ attend a class on reading multi-syllable words because they have demonstrated difficulty with this during reading.

Over the course of the next several weeks, I'd like to recommend a home reading activity. Have your child select a relatively difficult book on a topic of interest. Spend a few minutes—each day, if possible—reading the book aloud to your child. Stop at multi-syllable words and see if, using the context and the "chunking" strategy they are learning in class, your child can figure out these more challenging words. Chunking means to read the word part by part such as *mis-un-der-stand-ing*. Talk about the word meanings, too.

Your child will receive a certificate of participation upon completion of the class.

Sincerely,

Date _____

Dear Parent/Guardian,

My name is _____ and I am the reading specialist at _____ School. I am recommending that your child _____ attend this class because they demonstrated difficulty with using comprehension strategies (predicting, visualizing, and making connections) in their classroom.

Over the course of the next several weeks, I'd like to recommend a home reading activity. As your child reads to you (or you read to them), stop to ask questions such as, "What do you think will happen next and why? What picture can you make in your brain of what is happening? What has happened to you that is like what is happening in the story?"

Sincerely,

Date _____

Dear Parent/Guardian,

My name is _____ and I am the reading specialist at _____ School. I am recommending that your child _____ attend a class on comprehension monitoring because they demonstrated difficulty with making meaning from text during classroom instruction.

Over the course of the next several weeks, I'd like to recommend a home reading activity. Have your child select a relatively challenging book. Ask your child to read aloud about half a page. If they read something that doesn't make sense or if they self-correct just note it on a piece of paper. Ignore words that are inaccurate but still make sense in the sentence (e.g., *woods* for *forest*). After your child has finished reading that part, go back to your notes and compliment self-corrections. Point out just one word that should have been corrected because it didn't make sense in the sentence.

Sincerely,

Date _____

Dear Parent/Guardian,

My name is _____ and I am the reading specialist at _____ School. I am recommending that your child _____ attend a class on making inferences because they demonstrated difficulty with inferring ideas that are not directly stated in text during classroom instruction.

Over the course of the next several weeks, I'd like to recommend a home reading activity. Have your child select a relatively challenging book. Ask your child to read aloud about half a page. If they read something that doesn't make sense stop and help them. Ignore words that are inaccurate but still make sense in the sentence (e.g., *woods* for *forest*). After your child has finished reading that part, ask them about an idea that the text "hints at" but doesn't directly state. Then ask them to explain how they were able to understand it. For example, if the text says that a character has their head down and is crying, they could infer that the character is sad.

Sincerely,

Name _____ Date _____

Points of Confusion

Fix-ups for confusion:

1. Slow down
2. Read ahead a little
3. Re-read
4. Think about your own life
5. Look at or make a picture
6. Get help

There is an example listed:

Page Number	Word or Idea?	Fix-ups I Tried (write one or more numbers)
4	idea	2, 3

Date _____

Dear Parent/Guardian,

My name is _____ and I am the reading specialist at _____ School. I am recommending that your child _____ attend a class on retelling because they demonstrated difficulty with retelling a story on the fall reading assessment.

Over the course of the next several weeks, I'd like to recommend a home reading activity. Have your child select a relatively easy book. Have your child read a relatively small segment of text (say, a paragraph) and then tell you what happened. The next day, have them read a slightly larger segment (say, half a page) and retell. Keep expanding the amount of text each day.

Sincerely,

Date _____

Hi _____,

You are enrolled in my class on retelling because:

☐ You had difficulty retelling a story when you read with me
☐ You said that retelling was a challenge for you on the survey you filled out at the beginning of the year

On the retelling chart, you remembered ____/12 of the most important parts

Check the box below that tells how you think of yourself as a reteller:

☐ This is something I am very good at.
☐ This is something that is hard for me, but I notice that I am getting better.
☐ This is something that is really hard for me.

My goal for this class is to remember ____/11 of the most important parts on my last retelling

Date _____

At the end of class, you remembered ____/11 of the most important parts

Check the box below that tells how you think of yourself as a reteller:

☐ This is something I am very good at.
☐ This is something that is hard for me, but I notice that I am getting better.
☐ This is something that is really hard for me and I need more help.

Copyright material from Elizabeth L. Jaeger (2026), *Integrating Sophisticated Standards and Systems of Support for Elementary Readers*, Routledge

Retell Protocol: "The Ducks and the Fox"

Name _____ Date _____

Text	Major 3	Moderate 2	Minor 1
Two ducks/sisters		XXXXXXXXX	XXXXXXXXX
Going to the pond	XXXXXXXXX		XXXXXXXXX
Good road	XXXXXXXXX	XXXXXXXXX	
But find a new one for novelty		XXXXXXXXX	XXXXXXXXX
Many other roads to choose from	XXXXXXXXX	XXXXXXXXX	
No		XXXXXXXXX	XXXXXXXXX
Don't want to try a new way	XXXXXXXXX	XXXXXXXXX	
I feel comfortable	XXXXXXXXX	XXXXXXXXX	
Met a fox		XXXXXXXXX	XXXXXXXXX
Sitting near the road	XXXXXXXXX	XXXXXXXXX	
Good morning	XXXXXXXXX	XXXXXXXXX	
Heading to the pond?	XXXXXXXXX		XXXXXXXXX
Yes—every day	XXXXXXXXX	XXXXXXXXX	
Interesting	XXXXXXXXX	XXXXXXXXX	
With a smile	XXXXXXXXX		XXXXXXXXX
We'll meet the fox today		XXXXXXXXX	XXXXXXXXX
Didn't like his looks	XXXXXXXXX		XXXXXXXXX
Find another road		XXXXXXXXX	XXXXXXXXX
You're silly	XXXXXXXXX	XXXXXXXXX	
Fox smiled	XXXXXXXXX		XXXXXXXXX
He's a gentleman	XXXXXXXXX	XXXXXXXXX	
Went down same road		XXXXXXXXX	XXXXXXXXX
Saw fox		XXXXXXXXX	XXXXXXXXX
Had a sack	XXXXXXXXX		XXXXXXXXX
Lovely ladies	XXXXXXXXX	XXXXXXXXX	
Expecting you	XXXXXXXXX	XXXXXXXXX	
Opened sack		XXXXXXXXX	XXXXXXXXX

(Continued)

(Continued)

Text	Major 3	Moderate 2	Minor 1
Jumped on them		XXXXXXXXX	XXXXXXXXX
Quacked/screamed	XXXXXXXXX		XXXXXXXXX
Flew home		XXXXXXXXX	XXXXXXXXX
Bolted door	XXXXXXXXX	XXXXXXXXX	
Stayed home next day	XXXXXXXXX		XXXXXXXXX
Rested nerves	XXXXXXXXX	XXXXXXXXX	
Then searched for a new road	XXXXXXXXX		XXXXXXXXX
Took it the next day		XXXXXXXXX	XXXXXXXXX
They were safe	XXXXXXXXX		XXXXXXXXX

Retell Protocol: "Poor Old Dog"

Name _____ Date _____

Text	Major 3	Moderate 2	Minor 1
There was an old dog		XXXXXXXX	XXXXXXXX
Very poor		XXXXXXXX	XXXXXXXX
Ragged coat and shoes	XXXXXXXX		XXXXXXXX
Slept in the park	XXXXXXXX		XXXXXXXX
Looked for little things to sell	XXXXXXXX	XXXXXXXX	
Found a gold ring		XXXXXXXX	XXXXXXXX
Thought his luck had changed	XXXXXXXX	XXXXXXXX	
Thought it was magic	XXXXXXXX		XXXXXXXX
Rubbed the ring	XXXXXXXX	XXXXXXXX	
Made wishes such as		XXXXXXXX	XXXXXXXX
New coat/shoes	XXXXXXXX		XXXXXXXX
New home	XXXXXXXX		XXXXXXXX
Wants them to come true now	XXXXXXXX	XXXXXXXX	
Nothing happened		XXXXXXXX	XXXXXXXX
Felt wind and pebbles	XXXXXXXX	XXXXXXXX	
Slept in the park	XXXXXXXX		XXXXXXXX
Saw note		XXXXXXXX	XXXXXXXX
On lamp post	XXXXXXXX	XXXXXXXX	
Lost: gold ring		XXXXXXXX	XXXXXXXX
Name and address of terrier	XXXXXXXX		XXXXXXXX
Went there		XXXXXXXX	XXXXXXXX
Terrier was happy	XXXXXXXX		XXXXXXXX
Thanked dog	XXXXXXXX	XXXXXXXX	
Gave him money		XXXXXXXX	XXXXXXXX
Bought coat/shoes		XXXXXXXX	XXXXXXXX
Lots of money left	XXXXXXXX	XXXXXXXX	
Down payment on house		XXXXXXXX	XXXXXXXX
Moved in	XXXXXXXX	XXXXXXXX	
Never slept in park again	XXXXXXXX	XXXXXXXX	

Copyright material from Elizabeth L. Jaeger (2026), *Integrating Sophisticated Standards and Systems of Support for Elementary Readers*, Routledge

Retell Protocol: _____

Name _____ Date _____

Text	Major 3	Moderate 2	Minor 1

Dictation Graph for _____

15											
14											
13											
12											
11											
10											
9											
8											
7											
6											
5											
4											
3											
2											
1											
P?											
X	1	2	3	4	5	6	7	8	9	10	11	12

Dictation: Narrative Text

#1
I can't stand hunting. It doesn't seem right to me that men and boys should kill animals just for the fun they get out of it. I tried to stop Philip and William from doing it.

2
Mr. Gregg was the first to wake up. He opened his eyes. He was about to put his hand out for his watch, to see the time, but his hand wouldn't come out. "That's funny," he said. "Where is my hand?"

3
The nest began to grow. The boys brought many sticks. Mr. Gregg was very good at making the sticks stick together. After a while he said, "Now I want leaves and feathers and things like that to make the inside nice and soft."

4
All at once something strange happened. Everything went black before their eyes and they couldn't see. At the same time a funny feeling came over them all, and they heard a great wind blowing.

5
It must have been about half an hour later that I walked into the Greggs' garden. I had come to see how things were going. At the gate I stopped and stared. Mr. Gregg was smashing all three guns.

Which Words Go Together?

Name _____

Directions: The following words can be divided into three groups. Copy each word into the boxes below so that each box contains words which are closely related. Label each box to name the group.

corn, cake, orange, apple, cookie, carrot, pie, broccoli, cherry

This list is somewhat more challenging.

painting, dresser, chair, cupboard, bench, photograph, basket, drawing, sofa

Summary

Little Nino's Pizzeria is a book about _____.
    Lots of people come to the restaurant and enjoy the food. The son, Tony, is happy because he can help his father. One day, his father gets the chance to open a bigger restaurant called Big Nino so he can make more money. But everyone in the family is unhappy, so they sell Big Nino and open up Little Tony's.

Persuasive

It is a good idea _____.
These people are hungry, and they may starve if no one gives them any food. There is always leftover food in restaurants, and it will go to waste if it isn't eaten soon. Giving away the food is a kind thing to do.

Procedure

_____. First, you make the dough and carefully fit it in the pizza pan. Then you make the tomato sauce and spread it over the dough. Next you grate cheese and sprinkle it over the sauce. Choose some toppings to go on the pizza: maybe pepperoni or vegetables. Put it in the oven to bake. Finally, take it out and enjoy eating it.

Descriptive

Little Nino's is a lively place. _____

_____

_____

_____

_____

_____

_____

Response to Literature

I think Tony's dad did the right thing when he sold Big Nino and opened Little Tony's. Here are my reasons. _____

_____
_____
_____
_____
_____
_____

Cause and Effect

Nino's decision to open Big Nino caused several problems. ____

_____
_____
_____
_____
_____
_____

Paragraph Editing Checklist

Author _____ Date _____

Directions: Use a PEN to revise and proofread your paragraph. Check off each blank on the left as you go. When your teacher looks over your work, they will check the blank on the right if that element is in your paragraph.

Revision

_____ My writing makes sense. _____

_____ My topic sentence is _____ _____

_____

_____

_____

_____ I have at least three supporting sentences. _____

_____ All my supporting sentences relate to my topic. _____

Proofreading

_____ Each sentence begins with a capital letter. _____

_____ Each sentence ends with punctuation (usually a period). _____

_____ Each proper noun begins with a capital letter. _____

_____ I have circled all words I think might be mis-spelled _____ (and fixed them if I can).

_____ I have used correct paragraph form. _____

Cooking

I like to cook because it makes my family happy to ate tasty Food when I cook for them, I can be sure that they are getting the nutrients. that they need trying new recipes is interesting and fun I like to draw pictures, too.

Dictation: Expository Text

1
Alligators and crocodiles spend much of their lives in water. For swimming, they have streamlined bodies and webbed feet. They can cruise on the surface of a lake or river or dive below. The tail is used like a paddle.

2
In real life, unfortunate events happen. When they do, authorities often call in search and rescue dogs. They can search for hikers who don't return on time. They can find people trapped in the rubble of a collapsed building. They can find a child who has wandered off.

3
Some dogs are able to locate people with their sense of smell. People's scents are as unique as fingerprints. Wherever they go, people leave an invisible trail of scent behind them. Dogs, especially bloodhounds, can identify it easily.

4
The most famous dogsled race is the Iditarod. Run on an 1,100 mile course between Anchorage and Nome, Alaska the Iditarod takes between 11 and 21 days to complete. Drivers and dog teams face harsh winter weather, rugged terrain, and even wild animals.

Bats

Bats eat many different foods some bats. like to catch insects as they fly threw the air other bats ate big, juicy Fruits like mangoes and papayas vampire bats suck blud from cows and other animals bats sleep at night.

Appendix E
IRI and IELI Materials

Informal Emergent Literacy Inventory
for _____ **Date** _____

Introduction: "I want to find out what you know about books as I read this story to you."

What To Do	What To Say	Results
1.	What might happen in a story called "The Windy Day"?	
2. Show 1st picture.	Now what do you think?	
3. Read story through p. 7.	Now what do you think?	
4. Read to end of story.		
5.	Pretend I've never heard the story before. Tell me as much of the story as you can.	none inadequate adequate rich
6. Read last line on p. 2, pointing to the words as you read.	As I read this again, I'd like you to point to the words.	minimal close exact
7. Give child card with *said* on it.	Can you find this word on p. 3?	no yes, slowly yes, quickly
8. Read the last line on p. 4, pointing to words.	Can you find the word *he*? Can you find the word *cake*?	none one both
9. Read the last line on p. 6, pointing to words.	What is this word? (where) What is this word? (my)	none one both
	*********************************	
10. Give example(s).	I'm going to say a sentence and leave out a word. Tell me a word that could fit in.	I went to the ____ My _____ is broken.

(Continued)

(Continued)

What To Do	What To Say	Results
11. Give example(s).	Tell me a word that rhymes with…	car _____ sit _____ great _____
12. Give example(s).	Say the word I say and clap the syllables.	carpet pajamas underwater
13. Give example(s).	I will say some sounds. Try to squish them together to make a word.	so hop chat
14. Give example(s).	I will say some words. Try to split them into sounds.	go it cat stay past
15. Show students each of the letter cards. Notes Re Writing Sample:	What letter is this?	B S T R Y

IRI Example Passage: Grade 2 Narrative Text

EJIRI 2.0N1 Max's Magical Drawings 125 wds. (8; 3)

Name _____ Date _____

Max loved to draw. For his second birthday he was given a box of crayons. After that, he spent most of his time drawing pictures. He drew and drew. The more he drew the better he got.

One day Max was at the park. He was drawing a picture of a cloud.

"What a great drawing," said a lady. "May I have it?"

Max gave the lady the drawing. When she touched it, the cloud lifted right off the paper. It floated down the path.

"Wait!" cried the lady, as she ran after it.

"That was amazing!" said the man sitting next to Max on the park bench. "How did you do it?"

"I don't know," said Max. "Nothing like this has ever happened before."

R   Q
___ ___ (F) 1. What does Max love to do?
___ ___ (F) 2. Why did he get better at drawing?
___ ___ (F) 3. What did he draw at the park?
___ ___ (F) 4. What happened when he gave it to the lady?
___ ___ (V) 5. What does the word "amazing" mean?
___ ___ (I) 6. Why do you think the lady liked the drawing?
___ ___ (I) 7. How do you think Max feels at the end?
___ accuracy errors ___ comp errors ___ sentence errors
Retell: ___ rich ___ adeq ___ inadeq. Silent/Oral: ___ time ___ rate
Fluency: ___ smoothe ___ adeq ___ inadeq. Resp ___ rich ___ OK ___ none

Copyright material from Elizabeth L. Jaeger (2026), *Integrating Sophisticated Standards and Systems of Support for Elementary Readers*, Routledge

IRI Example Passage: Grade 2 Expository Text

EJIRI 2E Water for People and Animals 153 wds. (10 ½; 3) 20 sent. (8; 4)

Name _____ Date _____

People in the village of Moll need water to cook. They also need water to wash. They need water to grow their food. Animals, plants, and people can't live without it.

Where do you think they get their water? There is plenty of water in Moll because it rains a lot. There are also many creeks near the village. People take water from the creeks.

Sometimes people take animals to the creeks. They can drink there. Sometimes people bring water to the animals.

Plants in the fields of Moll get their water from rain. But plants also need water when it is not raining, so the people make small ponds. They do this by stopping up the water in the creeks. The ponds hold the water for the fields. Then a small people dig a canal from the pond to the field. Water runs through the canal and the plants have the water they need.

R Q I
___ ___ ___ (F) 1. Tell two things people need water for.
___ ___ ___ (F) 2. Where do the people of Moll get their water? (tell one)
___ ___ ___ (F) 3. How do animals get water? (tell one)
___ ___ ___ (F) 4. How do plants get water when it is not raining?
___ ___ ___ (F) 5. How do the people make the ponds?
___ ___ ___ (V) 6. What is a <u>canal</u>?
___ ___ ___ (I) 7. Why are the people so careful to be sure they have water?

_____ accuracy errors _____ comprehension errors _____ sentence errors
Retell: _____ rich _____ adeq. _____ inadeq. Silent/Oral: _____ time _____ rate
Fluency: _____ smoothe _____ adeq. _____ inadeq.

IRI Example Passage: Grade 4 Narrative Text

EJIRI 4N1 The Lazy Fox 164 wds. (10; 3) 14 sent. (5; 2)

Name _____ Date _____

There was once a fox who was known throughout the land for being a lazy scamp as well as a scheming rascal. He was too lazy to work on his own little farm. He was so scheming nobody would work for him. The fox was full of tricks. One morning he looked at his barren fields and said, "Unless my fields are planted, I shall go hungry. But what can I do?" He thought and thought. Finally, an idea popped into his head. "I'll get that slow, stupid armadillo to plant my fields for me and I'll promise him a share of the crops. Of course," the fox added slyly, "it will be a very small share." So the fox hurried down the road to the home of his neighbor. He found him sitting under a palm tree, telling stories to his children. "Good day, friend armadillo," the fox called. "I have been thinking about you this morning, and I want to help you."

```
  R     Q
____  ____ (F) 1. What is the fox like?
____  ____ (F) 2. What kind of work is the fox supposed to do?
____  ____ (F) 3. What is the fox's problem?
____  ____ (F) 4. What is his solution for it?
____  ____ (V) 5. What does barren mean?
____  ____ (I) 6. Why does the fox think the armadillo will help?
____  ____ (I) 7. Why do you think the fox tells the armadillo
                  that he wants to help him?
____  ____ (R) 8. Find the word that tells what kind of tree the
                  armadillo sits under.
```
_____ accuracy errors _____ comprehension errors _____ sentence errors
Retell: _____ rich _____ adeq. _____ inadeq. Silent / Oral: _____ time _____ rate
Fluency: _____ smoothe _____ adeq. _____ inadeq. Resp _____ rich _____ OK _____ none

Copyright material from Elizabeth L. Jaeger (2026), *Integrating Sophisticated Standards and Systems of Support for Elementary Readers*, Routledge

IRI Example Passage: Grade 4 Expository Text

EJIRI 4E What Good Is a Weed? 172 wds. (10; 3) 20 sent. (8; 4)

Name _____ Date _____

Few things are as unappreciated as weeds. Farmers, gardeners, and homeowners fight a constant battle against weeds. They spray weeds with poisons. They chop them with hoes. They cut them with machines. What's so bad about a weed? People dislike weeds because they grow in places where we don't like them. When a violet grows in the woods, it is called a wildflower. But when it grows in a cornfield, it is called a weed.

Weeds are important. They supply food for animals. Some weeds have seeds and berries that birds eat. The leaves of other weeds are eaten by insects, rabbits, cattle, and deer. Meadow mice and gophers eat the roots of some weeds. Many weeds protect the soil from wind and rain. Their roots make tiny holes in the soil. These holes let rain soak in instead of rushing over the land. Water rushing over the land makes gullies and washes away the topsoil. Topsoil is needed for growing crops. So the roots of weeds help hold topsoil in place.

R Q I
___ ___ ___ (F) 1. Tell two ways people try to get rid of weeds.
___ ___ ___ (F) 2. Why are weeds disliked?
___ ___ ___ (F) 3. Tell two animals that use weeds for food.
___ ___ ___ (F) 4. How do weeds protect the soil?
___ ___ ___ (V) 5. What is a <u>gully</u>?
___ ___ ___ (I) 6. Why do we need more than one way to get rid of weeds?
___ ___ ___ (I) 7. Why can the same plant be a weed in some places and not other places?

_____ accuracy errors _____ comprehension errors _____ sentence errors

Retell: _____ rich _____ adeq. _____ inadeq. Silent/Oral: _____ time _____ rate

Fluency: _____ smoothe _____ adeq. _____ inadeq.

Miscue Analysis Chart for _____
Date _____

P = problem   U = uncertain   N = not a problem

#	Reader	Text	Sight word?	Phonics?	Structural analysis?	Vocabulary?	Context?	Self-corrected?
1								
2								
3								
4								
5								
6								
7								
8								
9								
10								
11								
12								
13								
14								
15								
16								
17								
18								
19								
20								
21								
22								

(Continued)

(Continued)

#	Reader	Text	Sight word?	Phonics?	Structural analysis?	Vocabulary?	Context?	Self-corrected?
23								
24								
25								
26								
27								
28								
29								
30								
31								
32								
33								
34								
35								
36								
37								
38								
39								
40								

Appendix F
Tier 1 and 2 Research

Implementation of Common Core-Based Curriculum in a Fourth-Grade Literacy Classroom: An Exploratory Study (Abridged)

The full study can be found here: Jaeger (2017). Implementation of Common Core-based curriculum in a 4th-grade literacy classroom: An exploratory study. *Reading Horizons, 56* (1), 45–68.

Lack of teacher confidence in teaching the Common Core State Standards (CCSS) and concomitant low achievement levels have proved challenging for schools and districts. It is the purpose of this paper to describe an English language arts (ELA) curriculum I developed and implemented in collaboration with a 4th-grade teacher. I argue here that such a curriculum, based on the ELA CCSS and supported by in-class professional development, can increase teachers' expertise and confidence in their ability to provide appropriate instruction for their students. An increase in student achievement may follow.

In service of this effort, I collected a range of achievement data for all students and employed an interview protocol to focus on reading beliefs with six focal students who struggled with literacy. The study addressed three research questions:

- What were 4th-grade student ELA achievement levels and beliefs about literacy prior to and following the implementation of a CCSS-based curriculum?
- What was the collaborating teacher's response to participating in this implementation project?
- What roles did mediating tools play within this literacy learning system?

Method

The site of this Institutional Review Board (IRB)-approved study was Campbell Elementary School (school and participant names are pseudonyms), located in a rural community 20 miles outside of a large city in the southwest United States. Of the 534 students attending the K-8 school, 3% were African American, 1% American Indian, 2% Asian/Pacific Islander, 44% Hispanic, and 50% White; 41% of the population qualified for free- or reduced-price lunch when the study commenced in the fall of 2013. Traditionally, students at the school had done well on standardized tests, but over the past few years, scores had begun to decline. With more challenging CCSS testing on the horizon, the superintendent worried that Campbell students would not succeed, and teachers also expressed the pressure and uncertainty they felt moving forward. As a result, this site, and the participants involved, was appropriate for the study I conducted.

Participants

One student with an IEP received most of her literacy instruction in the resource room and was not included in the research. The remaining 4th graders ($n = 51$) participated in a range of ways:

- ♦ All students were taught using the new CCSS curriculum and assessed with unit tests and the state standards test. Data from the previous spring suggested that 23% of these students were reading well-above grade level on the Developmental Reading Assessment (DRA) (Beaver, 2011), 46% at or just above grade level, and 31% below grade level.
- ♦ In addition to the assessments noted above, I gave those students reading below grade level according to the DRA ($n = 16$), an adapted version of the Fountas and Pinnell Benchmark Assessment (Fountas & Pinnell, 2010). These students were eligible for extra support from the reading specialist (see Jaeger, 2016). In September, we sent home student assent and parent permission documents for each of these students.

- Few assents/permissions were returned (*n* = 6), but the students were quite diverse. Four were White and two were Latino, three were reading a year or more below grade level on the DRA, and three were reading slightly below their grade level, and there were an equal number of boys and girls. These focal students were interviewed as part of the study.

Working with a range of participants allowed us to consider the ways in which their learning was mediated in similar and distinct ways.

Katrina, one of the 4th-grade teachers, taught literacy to both classes while her colleague Elspeth provided instruction in math. Katrina responded with interest to my proposal to develop and co-teach a CCSS-based reading curriculum. She had taught for 28 years when the study began, 27 of them at this school. When I first met her, Katrina, like most of her Campbell colleagues, organized her reading instruction around a basal reader and demonstrated a skills-based orientation to literacy instruction (Dahl & Freppon, 1995). As she stated in her initial interview:

> I would do a typical introduction and have the kids have some kind of prior knowledge…and then do some kind of anticipatory set. But then basically introducing vocabulary, listening to the story on tape, then reading it aloud to me, discuss it, do worksheets together, and then typically culminate with a test. And it would take about a week.

Katrina believed this type of instruction worked relatively well for her average and above-average readers, but she noticed that the vulnerable readers[1] in her classes were often disengaged, did poorly on unit assessments, and lacked confidence. She feared that, with implementation of the more challenging CCSS, this curriculum would no longer effectively serve any of her students; new mediating tools were required. When presented with a well-structured curriculum and regular in-class support in the form of demonstration lessons and co-teaching, she was ready for a change. Katrina's responsibilities in the study were to observe my demonstration lessons with the first group of students she saw each day, teach the lesson to the other group, and continue to implement the curriculum on the days I was not present at the site. She also administered the unit assessments and collected student work such as drawings and written reflections (see list of curriculum units at the end of the article).

Researcher Positionality and Supports for Validity

My roles in this context were many and varied, including curriculum developer, professional development provider, and co-teacher, as well as researcher; this added complexity to my positionality. Having spent 25 years as a classroom teacher and reading specialist prior to becoming a researcher, the trials and tribulations of classroom teaching were always on my mind. It is possible that my familiarity with public school routines influenced the way I interacted with participants; for example, I may have been less than forthright with Katrina than a more neutral researcher would have been because I was cognizant of the realities with which she contended. On the other hand, I brought a certain sensitivity to the site born of my experience, and that sensitivity served as a tool of sorts in my efforts to build rapport. Supports for validity included intensive, long-term involvement at the site; respondent validation via student and teacher interviews; triangulation of data sources; and statistical tests of significance (Maxwell, 2013).

Description of Curriculum Implementation

The objective of the curriculum implementation was to increase literacy achievement. It was designed to address the 4th-grade CCSS for reading literature and information text, and foundational skills. Although not specified as CCSS content, units on reading strategies were also included in an effort to provide students with tools that would mediate their understanding by engaging them in metacognitive thinking about their reading processes (Afflerbach et al., 2008).

Data Collection

The following types of data were collected between August 2013 and May 2014.

Data collected 2013–2014

Instrument	Administered to ... and by ...	Instrument Description	Administration Dates	Purpose for Administration
Unit assessments	Given to all students (n = 51) by teacher	These researcher-developed assessments resembled CCSS-based classroom assignments rather than "tests"; average completion time was about 45 minutes	At the completion of each unit	Measured understanding of unit content
State Standards Test (AIMS)	Given to all 3rd graders in April 2013 and again in 4th grade (April 2014) by teacher; 12 students present in August of 4th grade (2013) had attended other schools in 3rd grade so their data were not included (n = 39)	AIMS is a criterion-referenced test designed to measure the state standards that preceded the CCSS; for the most part, it employs a traditional multiple-choice design	April 2013 (in 3rd grade); April 2014 (in 4th grade)	Served as a distal measure of overall reading achievement
Adapted Fountas & Pinnell Benchmark Assessment	Texts from the published version of this Informal Reading Inventory were used, but administration procedures were streamlined, given by researcher	Given to all students reading below level according to the DRA given in May 2013 (n = 16); all students assessed on the Fountas & Pinnell in the fall were also present in winter and spring	September 2013; February & May 2014	Proximal measure of overall reading achievement for vulnerable readers; information texts were used to reflect the CCSS's emphasis on this genre

(*Continued*)

(Continued)

Instrument	Administered to … and by …	Instrument Description	Administration Dates	Purpose for Administration
Student interviews	Researcher interviewed vulnerable reader focal students ($n = 6$); 3 boys and 3 girls, 4 Whites and 2 Latina/os, 3 near grade level in reading and 3 well-below	Interview questions were open-ended and addressed literacy beliefs (see interview protocol)	September 2013; February & May 2014	Surfaced vulnerable readers' beliefs about and experiences with literacy and detected changes that were, potentially, linked to the CCSS curriculum
Teacher interviews	Researcher interviewed Katrina, the 4th-grade literacy teacher	Interview questions were open-ended and explored teacher beliefs (see interview protocol)	October & December 2013; February & May 2014	Surfaced teacher beliefs about (a) teaching and learning, (b) the focal students, and (c) the CCSS implementation

Research questions were addressed as follows: In response to research question one (What were 4th-grade student ELA achievement levels and beliefs about literacy prior to and following the implementation of a CCSS-based curriculum?), achievement was defined in these ways:

- Percent of students demonstrating mastery on curriculum-based unit assessments. This measure reflected what students had been directly taught in the lessons we provided and approximated assignments given during the unit itself.
- Scaled score growth on the state standards test. Although this test did not yet reflect the CCSS, it served as the distal measure of reading growth.
- Grade level growth on a modified version of the Fountas and Pinnell Benchmark Assessment. Although the provided texts were used, the retell process was simplified and higher-level thinking questions (e.g., predicting, evaluation) were added. It was important to employ a measure like this that closely resembled the act of independent reading. Because the Fountas and Pinnell was time-consuming to administer, we reserved this assessment for below-level readers only.
- Evidence from focal student interviews of their reaction to instruction (see Appendix B, Part 1). These questions measured facile use of comprehension strategies and self-description of reading knowledge for the focal students.

In response to research question two (What was the collaborating teacher's response to participating in this implementation project?), the teacher's reaction to involvement was measured by quarterly interviews (see end of article). In response to research question three (What roles did mediating tools play within this literacy learning system?), the role of tools was assessed by analysis of curriculum unit plans, as well as student and teacher interviews.

Data Analysis

Data analysis varied by instrument. I rated student scores for the unit assessments as *high* (90% accuracy or higher), *passing* (70%–89%), or *not passing* (below 70%). Participants' AIMS scores for both third grade (2013) and fourth grade (2014) were available for 39 students, so a T-test was used to assess statistical significance on this measure. Due to the relatively small sample ($n = 16$), Fountas and Pinnell scores were analyzed using the Wilcoxon Signed Rank Test. Qualitative data from student interviews was analyzed by specific question (e.g., how do you choose something to read?). For teacher interview data, I employed data-driven coding (Gibbs, 2007). I read the transcripts, looking for patterns in the data: reading, re-reading, and re-coding as necessary to reach saturation. Finally, in working with interview transcripts and curriculum documents, I employed the theoretical construct of *mediating tool* for concept-driven coding (Gibbs, 2007); that is, I looked through all documents for instances of tool use and the level of sophistication of those tools. In sum, I employed assessment results, data-driven, and concept-driven coding to answer the research questions.

Findings

Findings from a range of collected data follow. I begin with achievement data from unit assessments, the state standards test, the Fountas and Pinnell inventory, and student reflections on learning. Then, I consider development in teacher confidence/commitment. Finally, I examine tool use.

Achievement: Assessments and Student Beliefs

All achievement-related measures—unit assessments, AIMS, the Fountas and Pinnell, and responsiveness to instruction among the focal students—offered evidence for the success of the implementation. Findings for vulnerable readers were as strong as or stronger than that of their higher-achieving peers.

Unit assessments. Pass rates for CCSS-based unit assessments averaged 90%. Although students reading at 6th-grade level or above on the previous spring's DRA had higher rates than others (98%), results for those reading below level (88%) were nearly identical to that of students reading at the 4th- or 5th-grade level (89%). Unit assessment pass rates tended to increase over the course of the school year.

AIMS. Of the 51 students participating in the study, 92% scored *meets* or *exceeds* expectations on the AIMS in 2014, and no scores fell *far below* expectations. Based on data of students for whom we had scores for the previous year ($n = 39$), the mean scaled score point gain between 3rd and 4th grade was 29 ($p = .01$). Students reading below level at the end of 3rd grade gained an average of 49 points ($p = .01$). This growth is remarkable given that the new curriculum addressed the CCSS while the AIMS test was developed to measure the previous state standards: a finding that speaks to students' ability to transfer their standards-based knowledge to other literacy assessments even when the specific standards measured differ. In comparison, growth in reading for those students who were in 5th or 6th grade in 2013–2014 (and therefore did not receive instruction using this type of curriculum) was not statistically significant, nor was growth in mathematics for the 4th graders who were involved in the study. Unfortunately, stronger readers failed to achieve hoped-for gains on AIMS. The scores of those students reading well-above grade level in fall 2013 and for whom we had spring 2014 data ($n = 6$) had increased, on average, by only six scaled score points; in fact, the scores of two students dropped by 13 and 20 points, respectively. It appeared that adjustments in the instructional protocol would be necessary to better support these strong readers.

Fountas and Pinnell assessment. Improvement on the Fountas and Pinnell Informal Reading Inventory (IRI) was substantial. The average gain among the 16 students who were assessed with this instrument (those reading below level in fall) was 2.3 years over the course of a nine-month school year ($p = .01$). There may, in fact, have been a ceiling effect with this calculation because, although five students successfully read the grade seven passage, I chose not to ask them to read beyond it because they were clearly more than able to negotiate text heading into fifth grade.

Focal student interview responses. The six focal students were interviewed at three points during the school year. As noted, the group was diverse in terms of ethnicity, gender, and reading level. I derived overall findings from transcripts from each student, but, to add depth and continuity to the interview responses presented here, I provide quotes from only two whose comments represent the range of those made by the group as a whole: Miguel, a Latino male reading well-below level in fall 2013 and Isabel, a White female reading just below level at that time. All focal students reacted positively to the new curriculum and demonstrated responsiveness to the instruction they received. Five of the six students said they felt reading was easier in May than in September; as Miguel put it, "You showed me more stuff to make it easier."

When asked to name something they had learned, focal student responses delineated the specific impact of the CCSS-based instruction. Four students employed new strategies before they began reading. Isabel's initial pre-reading strategy was to get a glass of water! By February, she was scanning the text for words that might cause her trouble, and in May, she added reading the blurb as a helpful approach.

By spring, five focal students had learned additional tools for understanding challenging vocabulary, grasped the need to vary rate while reading, and adopted new strategies for understanding and remembering what they read. In October, Miguel looked outside the text to deal with words he did not understand—asking for help or using a dictionary—but by February he was more likely to read on or re-read. He initially connected reading rate to mode (silent or oral) or to his feelings: "When I read silent, I read a little bit faster. I slow down when I get nervous." By May, he adjusted his rate based on text difficulty: "When it's a hard sentence, I take my time. When it's easy, I go fast." When asked about what she did when finished reading to remember what she had read, Isabel reported that her mom asked her questions and, when her mom was unavailable, she asked herself similar questions. Isabel nominated "the parts that say something has happened" as the most important information to remember. Four focal students gained in their ability to monitor comprehension.

Both Miguel and Isabel named re-reading as the best strategy for dealing with confusion and, to this, Miguel added asking someone who knows a lot about the topic.

Focal students also exhibited a change in their understanding of what it meant to be an effective reader. In general, this change involved a diminishing focus on accuracy and an increasing focus on meaning-making, beliefs supported by CCSS RF4.4: Read with sufficient accuracy and fluency to support understanding. In October and February, Miguel was uncertain about whether reading every word correctly is necessary, but in May he responded, "No, because you might figure out what that word is when you read ahead of it," a more efficient approach. He also viewed a strong reader as one who reads independently—"My mom helps me a little bit, but not all the time"—and who reads more challenging books. From early on, Miguel understood that a good oral reader like his mom "does excitement and all that and I have heard her read a lot and a lot." By May, he said reading clearly was also important. Focal students also recognized that good readers sometimes struggled. Isabel evidenced a growing understanding that even strong readers encounter trouble as they read and she became more specific and meaning-oriented in describing their strategies for dealing with difficulty. At first, she believed "they just try their best." By February, she said they used sounding out as a support. In May, however, she viewed herself as one of those effective readers, commenting that they behave "like I do sometimes … I re-read the sentence and fix what I messed up."

By May, each focal student had refined her/his process for selecting books, reflecting their awareness that reading materials may be appropriate for a range of reasons. Early on, Isabel simply looked at the cover, but in May she said, "I read the cover, and I look through the book, and I read the first page." Miguel replied that he looked for "not hard books and not easy books." Although the CCSS clearly support increasing text complexity in instructional situations, the ability to select appropriate books for independent reading is also important.

In sum, solid achievement data supported our general approach to instruction. Unit assessments demonstrated growth for all students; this finding indicated that the great majority of students were learning the curriculum based on the CCSS. AIMS offered a more global picture of improvement. Vulnerable readers exhibited strong progress on the Fountas and Pinnell as well as AIMS, suggesting that we were meeting their needs as well or better than those of average and stronger readers. Focal students offered evidence that they had gained greater expertise in strategy/tool use as well as constructing meaning from and discussing whole texts, major areas of focus in the curriculum. Changes in their beliefs about the activity of reading and about what it means to be a successful reader demonstrated their growing awareness of the complexity of the reading process (Engestrom, 1987).

Teacher Growth and Confidence

Katrina's experiences with and beliefs about the implementation evolved over the course of the school year. Initially, she did her best to implement the lesson tools as planned but found this to be tiring work. She felt "like a student teacher again" and she struggled with feeling far behind in the lessons she hoped to retain from her previous teaching. But then she noticed differences:

> I watch the kids ... being more engaged. With my struggling readers, I think they can be good thinkers. They have had difficulties with school before and it's nice to see how they ... are not giving up so easily because they have these specific strategies.

By December, Katrina was feeling more confident in the efficacy of the CCSS implementation and less reliant on old ways of teaching. In addition to the benefits for vulnerable readers, she referenced changes in her stronger readers who reported that they were enjoying reading more. Students were also beginning to transfer the tools they had mastered in lessons to other contexts, an example of appropriation. She quoted one student who referred to a science lesson during the unit on character analysis in which they had contrasted feelings (fleeting) with traits (more stable): "Oh, that reminds me of weather and climate and how the weather changes all the time. Climate can change, but it takes a lot to change it." I also noticed Katrina referring to previous CCSS units as she taught new ones, as if the curriculum was all one big learning process rather than units in isolation, another form of appropriation. Students began to do the same (e.g., "We can read ahead to know the word").

In February, Katrina talked about our work together. She felt she could ask about anything that confused her or tell me if she wanted to go in a different direction. For example, I developed a unit on following directions after she and her 4th-grade colleagues noted this to be a problem. When we spoke in May, Katrina reflected on the progress her vulnerable readers had made: "They really believe they are better readers, and I think that they are." Clearly, Katrina felt excited about and supported by learning new instructional tools.

I shared her enthusiasm. Her students participated actively in the lessons we taught and made headway toward mastering the ELA CCSS. In the end, my concerns were related less to what we had done but to what remained to do. There was room for further differentiation (McLaughlin & Overturf, 2012): more support for students who struggled and more challenge for students who grasped what we were teaching quickly and easily. A more regular system for collecting formative data would have supported this differentiation. To avoid overwhelm, the curriculum I wrote addressed the reading standards, but not those in writing. We agreed to work further in this area the following year. And the question of how this project might be expanded to other grade levels loomed large.

Conclusions

I have argued that a rich and engaging curriculum, based on the CCSS-ELA and supported by in-class professional development, can increase teacher expertise and confidence and support student achievement. In service of this argument, this report has provided answers to the proposed research questions related to reading achievement/beliefs, teacher confidence, and tool use.

Increased Reading Achievement and Richer Reader Beliefs

When an ELA CCSS-based curriculum was implemented in a 4th-grade classroom, student achievement levels were strong on the proximal (unit) assessments. Scores improved on the state standards test and, for vulnerable readers, the Fountas and Pinnell inventory. Students—vulnerable readers in particular—participated actively in the lessons and verbalized the positive experiences they had. And the teacher, although challenged initially, enjoyed teaching the curriculum and intended to maintain and expand implementation in ensuing years. An analysis of focal student interview responses added support for our belief that students were not only better readers but were also able, when given the opportunity, to reflect on the growth they had made. In addition, when asked what changes they would like to see in classroom activities, several focal students requested more time to read independently.

Teacher Confidence and Researcher Awareness

Over time, Katrina became more confident in her ability to help students construct meaning from text and to understand and apply sophisticated standards; she also demonstrated an increasing commitment to the changes we had made. From the discussions we had, I came to better understand the combination of tenacity and flexibility necessary to facilitate the implementation of a new curriculum in a new context, even with a willing and able teacher partner and interested students. In the end, we believed, along with Wertsch et al. (1993), that "the possibilities for following certain paths of action [had been] shaped by the mediational means employed" (p. 342) and that those means had contributed to positive outcomes.

Limitations

This study has five major limitations. The first relates to the student (and, potentially, the teacher) interviews; given my obvious enthusiasm for the project, it is possible that interviewees painted a rosy picture of their engagement in an effort to please me and their actual experiences were less positive than they appeared. The fact that we were unable to teach the Text Analyst aspect of the curriculum before the year ended was a second limitation. In future iterations, it will be important to both teach and assess this important literacy role, particularly considering the CCSS's greater emphasis on close reading and evidence-gathering. A third issue was the absence of a CCSS-based distal assessment. I used the AIMS as a general transfer measure, but this assessment was based on the state standards that preceded the CCSS; use of a CCSS-based assessment would likely alter the achievement findings. The fourth limitation relates to the potential for a more teacher-driven research protocol, often referred to as action research (Craig, 2009; McNiff & Whitehead, 2010). The motivating force for this study was my own interest and commitment. Had it originally emerged from Katrina's unease with her own teaching, her colleagues might have been more likely to turn to her for support and, therefore, difficulties with transferring to other classrooms would have been mitigated to some degree. Finally, and of greatest significance, the study occurred at one grade level in one context. Were it to have taken place in first grade or sixth grade, with a more diverse population, the outcomes might have been quite different. Because of these limitations, this study should be considered exploratory.

Implications

Even given these limitations, there are implications within this work for practice and future research. Implications for practice include lessons learned about ELA instruction in an era of Common Core. Implications for future research involve conducting concatenated exploratory studies with differing populations and, eventually, confirmatory experimental or quasi-experimental designs. As is common among exploratory studies, the work generated new questions and hypotheses as well as providing answers.

Instructional Practice

There are four key instructional implications of this study. First, when crafted with attention to what is known about teaching and learning (e.g., the benefits of using a gradual release of responsibility model of instruction), curriculum units that systematically address the CCSS mediated between readers and increased achievement. This is true for vulnerable readers, as well as their more successful peers. Additional curriculum development beyond a single grade level will be necessary to facilitate school-wide adoption.

A second implication is that an instructional protocol such as the one employed here needs to be adjusted as needed to suit a given situation. Rather than arranging the units per the Four Resources model, they could, for example, be structured differently to more fully integrate the reading of narrative and expository text. The employed distal measure (AIMS) provided some evidence that stronger readers failed to benefit from these lessons as much as their lower-achieving peers; they might benefit from more freedom, with the option to demonstrate mastery of content prior to the unit, followed by independent or small group studies of more challenging content.

Third, because stronger readers in this study failed to demonstrate the gains of mid-level and vulnerable readers, adjustments in the instructional protocol are necessary to better support these more advanced readers. One possibility is to give an optional pre-assessment prior to each unit. Students who were successful on the pre-assessment would then be allowed to complete an independent or collaborative project. For example, they might meet in Literature Circle groups to discuss texts of their own choosing (Barone & Barone, 2016; Cameron et al., 2012). These discussions could include some aspects of the unit underway in the classroom, such as predicting with narrative text or constructing their own text features for an information text.

Finally, in upcoming iterations of this work, either a 75-minute instructional block or integration of literacy curriculum across content areas seems necessary for students to experience the full breadth and depth of the curriculum. As currently organized, reading and writing lessons were almost entirely separated, and the only cross-curricular link occurred when the Text User part of the curriculum was taught in the context of a science research project.

Future Research

The research reported here was an initial exploratory study. As such, it offers only hints about what this curriculum, or something like it, may offer. Additional exploratory studies are necessary to investigate how this implementation would play out if alterations such as an extended literacy block were included. More importantly, such studies might examine a similar protocol employed in different contexts. For example, very few Campbell School fourth graders were English learners (ELs). ELs might benefit from a more explicit emphasis on English language development than is found in the current iteration of the curriculum. Younger children would likely require assignments involving less writing and more multi-modal and hands-on work. Older students would be likely to find the overall structure repetitive, and a fuller integration of standards would reflect the growing complexity of their thinking.

Eventually, one or more studies designed to test rather than generate hypotheses—so-called confirmatory studies—would prove useful. A series of exploratory studies would serve to eliminate a range of potentially promising, but ultimately fruitless, variables, solidifying our knowledge of what crucial aspects of curriculum and instruction underlie CCSS-based learning. Then a larger-scale design-based research project (Reinking & Bradley, 2007) could track outcomes in a school that embraces on-going change. Further down the line, a randomized control trial (Campbell & Stanley, 1963) could compare different approaches to Common Core-based teaching, ideally across a range of grade levels, allowing for the opportunity to confirm as well as explore.

Note

1 I use this term (Jaeger, 2015) to refer to readers who are particularly sensitive to disruptions in their literacy ecology: uninteresting texts, inauthentic tasks, stressed teachers, and potentially oppressive social structures related to class, race, gender, etc.

Bibliography

Afflerbach, P., Pearson, P.D., & Paris, S.G. (2008). Clarifying differences between reading skills and reading strategies. *The Reading Teacher, 61* (5), 364–373. doi: 10.1598/RT.61.5.1

Barone, D., & Barone, R. (2016). "Really," "not possible," "I can't believe it": Exploring informational text in literature circles. *The Reading Teacher, 70* (1), 69–81. doi 10.1002/trtr.1472

Barrett-Tatum, J. & Smith, J.M. (2018). Questioning reform in the standards movement: Professional development and implementation of Common Core across the rural South. *Teachers and Teaching: Theory and Practice, 24* (4), 384–412. doi: 10.1080/13540602.2017.1401534

Beaver, J. (2011). *Developmental reading assessment* (2nd ed.). Celebration Press.

Cameron, S., Murray, M., Hull, K, & Cameron, J. (2012). Engaging fluent readers using literature circles. *Literacy Learning: The Middle Years, 20* (1), 1–8.

Campbell, D.J., & Stanley, J.C. (1963). *Experimental and quasi-experimental designs for research*. Houghton Mifflin.

Craig, D.V. (2009). *Action research essentials*. Jossey-Bass.

Dahl, K.L., & Freppon, P.A. (1995). A comparison of innercity children's interpretations of reading and writing instruction in the early grades in skills-based and whole language classrooms. *Reading Research Quarterly, 30* (1), 50–74. doi: 10.2307/747744

Engestrom, Y. (1987). *Learning by expanding*. Orienta Konsultit.

Fountas, I., & Pinnell, G.S. (2010). *Benchmark assessment system* (2nd ed.). Heinemann.

Gibbs, G.R. (2007). *Analyzing qualitative data*. Sage.

Jaeger, E.L. (2015). Literacy and vulnerability: Shame or growth for readers who struggle. *Talking Points, 26* (2), 17–25. doi: 10.58680/tp201527200

Jaeger, E.L. (2016). Intensity of focus, richness of content: Crafting tier 2 response to intervention an era of the common core. *The Reading Teacher, 70* (2), 179–188. doi: 10.1002/trtr.1495

Jaeger, E. (2017). Implementation of common core-based curriculum in a fourth-grade literacy classroom: An exploratory study. *Reading Horizons, 56* (1), 45–68.

Maxwell, J.A. (2013). *Qualitative research design: An interactive approach* (3rd ed.). Sage.

McLaughlin, M., & Overturf, B. (2012). The common core: Insights into the K-5 standards. *The Reading Teacher, 66*, 153–164. doi: 10.1002/TRTR.01115

McNiff, J., & Whitehead, J. (2010). *You and your action research project* (3rd ed.). Routledge.

Reinking, D., & Bradley, B. (2007). *On formative and design experiments.* Teachers College Press.

Richardson, V. (1994). The consideration of teachers' beliefs. In V. Richardson (Ed.), *Teacher change and the staff development process* (pp. 90–108). Teachers College Press.

Wertsch, J., Tulviste, P., & Hagstrom, F. (1993). A sociocultural approach to agency. In E.A. Forman, N. Minick, & C.A. Stone (Eds.), *Contexts for learning: Sociocultural dynamics in children's development* (pp. 336–356). Oxford University Press.

Appendix G
Tier 3 Research

Learning through Responsive and Collaborative Mediation in a Tutoring Context (Abridged)

The full study can be found here: Jaeger (2017). Learning through responsive and collaborative mediation in a tutoring context. *Australian Journal of Language and Literacy*, *40* (3), 210–224.

  The purpose of this paper is to describe a tutoring study conducted in an urban primary school with three 4th-grade students who exhibited key strengths in reading, but also important challenges. This article focuses, in particular, on one child who was a fluent decoder, but struggled to make meaning from text. I argue that this partnership was effective for two major reasons: the tutor developed a curriculum in response to the specific needs of the child and collaborated with the learner to decide what objectives and practices would best meet his needs, what instructional tools would mediate his learning (Vygotsky, 1978), and how they would measure progress. Evidence suggests that the tutoring the child received as part of this study supported his literacy growth. The research question that served as the foundation for this exploratory study was: Did a vulnerable reader's literacy develop as he experienced instruction explicitly aligned with his individual needs? If so, in what ways?

Method

The site for this Human Subjects Internal Review Board-approved study was a primary school in a large urban district in a western state. Of the school's 350 students, 52% were Latino, 20% African American, 12% Asian, and 16% other ethnicities/no response given; 59.8% were English learners and 92.7% of students received free or reduced-price meals. The school was selected because I had been the student teaching supervisor of one of the teachers with whom I would be interacting during the study. I chose to work with 4th graders because they are likely to exhibit both strengths and challenges in their reading and tend to be more metacognitive than younger children. In the sections that follow, I describe the participant who is the focus of this study, the tutoring protocol employed, and data collection and analysis procedures.

Participant

Because vulnerable readers who also exhibited clear strengths were of particular interest to me, 4th-grade teachers referred for assessment students who fit this profile. I used a series of leveled passages to screen 42 fourth graders. The three students whose reading profiles showed the most dramatic contrasts between strengths and challenges (e.g., they decoded fluently but struggled to understand or vice versa) were selected to participate.

Sam, a Chinese American child who had recently been reclassified as English proficient, was one of these children. At the beginning of the study, he was a fluent decoder but exhibited minimal awareness of comprehension strategies and struggled to make meaning from text. Sam was selected as the focal child for this manuscript because less research has been conducted with students like Sam than, say, those who struggle with decoding (Geva & Massey-Garrison, 2012). Details about Sam and his reading profile are provided in the Findings section.

Sam's difficulty with reading may have been rooted in his long-term English learner status (Al Otaiba, 2005). It appears, however, curriculum materials may also have played a role. The reading adoption during Sam's first four years of school was *Open Court Reading* (Bereiter et al., 2002). *Open Court* instruction is focused more on decoding than comprehension strategy instruction (Pilonieta, 2010) and is relatively inattentive to the needs of English learners (Bello et al., 2003). The *Open Court* lesson scripts, rather than the stories and articles or teacher/student relationships, served as the most important mediating tool in this learning environment.

Instructional Design

The tutoring process. I incorporated three major elements in the tutoring design: it was responsive to Sam's needs, collaborative, and goal-oriented. I began by interviewing Sam to establish rapport as well as to collect data. Then I administered a battery of assessments that will be described in greater depth in the Data Collection section. The content of the tutoring sessions reflected findings from assessment and interview information, allowing for differentiation of instruction based on student need and interest (Watts-Taffe et al., 2012/2013). After collecting baseline data, I filled out a reading checklist (see end of article). The checklist included aspects of reading ranging from using letter sounds for decoding to grasping the author's theme; I marked each item as a strength or challenge for Sam, and he also filled out the checklist without looking at the ratings I had selected.

Choice is an important support for student engagement (Turner & Paris, 1995). Sam and I began by focusing on areas of reading that we both agreed were challenges (see example unit plan at the end of the article). Texts were also chosen collaboratively. Goal-setting offers students some control over their school lives: what tasks they do, how they do them, and how the work is assessed (Kohn, 1993). This activity is particularly important for students who struggle (Sanacore, 1999). Once we agreed on what we would work on, Sam set goals for improvement (e.g., to learn the meaning of 20 new words).

Session protocol. Tutorial sessions occurred two times per week for 40 minutes each over 30 weeks, totaling 40 hours. Although the details of instruction were adjusted as needed (Massey, 2007), the structure of the sessions remained relatively constant. A typical tutoring session had three parts:

Part 1. For the first 15 minutes or so, we worked on the goal we had both agreed to, employing a strategy-instruction model. Strategy instruction is well-supported in the literature, especially for readers who struggle (Robertson, 2014) and English learners (Al Otaiba, 2005; Jimenez et al., 1996; Martinez-Alvarez et al., 2012). Unless the strategy was appropriate only for narrative text (e.g., predicting), I provided expository texts from which Sam selected. He struggled more with expository texts, but the primary reason for choosing them was because it was difficult to find stories at the primary level that seemed appropriate for his age.

The initial few lessons followed a model similar to that developed by Baumann et al. (1993): define the strategy; explain how it is useful; model how to use it; activate Sam's prior experience ("Do you remember using this in the past?"); support him to use what he learned with step-by-step directions; support Sam to use what he learned with hints only; explain the circumstances under which the strategy is/is not useful and how to know if it has been used effectively; and provide a bookmark with hints listed to assist with transfer to home and classroom. Additional lessons facilitated growing independence and continued until Sam had reached his goal, at which point he selected a new strategy and set a related goal.

Part 2. In the second part of the lesson (also about 15 minutes), I followed the same structure but focused on an area that I believed Sam needed, even if he disagreed. This element allowed me the flexibility to address a limited number of issues that had not originally seemed necessary to him, such as comprehension monitoring.

Part 3. Finally, about ten minutes' time was allotted for self-selected reading (SSR). Because Sam did not have a regular SSR time in his classrooms, I felt it was important to provide such a time during our tutorial sessions to support his independent reading.

Data Collection

The emphasis on ongoing qualitative data reflects the emerging character of the study and my desire to generate data rich in detail and embedded in context. The quantitative data is an appropriate supplement to gauge student progress and was collected primarily in the week before tutoring began, two days at the mid-point, and the week after tutoring ended.

Primary data sources included transcripts from audio-recordings of interactions—formal and informal interviews and tutorial sessions—as well as initial and ensuing assessments. Once Sam was selected as a participant, I administered the Critical Reading Inventory (CRI) (Applegate, Quinn, & Applegate, 2002). The CRI measured oral reading accuracy, fluency, and comprehension, as well as silent reading comprehension, and included both narrative and expository texts. Two measures were used to evaluate reading strategy use. During a think-aloud activity, Sam read segments of text, stopping to discuss his ongoing processing of that text, while the Metacomprehension Strategies Index (MSI) (Schmitt, 1990) prompted him to select appropriate strategies to employ in particular reading situations. I also had access to California English Language Development Test (CELDT) and California Standards Test (CST) data as distal measures.

I also conducted audio-taped, in-person interviews with Sam at the beginning and end of the study. The interview questions—focusing on beliefs about and attitudes toward reading, text preferences, and reading strategies—were identical at each administration. I began informal interviews midway through the study, probing for his opinions about the work we were doing together.

Audio-recordings of tutorial sessions captured the process of instruction, beginning from the point at which a strategy was quite new to Sam and continuing until he had achieved the established goal and felt comfortable applying the strategy independently. Because I was the teacher in this study as well as the researcher, these tapes provided a rich source of data that allowed me to see and hear aspects of the interaction of which I might otherwise have been unaware.

I re-administered the CRI and asked Sam for his opinions about our collaboration at mid-year. I conducted post-testing using all assessments and interview questions at the end of the school year.

Data Analysis

Analysis of data began almost immediately in order to facilitate decisions about lesson planning. I listened to audio within a day or two of each session, kept a content log that tracked what was taught when, and developed upcoming lesson plans based on what I heard and saw. After data collection was complete, I transcribed the interview and lesson audio.

Further analysis suited the type of data in question. Data matrices (Miles et al., 2014) allowed me to condense the quantitative data, representing change over time on assessments using simple calculations and summarizing these in a table format. For the qualitative data, I conducted concept-driven coding (Gibbs, 2007) for all transcripts. In this process, terms related to a theoretical frame are employed to code the data; in this case, those codes were mediation-based terms (e.g., subject, tools [material, symbolic, and human/relational], object, and outcome). This process allowed me to address the research questions by tracking the mediation process and the tools facilitating that process, as well as tutoring outcomes. Sam worked on several goals over the course of the tutorial, but I focus here on the goal that was central to his development, and which has considerable support in the research literature (Oakhill et al., 2005; Wassenburg et al., 2015): comprehension monitoring.

Findings and Discussion

Three aspects of this study findings are reviewed in this section. First, I provide a description of how Sam functioned as a reader, and how he assessed his own abilities, when the study began; these findings reflect data from assessments and interviews. Following that, an analysis of session audio and informal interviews demonstrates the ways in which material, symbolic, and human/relational tools facilitated his literacy learning across the time of the tutoring project. Finally, I evaluate the extent to which Sam became more skilled at constructing meaning from text. In addition to more traditional measures of reading growth such as assessments, success in this context was also defined by change in observed behavior around tool use: increase in the number and variety of tools employed, engagement with tools of greater mediational potential, and increased level of tool internalization (Cole, 1996).

Sam as He Emerged from Third Grade

On both distal and proximal measures, Sam exhibited strengths and challenges as he entered fourth grade. At the beginning of the study, Sam's CELDT scores averaged in the Early Advanced range with similar scores across the four domains of listening, speaking, reading, and writing. He was ranked at the Basic level in English language arts and Proficient in mathematics on the CST. Based on the CRI, Sam's reading instructional level was somewhere between late first and late second grade, depending on the genre of the text (narrative stronger than expository) and the method of reading (oral reading stronger than silent—although not preferred).

In analyzing Sam's miscues and understanding of text, more specific strengths and challenges emerged. Relative strengths included sight vocabulary, decoding, and fluency. Relative challenges included all levels of comprehension (low inference/retell, high-inference, and critical/creative) and making personal connections to text. As the think-aloud protocol demonstrated, Sam was sometimes aware that he had failed to understand what he was reading, but was unable to name what was causing the problem. Results from the MSI showed that Sam had great difficulty selecting useful approaches to accessing text before, during, and after reading; he correctly answered only 28% of the questions. Sam was not strongly engaged by books; he had neither a favorite book nor a favorite author and, when asked, did not suggest a topic he wanted to read about. Overall, Sam exhibited the characteristics of readers who decode fluently, but who fail to construct meaning from text (Oakhill & Garmson, 1988): demonstrating both an over-reliance on bottom-up strategies for decoding and difficulties with planning for and organizing the use of comprehension strategies.

Insisting he rarely experienced difficulties with reading, Sam seemed to have no real sense that he was not a strong reader—or failed to admit it if he did; this is another characteristic common to readers with weak comprehension (Oakhill et al., 2005). He also claimed to enjoy reading, despite his inability to name a book he had read for pleasure in the previous month. Sam was, in fact, a weaker reader than he believed himself to be.

The Change Process: An Analysis of Tool Use

Provided here is an analysis of interactions focusing on comprehension monitoring, Sam's greatest challenge. The instruction followed a gradual release of responsibility model (Pearson & Gallagher, 1983): initially, I did the preponderance of the work, with Sam contributing more as time went on and as he evidenced a greater internalization of the strategy. Similarly, our initial sessions focused on reading brief bits of text such as sentences and progressed to longer texts. Finally, tools played an important role over the course of our work together.

In what follows, I quote from and analyze transcripts spanning eight sessions occurring over a period of five weeks in order to demonstrate the way tool use evolved over the course of our interactions. The tools served to facilitate Sam's ability to notice and, ultimately, address his own confusion. Material and symbolic tool use characterized the tutoring sessions from the beginning, but, as time went on, texts were more authentic (from specially crafted sentences to extended texts), material/symbolic tools use shifted from a product orientation (progress-monitoring graphs) to a transferrable-process orientation (strategy process list), and responsibility for symbolic tool use was more collaborative (from direct explanation to probing questions). Tools related to the tutor/child relationship emerged at about the mid-point of the sessions and appeared to have a particularly catalytic effect.

Material/symbolic tools: Strategy introduction and practice. In an attempt to help Sam understand that the real purpose of reading was meaning-making, the sessions began with "consciousness-raising" conversations; these conversations were characterized by the use of symbolic tools such as direct explanation of strategies and of sources of confusion.

Strategy use. In the first session, I explained that we would focus on comprehension monitoring and provided examples; Sam often responded tentatively, as noted by rising intonation at the end of many of his replies.

> *Elizabeth:* Monitoring is when you are reading and you're always paying attention to whether you understand

> what's going on or you don't. I'm going to give you a sentence that I think will be confusing to YOU: *The man had a goatee.* Do you understand that sentence?
>
> *Sam:* Uh, I don't know what it is?
>
> *Elizabeth:* Is it a word that's confusing you or the whole sentence?
>
> *Sam:* It's the word? Goatee?
>
> *Elizabeth:* If I tell you that a goatee is a little pointed beard that's only on your chin, then would you understand the sentence?
>
> *Sam:* (nods)

This vignette demonstrates the way I (a) was initially responsible for most of the work, (b) began with sentences intended to surface challenges rather than authentic, whole texts, and (c) used symbolic tools—direct explanation of strategy use, followed by a conversation structured with specific probing questions—to initiate teaching and learning.

Sources of confusion: Words and ideas. We continued working with sentences, shifting from word-based to idea-based difficulties. I introduced this distinction by noting that individual words can cause problems, but even if the reader understands all of the words in a passage, ideas can still be confusing. In the second session, my probing questions encouraged his thinking:

> *Elizabeth:* We were hoping this would be a bad day to travel. Is that clear or confusing?
>
> *Sam:* (long pause) Uh, clear?
>
> *Elizabeth:* (after re-reading the sentence) Is there anything about that that seems kind of weird?
>
> *Sam:* Uh, they hope?
>
> *Elizabeth:* Yeah, hope. What is it that doesn't fit with hope?
>
> *Sam:* (long pause) Uh, they were hoping that it would be a bad day?

This excerpt demonstrates that when provided with material/symbolic tools such as structuring statements/questions, Sam gained proficiency in noting confusion. He also paused for longer periods of time during this interaction, possibly indicating that he was assuming a more reflective stance.

Material/symbolic tools: More authentic texts and "code" words. At this point, we switched from working with single sentences to reading complete books. To facilitate this transition, I introduced another symbolic tool: the terms *click* (meaning understanding) and *clunk* (meaning confusion) (Babbs, 1984). I modeled the process by reading aloud, stopping after every sentence to say *click* or *clunk,* and explaining my reasoning. After listening to and observing my process, Sam took over the role of reader, supported by the symbolic tool of probing questions. Initially, this new responsibility was a struggle for Sam.

> *Sam:* The rest of the country is mainly covered in deserts, mountains, and highlands.
> *Elizabeth:* OK, so click or clunk?
> *Sam:* Uh, click?
> *Elizabeth:* Do you know what highlands are?
> *Sam:* (pause) No.

Even in a case like this where the problem was word-based, Sam failed to grasp his confusion.

Although Sam continued to focus on word-based confusion only, he self-monitored more accurately over the remainder of the session and the next, even when we shifted from reading one sentence at a time to full pages. By the end of this session—employing the click/clunk symbolic tool as he read authentic texts—Sam either knew the meanings of challenging words or recognized the difficulty they caused him.

A key human/relational tool: Hitting the wall. Nevertheless, Sam's progress was erratic. He would successfully evaluate his understanding for two or three pages in a row and then regress, repeatedly failing to self-monitor. I eventually lost my patience.

> *Elizabeth:* Each time when you read a page, you always say click, but then when we go back and look at particular things, you sometimes say that you don't know what it

means. So, why do you say click if there are things that you don't understand.

Sam: Uh, because, because, I think that uh (long pause)

Elizabeth: Is it that you're having trouble noticing when you don't understand something? Or…maybe you didn't think that was IMPORTANT?

Sam: I didn't think that was important.

This conversation was somewhat of a turning point for us. The "tool" of transparency served as a mediator of teaching as well as learning. This exchange accomplished two things. It alerted me to the possibility that, at least on some occasions, Sam and I differed in our conceptions of what was important in a text. It also raised the possibility that Sam was reluctant to admit a lack of understanding because such an admission undermined his belief in himself as a reader. Yet another contradiction surfaced: between my desire for Sam to acknowledge confusion and the fact that he received no clear recognition for doing so. This interaction highlighted the need for a change in plans: adjusting our interaction to elevate an admission of *difficulty* with meaning-making to the same level as meaning-making itself and including activities that would more fully engage Sam in our collaborative efforts.

Material/symbolic tools: Altering the protocol. In the following session, three adjustments were implemented. In an effort to simplify the process, we briefly returned to working with one or two sentences at a time. In addition, when Sam replied *click*, I asked him to explain what the sentence meant, and after each *clunk*, I asked him to tell me whether it was a word or an idea that interfered with his comprehension. This change was intended to assist Sam in becoming more conscious of his thought processes and promoting internalization of strategy use. Finally, each time he said *click* and could demonstrate understanding, OR each time he said *clunk* and enumerated the problem, we added a point to a graph of improvement. In this scenario, Sam received reinforcement for admitting difficulty, as well as for demonstrating success. Returning to a simpler task, requesting explanations as well as answers, and graphing his progress served as useful tools in this context, but none of these changes completely solved the problem.

At this point, I began admitting to Sam that I myself was confused by some sentences, another form of the "transparency tool." Whether or not my admission directly affected him, Sam began to improve. In fact, in this example, Sam spontaneously re-read to better process the text, a behavior he had never before demonstrated. He not only grasped the literal meaning but also made an inference by connecting back to a fact he had read earlier—that one is weightless in space. When invited, he noted his confusion and spontaneously re-read to resolve the problem.

> *Sam:* She practiced on a model of a telescope in a swimming pool. Being underwater is a bit like being in space.
> *Elizabeth:* I think it's POSSIBLE that there's something confusing in there, but maybe it wasn't to you.
> *Sam:* Can I see it again? (re-reads silently) Uh, she goes in a swimming pool and practices how to be weightless? Because in the water it feels like you're floating?
> *Elizabeth:* I like the way you made the decision to re-read when you weren't sure. I could really see you THINKING and figuring out what you knew and what you didn't know.

The symbolic tool strategically employed in my comment might be termed *naming of intelligent behavior*. Over the next couple of sessions, Sam demonstrated his ability to manage his comprehension for segments of text extending over several pages.

Integration of tool use: Internalization. My hope was that Sam would begin to internalize the comprehension monitoring strategy and apply it spontaneously: the object of this series of lessons. Evidence for internalization surfaced during the last session we spent working on this goal when my expectations were adjusted upward. In this extended segment, Sam himself stopped the reading to note confusion.

> *Elizabeth:* I'm going to have you read the whole page, but let's say you get to here and it's clunk. You can tell me before I ask you. Make sense?

Sam: Fortune seekers, scientists, and monster enthusiasts swarmed…Uh, clunk.
Elizabeth: What are you clunking for?
Sam: This word?
Elizabeth: Enthusiasts? So, first you're going to…[points to strategy tip on card]
Sam: Read ahead…enthusiasts swarmed.
Elizabeth: OK, did that help you know what monster enthusiasts are?
Sam: (pause) uh (pause) um (pause) um, no?
Elizabeth: OK, so let's try this. Start from here and when you get to *scientists*, just go to *swarmed*.
Sam: (reads ahead, skipping *monster enthusiasts*)
Elizabeth: OK, were you able to understand that sentence if we skip that part?
Sam: Uh-hmm
Elizabeth: Yeah, you actually can…*Monster enthusiasts* are just people who get interested in and enthusiastic about monsters. OK? But as you noticed, if we just drop that, the sentence still makes sense. So, you were able to skip and still understand…Wow, Sam! This is the first time that I remember that you actually stopped YOURSELF and let me know that you didn't understand something. That's really important because good readers, all of them, run into things they don't understand.

In addition to naming his intelligent behavior, I reinforced how common it is for readers—even effective ones—to struggle with text.

New material and symbolic tools for advanced expectations: Knowing when to move on. It would be inaccurate to imply that Sam never regressed to a more passive reading style, choosing to ignore rather than confront difficulty. He most certainly did. But he had made enough progress that it was time to move on to the next logical step.

Fix-ups. Our new focus was on learning and applying strategies for dealing with acknowledged difficulty, strategies that we termed "fix-ups." We did this by returning to a sentence we had worked on previously; the activity was expanded to include context clues, another symbolic tool.

> *Elizabeth:* When we first talked about noticing when you don't understand, the sentence I gave you was: *The man had a goatee.* So, here's a similar sentence. It says, *The man combed the goatee on his chin.* What clues do you notice in that sentence that would help you know the meaning of that word?
>
> *Sam:* Uh, *combed*.
>
> *Elizabeth:* Combed, right? Whatever a goatee is, it has to be something you can comb. So, if that's as far as we read, we might think that goatee is hair because hair is what we usually comb. Is there another clue in the sentence that helps us know that it's not hair on your head?
>
> *Sam:* Chin?

In this example, Sam exhibited an ability to employ context clues to deal with comprehension breakdown.

Strategies, step by step. Knowing Sam's academic strength was in mathematics, his teacher and I mused early on that if we could make reading more like mathematics, it might be easier for Sam. I developed a series of "strategy algorithms"—step-by-step processes for each goal—and these algorithms were important symbolic tools. For example, fix-up strategies were listed for Sam from most (read ahead) to least (ask for help) efficient. At the end of each unit, I provided Sam with two 3 × 5 cards, one for home and one for his classroom, listing the steps or options. He told me that he regularly referred to them while reading. These cards were material versions of the symbolic tools he had learned and served to support him until such time as he internalized the strategy, and the tool could be converted back from material to symbolic.

Sam as He *Became* the Reader He had *Thought* He Was

End-of-year assessment and interview data, when triangulated with lesson quotes, highlighted day-by-day change and demonstrated Sam's literacy development. In late spring, Sam's instructional level was somewhere between third and fifth grade, depending on the genre of the text (narrative still stronger than expository), although no longer on the method of reading (oral and silent reading equally effective).[1] In analyzing Sam's miscues and understanding of text, he had no clear difficulties, and comprehension for both narrative and expository texts was much improved. His think-alouds were richer and he was more willing to admit confusion, and his score on the MSI increased. He scored within a few points of the Advanced level on the CST.

Sam believed that he had learned a number of new things. He said he knew more words, could figure out the topic of a passage, and remembered what he had read. He viewed "getting the words to make sense," remembering facts, and learning as the primary purposes for reading, and, when provided with several other choices, added enjoyment and talking with others about books as additional reasons to read. Sam explained that he now had strategies for determining word meanings (reading ahead), for dealing with overall confusion (re-reading), and for remembering what happened (repeating the plot aloud). Even good readers sometimes have trouble, Sam noted.

Sam's reading engagement also improved. His connection to books grew stronger. He mentioned the *Scary Stories* and *Wayside School* series as favorites, and, despite his usually reserved nature, provided a laughter-filled retelling of a story from the latter series in a late-spring session. He stated that he had read six books for pleasure in the previous month.

Conclusion

Findings from a range of traditional academic measures support the claim that Sam's literacy achievement and engagement improved. On the CRI, he gained between two and three levels. The greatest growth occurred in silent reading, a necessary transition for a student approaching middle school age. Although strategy use remained an area of challenge for him, his MSI score nearly doubled. Sam now understood that meaning-making was the point of reading, with learning new information and enjoyment emerging as primary motivating forces. He now named both favorite books and authors.

This improvement was facilitated by a mediation process involving a range of tools unknown and unavailable to Sam in earlier literacy environments. Material tools included cards with a breakdown of steps for strategy use. These cards supported independent application of strategies at home and in the classroom, and the graphs provided tangible evidence of success. Of greater importance, however, were the range of symbolic tools that made up the overall lesson structure and the responsive interactions that occurred within it. The unit described here began with a direct explanation of the *what, how, when*, and *why* of strategy use, followed by structured conversations. The memorable *click/clunk* trope served as a method for crystallizing Sam's ability to differentiate between what he understood and what he did not. And the naming of intelligent behavior alerted Sam to his ongoing progress. This lesson's evolution came in response to what Sam said and did in the moment.

It is important to note the interaction in which I lost my patience: an occasion that ultimately showed itself to be a human/relational tool. I suspect my forthrightness may have influenced Sam's subsequent behavior, but it most certainly catalyzed my decision to set a somewhat different course. It was at this point that I adjusted the protocol to include demonstrating more explicitly my own confusion, acknowledging Sam's willingness to admit difficulty as equal in importance to demonstrating understanding, and adding flexibility to the protocol by providing further direct explanation and returning to word-focus and single sentences as needed for clarification.

Over time, Sam's tool use exhibited greater mediational potential. The material tools (e.g., list of strategy steps), symbolic tools (e.g., probing questions), and human/relational tools (e.g., transparency) that characterized this study served to mediate his literacy learning. In addition, Sam further internalized tool use; he no longer waited for me to prompt him with *click/clunk* but stopped in mid-sentence to express a lack of understanding. Sam progressed on a range of traditional assessments. But this study also demonstrates how vulnerable readers can learn to employ additional and more sophisticated mediating tools.

Limitations and Implications

The research reported here is a case study of a single student and, as such, findings are not widely generalizable. It is also not possible to establish a causal link between Sam's participation in tutorial and the positive outcomes he experienced. Other aspects of Sam's schooling, such as improved classroom instruction that occurred between third and fourth grade, may have facilitated his improvement.

Nevertheless, at a time when more sophisticated standards are likely to create greater disparities in educational outcomes (Wixson & Lipson, 2012), this study has implications for both practice and research. The implemented protocol (see end of article) offers a potential model for tutoring: highlighting the material, symbolic, and human/relational tools required to mediate a literacy learning process that has stymied many students. It is important to begin with a re-visioning of core curriculum (Jaeger, 2024), supplemented by rich and flexible small-group support (Jaeger, 2016). It is unlikely, however, that these changes will be enough to accelerate achievement for our most vulnerable readers. They require the type of intense and responsive instruction that characterizes the protocol described here, a tutoring process in which "the path from object to child and from child to object passes through another person" (Vygotsky, 1978, p. 30). This protocol supported Sam's literacy growth and that of the other two students with whom I worked, but it will be important for other researchers to investigate its applicability with students of other age groups and in other contexts, studying the extent to which such tutor/child interactions can allow these readers to "mediate [their] comprehension of the world through print" (Cole, 1996, p. 274).

Reader Skill Assessment

Name _____ Date _____

For each reading skill, write one of the following codes:

S = This is a reading strength for me; I'm very good at it.
OK = This is not really a strength or challenge for me; I'm OK at it.
C = This is a reading challenge for me; I need to get better at this.

Child		**Tutor**
_____	Reading little words (such as *the, from, were*) correctly and easily	_____
_____	Using letter sounds to figure out words (such as *plant, story, happen*)	_____
_____	Using word parts to figure out longer words (such as *everyone, unhappily*)	_____
_____	Using the words around a word to figure out what it is	_____
_____	Noticing when I don't understand	_____
_____	Using "fix-ups" when I get confused (such as reading ahead, slowing down)	_____
_____	Correcting reading mistakes so the sentence makes sense	_____
_____	Paying attention to punctuation marks (such as.? and!)	_____
_____	Reading at the correct speed – not too fast and not too slowly	_____
_____	Reading smoothly and with expression	_____
_____	Using what I already know to help me understand	_____
_____	Predicting what may happen in a story and giving a reason for my prediction	_____

Copyright material from Elizabeth L. Jaeger (2026), *Integrating Sophisticated Standards and Systems of Support for Elementary Readers*, Routledge

_____ Asking questions about what information might be in an article   _____

_____ Figuring out the meaning of difficult words   _____

_____ Making pictures or movies in my mind as I read   _____

_____ Making connections to my own life as I read   _____

_____ Getting the main idea of an article (1–2 sentences)   _____

_____ Answering questions about what information might be in an article or story   _____

_____ Looking back to quickly find information I didn't remember   _____

_____ Retelling the most important events in the correct order   _____

_____ Figuring out ideas that aren't stated in the story   _____

_____ Stating my opinion and giving a reason for my opinion   _____

_____ Figuring out and questioning the author's theme or message   _____

_____ Noting voices in the story which are minimized or unheard   _____

Comprehension Monitoring Unit Plan

Define/describe	Noticing when there is a word or idea you don't understand
Why important to be a better reader	Readers need to notice when they don't understand so they can fix their comprehension
Model	Word example: The man had a goatee. Idea example: The dogs at Leo's house had always belonged more to his father than anyone else.
Activate prior experience	Have you ever been reading and noticed that you didn't understand? What did you do?
Student does with explicit teacher direction step-by-step	Read the title and cover picture for _____ I notice that I don't understand _____
Student does with initial hints from the teacher	Hints: Read. Notice not understanding. Word or idea?
When to use/not use	Use: When you are reading difficult text or text about a topic you aren't familiar with. Don't use: When everything seems clear.
How to know if it's effective	If you feel you understand what is going on
How to transfer to class/home	Bookmark with hints
Independent practice and debrief	Use of *click/clunk* (led by student) Request that student explain what has been learned

Note

1 While I focus here on Sam, CRI progress for the other two students was also about one year per semester.

Bibliography

Al Otaiba, S. (2005). How effective is code-based reading tutoring in English for English learners and preservice teacher-tutors. *Remedial and Special Education, 26* (4), 245–254. doi: 10.1177/07419325050260040701

Applegate, M.D., Quinn, K.B., & Applegate, A.J. (2002). Levels of thinking required by comprehension questions in informal reading inventories. *The Reading Teacher, 56* (2), 174–180.

Babbs, P.J. (1984). Monitoring cards to help improve comprehension. *The Reading Teacher, 38* (2), 200–204.

Baumann, J.F., Jones, L.A., & Seifert-Kessel, N. (1993). *Monitoring reading comprehension by thinking aloud* (Instructional Resource # 1). National Reading Research Center.

Bello, M., Fajet, W., Shaver, A.N., Toombs, A.K., & Schumm, J.S. (2003). Basal readers and English language learners: A content analysis study. *Reading Research and Instruction, 42* (1), 1–16.

Bereiter, C., Adams, M.J., Pressley, M., Roit, M., McKeough, A., Hirshberg, J., & Scardamalia, M. (2002). *Open court reading.* SRA/McGraw-Hill.

Cole, M. (1996). *Cultural psychology: A once and future discipline.* Harvard University Press.

Geva, E. & Massey-Garrison, A. (2012). A comparison of the language skills of ELLS and monolinguals who are poor decoders, poor comprehenders, or normal readers. *Journal of Learning Disabilities, 46* (5), 387–401.

Gibbs, G.R. (2007). *Analyzing qualitative data.* Los Angeles, CA: Sage.

Jaeger, E.L. (2016). Intensity of focus, richness of content: Crafting Tier 2 response to intervention an era of the Common Core. *The Reading Teacher, 70* (2), 179–188. doi: 10.1002/trtr.1495

Jaeger, E.L. (2017). Learning through responsive and collaborative mediation in a tutoring context. *Australian Journal of Language and Literacy, 40* (3), 210–224. doi: 10.1007/BF03651999

Jaeger, E.L. (2024). The potential for Common Core and response to intervention as intersecting initiatives: Supporting readers who struggle with high-level standards. *Reading and Writing Quarterly, 40* (2), 87–102. doi: 10.1080/10573569.2023.2172496

Jimenez, R.T., Garcia, G.E., & Pearson, P.D. (1996). The reading strategies of bilingual Latina/o students who are successful readers: Opportunities and obstacles. *Reading Research Quarterly, 31*, 90–112. doi: 10.1598/RRQ.31.1.5

Kohn, A. (1993). Choices for children: Why and how to let students decide. *Phi Delta Kappan, 75* (1), 8–16 & 18–20.

Martinez-Alvarez, P., Bannan, B., & Peters-Burton, E.E. (2012). Effect of strategy instruction on fourth-grade dual language learners' ability to monitor their comprehension of scientific texts. *Bilingual Research Journal, 35* (3), 331–349. doi: 10.1080/15235882.2012.734005

Massey, D.D. (2007). "The Discovery Channel said so" and other barriers to comprehension. *The Reading Teacher, 60* (7), 656–666. doi: 10.1598/RT.60.7.6

Miles, M.B., Huberman, M., & Saldana, J. (2014). *Qualitative data analysis: A methods sourcebook* (3rd ed.). Sage.

Oakhill, J., & Garmson, A. (1988). *Becoming a skilled reader*. Basil Blackwell.

Oakhill, J., Hartt, J., & Samols, D. (2005). Levels of comprehension monitoring and working memory in good and poor comprehenders. *Reading and Writing, 18*, 657–686. doi: 10.1007/s11145-005-3355-z

Pearson, P.D., & Gallagher, G. (1983). The instruction of reading comprehension. *Contemporary Educational Psychology, 8*, 317–344. doi: 10.1016/0361-476X(83)90019-x

Pilonieta, P. (2010). Instruction of research-based comprehension strategies in basal reading programs. *Reading Psychology, 31* (2), 150–175. doi: 10.1080/02702710902754119

Robertson, D.A. (2014). Teacher talk: One teacher's reflections during comprehension strategy instruction. *Reading Psychology, 34* (6), 523–549. doi: 10.1080/02702711.2012.660303

Sanacore, J. (1999). Encouraging children to make choices about their literacy learning. *Intervention in School and Clinic, 35* (1), 38–42. doi: 10.1177/105345129903500107

Schmitt, M.C. (1990). A questionnaire to measure children's awareness of strategic reading processes. *The Reading Teacher, 43* (7), 454–461.

Turner, J., & Paris, S. (1995). How literacy tasks influence children's motivation for literacy. *The Reading Teacher, 48* (8), 662–673.

Vygotsky, L.S. (1978). *Mind in society: The development of higher psychological processes.* Harvard University Press.

Wassenburg, S.I., Bos, L.T., de Koning, B.B., & van der Schoot, M. (2015). Effects of an inconsistency-detection training aimed at improving comprehension monitoring in primary school children. *Discourse Processes, 52*, 463–488. doi: 10.1080/0163853X.2015.1025203

Watts-Taffe, S., Laster, B.P., Broach, L., Marinak, B., Connor, C.M., & Walker-Dalhouse, D. (2012). Differentiated instruction: Making informed teacher decisions. *The Reading Teacher, 66* (4) 303–314. doi:10.1002/TRTR.01126

Wixson, K.K., & Lipson, M.L. (2012). The CCSS and RTI in literacy and language. *The Reading Teacher, 65* (6), 387–391. doi: 10.1002/TRTR.01058

Index

Note: **Bold** page numbers refer to tables.

Aldrich, C.K. 3
answering questions 6, 79; structures for, Tier 3 **104**
Applegate, M.D. 144
Arizona 9
Ascenzi-Moreno, L. 55
asking questions: fourth-grade unit for research project and oral report, Tier 2 137; second-grade unit for research project and oral report, Tier 1 140; structures for, Tier 3 **105**
assessment: foundational skills standard 2.4c, Tier 1 111; informational text standard RI 2.5, Tier 1 108; informational text standard RI 4.2, Tier 1 120; prior knowledge, structures for, Tier 3 179, **179–180**
Assessment and Student Success in a Differentiated Classroom (Tomlinson) 36
assisted reading 5, 67, 75, 103, 119, 129
Aukerman, M. 29
Austin, C.R. 18

Bajtelsmit, L. 63
Balu, R. 13
Barone, D. 58
Barone, R. 58
Barrett-Tatum, J. 13, 29
Beck, I. 43
Beecher, C.C. 29
Berry, G. 3
Bester, S. 13
Bhowmik, S. 60
Bickford, R. 10, 14

Big Book 49–50, 150–152
Blackburn, B.R. 14
Bleiberg, J. 14
Book Auction 48
Book Group-like interaction 55
Brabham, E.G. 55
Brown, J.E. 10, 30, 33
Brown-Chidsey, R. 10, 14
Buly, M.R. 17, 31, 145
Burke, P. 29
Burkins, J. 55
Burns, M.K. 13

Calfee, R. 29
California Department of Education 11
Candler, L. 46
Capelli, R. 60
Carrison, C. 58
character unit, reading specialist plans for: at Tier 2 78–79; at Tier 3 81–82
character unit, teachers plan for: at Tier 0 84; at Tier 1 74–76
Chen, C-H. 28
Chiu, C-H. 28
Ciampa, K. 65
Clausen-Grace, N. 31, 106
close reading protocol 5, 67, 75, 101, 107, 119, 124, 171
Cohan, A. 30
Common Core State Standards (CCSS) 2–4, 9; aligned classroom instruction 12; barriers 14; based instructional materials 9; based lessons and assessments 4; comprehension monitoring and fix-ups unit 168; for curriculum 3, 28, 188; emergent auditory unit,

IELI 152; emergent meaning unit, IELI 148; emergent print unit, IELI 149–150; emergent writing unit, IELI 155–156; fourth-grade unit for research project and oral report 135–136; for gifted learners 19, 20; implementation of 13; inference unit 172; information about 4; integration of ELA 17, 29; knowledge of 13; metacognition unit 167; multi-syllable decoding unit 165; oral retell unit 172; paragraph writing unit 174–175; second-grade unit for research project and oral report 139; sight words unit, IRI 156; simple decoding unit, IRI 158; sophisticated standards 2; Tier 2 classes 32; and variants 187
comprehension monitoring: IRI and writing, Tier 2 169–172; structures for, Tier 3 **116**, 178, 183, **183–184**
Conway, M. 13
Council of Chief State School Officers (CCSSO) 9
Croft, M. 55
Cunningham, J.W. 165
Cunningham, P.M. 33, 165, 166
curriculum 15; CCSS for 3; development of 86, 95, 143; ELA *see* English language arts (ELA); MTSS 4, 20, 27, 42; for reading instruction 5; for Simple Blending level 165; standards-based 27; Tier 0 35–36; Tier 1 5, 28–30, 42, 59; Tier 2 30–33, 78; Tier 3 33–35, 81, 95; units 5, 42, 59, 85; weak materials 15; for writing instruction 5–6, 88–89

Dean, J. 13, 15
Dietrichson, J. 18
The Differentiated Classroom: Responding to the Needs of All Learners (Tomlinson) 36
Dollins, C.A. 59
Dombey, H. 31
Doolittle, J. 10, 30, 33

Dorfman, L.R. 60
Doult, W. 63
Dunham, H.R. 14

education/educational: content and structure 2; conversation 10; MTSS and placement in special education 3
Elijah, D. 144
emergent auditory unit, IELI, Tier 2 152–155
emergent meaning unit, IELI, Tier 2 148–149
emergent print unit, IELI, Tier 2 149–152
emergent writing unit, IELI, Tier 2 155–156
English language arts (ELA) 13–15, 17, 29, 35, 72
Ensley, A. 67
Ernst-Slavit, G. 58
Estes, T.H. 145
exit slips 5, 64, 66–67, 74, 75, 78, 101, 106, 110, 118, 119, 123, 124, 176

Faggella-Luby, M. 17
Finger Flash vocabulary practice 5, 68, 129, 130, 176
Fisher, D. 28, 34, 43, 44, 49, 50, 61
"Five Finger Method" 47
"Five Page Method" 47
fix-ups unit: IRI and writing, Tier 2 169–172; structures for, Tier 3 183, **183–184**
Fletcher, R. 63; *Writing Workshop: The Essential Guide* 63
foundational skills standard 2.4c, Tier 1: assessment 111; guided reading 110–111; introduction and interactive read-aloud 110; reading workshop 110; shared reading 110
foundational skills standard 2.4c, Tier 2: daily plan 111–115; progress monitoring assessment 111
foundational skills standard RF4.4b, Tier 1: guided reading 125; introduction 123; reading

workshop 123–124; shared reading 124
foundational skills standard RF4.4b, Tier 2: daily plan 126–128; progress monitoring assessment 126
foundational skills standard RF4.4b, Tier 3 128
Fountas, I. 54
Four Resources Model of literacy practice 30
fourth-grade unit for, research project and oral report: Tier 1 135–138; Tier 2 138; Tier 3 138
Freebody, P. 29
Frey, N. 28, 34, 61
Fu, D. 65

Gersten, R. 18
Giouroukakis, V. 30
Gojak, L.M. 3
Gomez-Najarro, J. 14
Gonzales, P. 144
Goodman, S. 2, 3
Graham, S. 28, 29
Greenstein, L. 29
Grindon, K. 30
guided reading 5; additional resources 54–55; foundational skills standard 2.4c, Tier 1 110–111; foundational skills standard RF4.4b, Tier 1 125; informational text standard RI 2.5, Tier 1 107–108; informational text standard RI 4.2, Tier 1 120; simplest version (especially for young children) 51–54

Haager, D. 14
Hagerty, P. 46; *Readers' workshop: Real reading* 46
Hall, S.L. 2, 10
Hannigan, J.D. 1, 3
Hannigan, J.E. 1, 3
Hattie, J. 29
Heflebower, T. 16
Hershberger, K. 31
Hinton, M. 10
Hodge, E.M. 14

Hoffman, J.L. 44
Hubbard, R.S. 65
Hughes, C.E. 19
Hunt, C.S. 29

Individuals with Disabilities Education Act (IDEA) 10, 12–13
inference unit: based on IRI and writing, Tier 2 172; structures for, Tier 3 184, **184–185**
informal data, for developing and teaching: Tier 2 147–148; Tier 3 147–148
Informal Emergent Literacy Inventory (IELI), Tier 2: emergent auditory unit 152–155; emergent meaning unit 148–149; emergent print unit 149–152; emergent writing unit 155–156; meaning, print, and sound skills 145–147
Informal Emergent Literacy Inventory (IELI), Tier 3: comprehension monitoring and fix-ups 183, **183–184**; inference 184, **184–185**; making connections sub-unit 182, **182–183**; meaning, print, and sound skills 145–147; oral retelling 185, **185**; prediction sub-unit 180, **180–181**; prior knowledge sub-unit 179, **179–180**; units based on 178–179; visualization sub-unit 181, **181–182**
Informal Reading Inventory (IRI) 33, 143–145
Informal Reading Inventory (IRI), Tier 2: comprehension monitoring and fix-ups unit 169–172; inference unit 172; metacognition unit 167–169; multi-syllable decoding unit 165–167; oral retell unit 172–174; paragraph writing unit 174–178; sight words unit 156–158; simple decoding unit 158–165
Informal Reading Inventory (IRI), Tier 3: units based on 178–179
informational text standard RI 2.5, Tier 1: assessment 108; guided

reading 107–108; introduction and interactive read-aloud 106; reading workshop 106; shared reading 107
informational text standard RI 2.5, Tier 2: visuals with captions 108
informational text standard RI 4.2, Tier 1: assessment 120; guided reading 120; introduction and interactive read-aloud 117–118; reading workshop 118; shared reading 118–119; summarizing from shared reading 119
informational text standard RI 4.2, Tier 2: daily plan 120–121; final session 121; progress monitoring assessment 120; second-to-last session 121; third-to-last session 121
intended readership 4
interactive read-aloud 5; defined 43; foundational skills standard 2.4c, Tier 1 110; informational text standard RI 2.5, Tier 1 106; informational text standard RI 4.2, Tier 1 117–118; simplest version 43–45

Jaeger, E.L. 14, 28, 63
Johnsen, S.K. 19
Juel, C. 18

Kane, T.J. 13, 15
Kasten, L. 19
Kelley, M.J. 31, 106
Kennedy, E. 29
Kern, D. 28
Korn, S. 9
Kramer, S.V. 17, 33

Lachowicz, B.L. 62
Laman, T. 65
Langer, J.A. 60
Lee, J. 13, 14
Lipson, M.Y. 30, 33
Literature Circles 5, 43, 45; additional resources 58; simplest version 55–58

literature standard RL 2.1: Tier 1 100–102; Tier 2 102–103; Tier 3 **104–105**
Lobel, Arnold 103, 126, 172
Lose, M.K. 28
Loveless, T. 12, 13, 15
Luke, A. 29

Manzo, A.V. 145
Manzo, U. 145
Marcell, B. 34
Mather, N. 62
Matos, F. 62
McEneaney, J.E. 28, 31
McInnes, A. 36
McIntosh, K. 2, 3
McKenna, M.C. 144
McKeown, M. 43
McLaughlin, M. 29
metacognition unit, IRI and writing, Tier 2 167–169
Miles, R.H. 3
modeled writing 5, 59–61, 89–91
Mohr, K.A.J. 60
Morgan, D.N. 51, 59, 60
Morris, D. 18
Morse, T.E. 14, 33
Moustafa, M. 31
Mo, Y. 30
multi-syllable decoding unit, IRI and writing, Tier 2 165–167
multi-tiered systems of support (MTSS) 2–3, 16, 18, 85, 99; complexity of 13; definition of 10; in educational conversation 10; ELA standards 14, 15; and placement in special education 3; and RtI, differing ways 11–12; and RtI, similar ways 11; at school or district level 4; and sophisticated standards 4, 143, 188; standards-based curriculum 20, 27, 42; and state literacy standards 4; structures of 42; Tier 0 instruction *see* Tier; Tier 1 for classrooms *see* Tier 1; Tier 2 for small groups *see* Tier 2; Tier 3 for one-on-one instruction *see* Tier 3 0
Muschla, J. 3

Naab, H. 63
National Assessment of Educational Progress (NAEP) 12–13
National Governors Association Center for Best Practices (NGACBP) 9
Neitzel, A.J. 14
Nichols, S.L. 13
Nickow, A. 17
Nilsson, N.L. 144
Novak, K. 3

O'Day, J.A. 9, 10
Opfer, V.D. 13, 15
oral retelling 144; structures for, Tier 3 178, 185, **185**; unit, IRI and writing, Tier 2 172–174
Al Otaiba, S. 13
Overturf, B. 29

paired/collaborative writing 5; additional resources 63; simplest version 62
Pak, K. 15
Pandaya, J.Z. 29
paragraph writing unit, IRI and writing, Tier 2 174–178
Paris, S. 34
Pearson, P.D. 14, 28, 34
personal narrative unit, teachers plan for: at Tier 0 97–98; at Tier 1 90–91; at Tier 2 92–94; at Tier 3 95–96
picture book read-aloud plan 149
Pinnell, G.S. 54
planning conversation 72–74
Polikoff, M.S. 12–15
Portalupi, J. 63; *Writing Workshop: The Essential Guide* 63
Positive Behavioral Interventions and Supports (PBIS) 10
prediction sub-unit, Tier 3 180, **180–181**
progress monitoring assessment: foundational skills standard 2.4c, Tier 2 111; foundational skills standard RF4.4b, Tier 2 126; informational text standard RI 4.2, Tier 2 120

Provost, M.C. 147
Pullen, P.C. 10
Pytash, K.E. 59

Quinones, R. 55

Readers' workshop: Real reading (Hagerty) 46
reading, structures for 42–43; guided reading 51–55; interactive read-aloud 43–45; Literature Circles 55–58; reading workshop 45–48; shared reading 49–50; Tier 3 65, **65–66**
reading specialist plans, for character unit: at Tier 2 78–79; at Tier 3 81–82
Reading Workshop: additional resources 46–48; foundational skills standard 2.4c, Tier 1 110; foundational skills standard RF4.4b, Tier 1 123–124; informational text standard RI 2.5, Tier 1 106; informational text standard RI 4.2, Tier 1 118; simplest version 45–46
response to intervention (RtI) 2–3, 10; implementations 13; and MTSS, differing ways 11–12; and MTSS, similar ways 11; protocol for Tier 1, Tier 2 and Tier 3 10
Reyes, J. 14
Reyes, M.R. 28
Rodriguez, K. 3
Rodriguez, S.C. 67
Rosenshine, B. 34
Rupley, W.H. 34

Santangelo, T. 36
Scharlach, T.D. 34
Schwartz, R.M. 28
second-grade unit for, research project and oral report: Tier 1 139–142; Tier 2 142; Tier 3 142
second-to-last session, informational text standard RI 4.2, Tier 2 121
Senn, G.J. 29
Shanahan, T. 18

shared reading 5, 28, 43; additional resources 50; comprehension monitoring and fix-ups unit 171; foundational skills standard 2.4c, Tier 1 110; foundational skills standard RF4.4b, Tier 1 124; informational text standard RI 2.5, Tier 1 107; informational text standard RI 4.2, Tier 1 118–119; literature standard RL 2.1 101; simplest version for big books 49–50; simplest version for other texts 50; teachers plan for character unit, Tier 1 75; teachers plan for personal narrative unit, Tier 1 90
shared writing 5, 59, 91, 96–97, 131; additional resources 61–62; simplest version 61
Shelton, N. 65
Shifflet, R. 29
Shingles, B. 13
Shorey, V. 65
sight words unit, IRI and writing, Tier 2 156–158
simple decoding unit, IRI and writing, Tier 2 158–165
Slaughter, J.P. 50
Smith, J.M. 13
Smith, M.S. 9, 10
Smith, R. 31
sophisticated standards 2; within CCSS *see* Common Core State Standards (CCSS); within MTSS *see* multi-tiered systems of support (MTSS); teaching of 7, 27, 67
Spear-Swerling, L. 3
Stephens, D. 30
Stratigou, K. 62

Tampio, N. 10
Tassel-Baska, J. Van 19
teacher self-assessment 86
teachers plan, for character unit: at Tier 0 84; at Tier 1 74–76
teachers plan, for personal narrative unit: at Tier 0 97–98; at Tier 1 90–91; at Tier 2 92–94; at Tier 3 95–96

teaching: at Tier 0 84–85, 98–99; at Tier 1 76–78, 91–92; at Tier 2 80–81, 94–95; at Tier 3 82–84, 96–97
text features, structures for using, Tier 3 108, **109**
third-to-last session, informational text standard RI 4.2, Tier 2 121
Tier 0: curriculum 35–36; issues 19–20; teachers plan for character unit at 84; teachers plan for personal narrative unit at 97–98; teaching at 84–85, 98–99
Tier 1 5–7, 10; for classrooms 4; curriculum 28–30; foundational skills standard 2.4c 110–111; foundational skills standard RF4.4b 123–125; fourth-grade unit for research project and oral report, CCSS 135–138; informational text standard RI 2.5 106–108; informational text standard RI 4.2 117–120; issues 15–16; literature standard RL 2.1 100–102; second-grade unit for research project and oral report, CCSS 139–142; teachers plan for character unit at 74–76; teachers plan for personal narrative unit at 90–91; teaching at 76–78, 91–92; Writing Standard W4.1A, B, & D 128–132
Tier 2 5–7, 10; curriculum 30–33; foundational skills standard 2.4c 111–115; foundational skills standard RF4.4b 126–128; fourth-grade unit for research project and oral report 138; informational text standard RI 2.5 108; informational text standard RI 4.2 120–122; issues 16–17; literature standard RL 2.1 102–103; reading specialist plans for character unit at 78–79; second-grade unit for research project and oral report 142; for small groups 4; teachers plan for personal narrative unit at 92–94; teaching at 80–81, 94–95; units

based on IELI and writing analysis 148–156; units based on IRI and writing 156–178; use of informal data for developing and teaching 147–148; Writing Standard W4.1A, B, & D 132–133

Tier 3 5–7, 10; answering questions, structures for **104**; asking questions, structures for **105**; comprehension monitoring, structures for **116**; curriculum 33–35; determining main idea, structures for 121, **122**; foundational skills standard RF4.4b 128; fourth-grade unit for research project and oral report 138; informal data for developing and teaching 147–148; issues 17–19; for one-on-one instruction 4; reading and writing, structures for 65, **65–66**; reading specialist plans for character unit at 81–82; second-grade unit for research project and oral report 142; teachers plan for personal narrative unit at 95–96; teaching for integration at 82–84, 96–97; text features, structures for using 108, **109**; Writing Standard W4.1A, B, & D 133

Tobin, R. 36

Tomlinson, C.A. 19; *Assessment and Student Success in a Differentiated Classroom* 36; *The Differentiated Classroom: Responding to the Needs of All Learners* 36

Tucker, C.R. 3

Turner, J. 34

units based on IELI and writing, Tier 2: emergent auditory unit 152–155; emergent meaning unit 148–149; emergent print unit 149–152; emergent writing unit 155–156

units based on IELI and writing, Tier 3 178–179

units based on IRI and writing, Tier 2: comprehension monitoring and fix-ups unit 169–172; inference unit 172; metacognition unit 167–169; multi-syllable decoding unit 165–167; oral retell unit 172–174; paragraph writing unit 174–178; sight words unit 156–158; simple decoding unit 158–165

units based on IRI and writing, Tier 3 178–179

Valencia, S.W. 17, 31, 145
VanDerHeyden, A.M. 13
Vaughan, Jr. J.L. 145
Vaughn, S. 14, 17
Venegas, E.M. 58
Villaume, S.K. 55
visualization sub-unit, Tier 3 181, **181–182**
visuals with captions, informational text standard RI 2.5, Tier 2 108

Walker, S.A. 63
Walker-Dalhouse, D. 36
Wanzek, J. 17, 19
Watts-Taffe, S. 31
Werts, M.G. 13, 14
Wheel of Fortune game 5, 68, 78, 80, 102, 111–115, 120–121, 160–163, 165, 170, 171, 173–174
Williams, C. 62
Witzel, B.S. 14
Word Wall 150, 152
writing analysis, Tier 2: comprehension monitoring and fix-ups unit 169–172; emergent auditory unit 152–155; emergent meaning unit 148–149; emergent print unit 149–152; emergent writing unit 155–156; inference unit 172; metacognition unit 167–169; multi-syllable decoding unit 165–167; oral retell unit 172–174; paragraph writing unit 174–178; sight words unit 156–158; simple decoding unit 158–165
writing, structures for 59; mentor texts within genre study 59–60; modeled writing 60–61; paired/

collaborative writing 62–63; shared writing 61–62; Tier 3 65, **65–66**; writing workshop 63–65
writing analysis, Tier 3: comprehension monitoring and fix-ups 183, **183–184**; inference 184, **184–185**; making connections sub-unit 182, **182–183**; oral retelling 185, **185**; prediction sub-unit 180, **180–181**; prior knowledge sub-unit 179, **179–180**; structures for 65, **65–66**; units based on 178–179; visualization sub-unit 181, **181–182**

writing standard W4.1A, B, & D: Tier 1 128–132; Tier 2 132–133; Tier 3 133
Writing Workshop 5, 59, 62, 91; additional resources 65; simplest version (over several days) 63–65
Writing Workshop: The Essential Guide (Fletcher and Portalupi) 63
Wu, Y. 13

Yopp, H.K. 153
Young, N. 43, 45

Zohbie, A. 60

For Product Safety Concerns and Information please contact our EU
representative GPSR@taylorandfrancis.com
Taylor & Francis Verlag GmbH, Kaufingerstraße 24, 80331 München, Germany

Integrating Sophisticated Standards and Systems of Support for Elementary Readers

This book supports elementary school teachers and other school leaders in considering the ways in which sophisticated standards (e.g., the Common Core State Standards [CCSS]) and multi-tiered systems of support (MTSS) can be effectively integrated to raise student reading and writing achievement. This book provides practical instructions to guide professional development for teachers and administrators to assess students for MTSS placement and develop standards-based lessons and assessments at all levels of MTSS.

The CCSS and other such standards were developed and marketed as a mechanism for raising expectations and enriching instruction for all students. MTSS offers a foundational structure for supporting children who struggle with literacy—providing increasingly intense levels of intervention for students who need it. This book argues that integration of sophisticated standards and MTSS is necessary if we expect children who struggled with less sophisticated standards to navigate these more challenging standards effectively. It reviews the two initiatives and the potential for integration, proposes professional development opportunities for crafting curriculum that reflect this integration, and offers examples of what standards-based units might look like for classroom instruction (MTSS Tier 1), small-group instruction (Tier 2), and one-on-one tutoring (Tier 3).

With examples of lessons and assessments, this book is ideal for elementary school teachers, academic coaches, school administrators, and other professionals who lead literacy initiatives.

Elizabeth L. Jaeger is Associate Professor emerita in the Department of Teaching, Learning, and Sociocultural Studies at the University of Arizona. She has taught reading and writing methods courses for undergraduates and qualitative research methods courses for graduate students.